<u>Scoring Points:</u>

Love and Football in the Age

of AIDS

By

Gary D. Gerson

For Mrs. Quarles, Mrs. Lafever, and Mr. Claborn:
Artists all who painted beautiful pictures.

ISBN 978-0-6152-4457-0

Acknowlegements:

With great affection, I thank my wonderful co-workers at Cranbrook Kingswood for making our jobs so worthwhile. I especially thank my fellow science department members, particularly Greg Miller for his support of this project. Thank you to my office mates, Bob, Russ, John, Audrey, and Matt, for putting up with the jokes and mess. Thank you forever to Randy and Ellen Tufts, as if you need to know why.

Thank you to every young man who ever played football at Cranbrook, for every drop of sweat you have given. Thank you to every young man who ever played football at Windsor, especially those in 1993 and 1994 who let me into your precious fold. Thank you to all my coaches, each of whom gave a little of themselves for so many of us.

And of course, thank you to Shelley, for showing me the way.

Chapter 1: Morristown

If only I could have been the explosive band of fibers that was Doby Boseman, commanding the field for the West High Trojans, dazzling all the good old boys in Morristown, taking us to the playoffs and single-handedly bringing Elizabethton down with 220 yards in the first round. He was 5-foot-6 if he was anything, had not an ounce of body fat, rippled at all corners of his lithe self with muscles and grace and confidence. With jets on his feet Doby took touchdowns from feeble country-boy opponents, faking foolish tacklers, arms outstretched and empty, onto their own surprised faces. He did whatever he wanted on the field, anytime, and quickly. I wanted to be him.

As if that field wasn't enough, Doby dominated the school hallway with his lazy smile, his presence sufficing magnificently, never saying much except the occasional "hey". Even with his tiny size and average grades, his greatness on the field was so obvious that he got a full ride up at East Tennessee State University in Johnson City. A scholarship just to play football, because that's the way the game works. They say if he'd been any bigger he'd have worn Tennessee Orange instead. How great to have been Doby, showing off so effortlessly in front of all the girls and making the grown men proud, leaving them shaking their heads and looking at each other in that knowing way. With every headfake and score, they stood high up in the stands chuckling and saying with a slight head turn in hillbilly understatement, "Yup. He's a good 'un."

I grew up there, snuggled in the Appalachian fold with people who love the football player and rave with reverence and loyalty about the rare true athlete on the hometown team. It is sad to leave them on returning up here to my home up North, though I love just about everything about Michigan; it is home to me now. But Michigan is not Tennessee, and the Maize-and-Blue car army that clogs into Ann Arbor on fall Saturdays to cheer on the massive Midwestern linemen and blue-chip running backs are very different from the southern Orange-and-White throng that descends on Knoxville to yell for their thick farmboys and South-Florida-imported speedsters.

They do have that in common, the fans do, that football-as-prayer salvation and fierce loyalty to all that is right on the field on any given weekend. I have seen and felt that in person in both places, but especially while growing up in East Tennessee. I can still feel the vibrations of John Ward's mystical, lyrical voice on Morristown's WCRK (We Can't Reach Knoxville) as he told of the magic of Condredge Hollaway running the option and little Bill Bates saving the game with a crazy tackle. As little boys we lived it and loved it and wanted to *be* it, John Ward announcing our own names with astonishment as we skipped across the goalline.

It's easy to look back and feel comfort on the sounds of youth, but every thought of my past leads me to present thoughts of my beautiful Shelley, and I have to pay attention to my love for her right then, so strong is her pull.

> She is sleeping on the fat green couch, the one we bought that summer in Tennessee and brought back up with us after. She has the most beautiful face these eyes have ever spoken to, soft yellow hair framing her pale gentle blossom of lips. I walk over quietly and touch her cheek with the full of my open hand and there is a light flinch, a faint smile. I ask in low tones if she wants to get up and go to dinner now. Trying hard not to sound grumpy, having been brought from that far-off place of sleep so suddenly, where she is safe, she cutely croaks for "just a few more minutes." I sit down across from her in the matching fat green easy chair and stare at her until the dog sighs and puts her insistent muzzle in the cup of my hand, lifting my fingers to have her ears gently pulled. The dog, Gypsum, loves us both so much, telling us often with her stare and the way she softly stamps her feet. She sits nice while I gaze at my wife.

My father and mother, never shy, fought to give me and my brother and sister a Jewish home smack in the middle of a determined Bible Belt. Never mind the illogic of Mom's kosher-ness: we could have bacon in the house but not country ham, which I craved constantly ("There have to be some limits!" she would say, making me furious with her millionth insane rationalization). Mom had been transplanted in the South by my charmingly huge father, Allan, in 1960 after he was floored by her brash New England shield on a blind date in New York. Bunny Misner was from the mean streets of Beverly Mass, and you had better not mess with her.

Being Jewish was its own story in East Tennessee since there were only about 10 Jewish houses in Morristown, and there were many forms Judaism took for us kids. It meant taking that hour-long drive into Temple Beth El in Knoxville every Sunday and Friday night for Hebrew school and Sabbath services. Dad tried to make that endless trip fun by having us sing silly songs about the cows and pigs by the side of the road, and for a long time that was our best relationship with him, singing all the way to Temple about farm animals in our funny voices. That, and dreaming about the rare visit to the one Knoxville McDonald's after religious school for addictive burgers and fries not yet available in Morristown or anywhere else in all of East Tennessee.

Being Jewish meant that we never went to regular school on the High Holidays and were guilted into maintaining a 24-hour fast on Yom Kippur. Going hungry was never fun, particularly when you were 12, but you didn't want to be the one who ate the A&P oatmeal cookie while everyone else frowned at you and shook their heads. The cookies called to me, fueling my guilty mind.

We lit the candles for every Sabbath, and our family never missed a Friday night meal together, not ever, while we still lived at home. It was orchestrated: Mom welcoming the Sabbath, Dad blessing the wine, Marty singing a prayer for the bread (often a defrosted *challah* lovingly stockpiled from Atlanta, sometimes Ry-Krisp since mom thought the rye gave it Jewish connotations), me working my way through the *Shema* prayer, and little Hillary telling us that God is great, God is good, because that was the only prayer she knew, the one we had all started with. We learned "God is Great" at the Methodist kindergarten, where we also sang songs about the mysterious Jesus. We never said "Jesus" in our house, as if he provided some source of wariness and conspiracy.

There were days when I got to be the star at Rose Elementary School, bringing in the *matzo* at Passover time so my classmates could taste the flat bread of our deliverance that kept all Jews so constipated and irritable for those eight days. My schoolmates thought I was so lucky to eat such wonderful things (and boy could I play that up). And then some of them would tell me that they had prayed for me in their churches because their pastors had told them that I would burn in Hell with my unsaved relatives, simply because I did not know Jesus. Some of my little friends even insisted to my face that I was the one who had *killed* their Lord. It took a while to get past that. When you were 7, it was hard to gather a reasonable comeback for the idea that your forebears had caused so much strife.

Mom could be fierce when it came to protecting what we were in our makeshift, almost desperate, Jewish-ness, and it was known around town that she would have no tolerance for anyone who tried to infuse any small sneaky bit of Christianity where it did not belong. I found this very convenient at times, such as when lovely and proper Mrs. Quarles, my wonderful gray-haired English teacher, sent home a note in eighth grade telling Mom that I had not read *To Kill a Mockingbird* as assigned. I had tried to fake a book report in front of the class. And then I tried to fake it a second time, like Mrs. Quarles wouldn't know. That was the kind of kid I was then.

Now Mrs. Quarles was about the best teacher there was in East Tennessee, patient and demanding, able to teach the heck out of English grammar. But when Mom scowled at me with that note from Mrs. Quarles clenched in her small tight fist (those veins in her little hand could get awfully blue, let me tell you), I trembled for a few moments, but then I played my trump card.

I told Mom that, well, Mrs. Quarles had used New Testament characters when illustrating conjugation ("Mary and Joseph *walked* down the Jerusalem street..."). Oh boy, did that force my Mom's rage away from me and onto poor Mrs. Quarles!

It was fierce the way Mom got Mrs. Quarles back in the follow-up note, telling the good teacher not to dare use the Bible again in class while I was in there, all huffy and hot about "separation of church and state", and hardly acknowledging my own shortcomings in the undone book reports. When I handed that note to my teacher, I thought I was about the cleverest boy that ever walked into a classroom, all smug and smart. Mrs. Quarles read it while I stood smirking at her in front of her desk. Then I watched her face fall.

As my mother's words registered in her mind and a sharp look of victory appeared on my face, Mrs. Quarles just pressed her lips together, folding the note while her eyes never reached mine, and told me that she did not care if I *ever* read that book. Well, I'd never had a teacher not look at me. It was clear that she was hurt, and I instantly felt like a pile of garbage.

Incidentally, I have read *To Kill a Mockingbird* five times since then. And this past spring, when a parent blasted me over the phone for not inspiring her child to a grade better than B even though she really deserved a D, I sent Mrs. Quarles a dozen fine roses, 25 years after my transgression, knowing now what she knew then.

> The tears come out onto her cheeks again, sobbing while still trying to finish the conversation on the phone, and my heart breaks one more time. I go to hug her but she is impatient with me, and I know that she must be left alone. This evening it is Jim who is dead. His liver could not stand any more drugs, and the unexplainable tumor in his back was inoperable, so his body finally quit after enough of the good struggle. We knew he would die, though he had gone surprisingly quickly. Jim and Shelley had gone to the hemophilia camp together as they had grown up, sharing the burden of painful joint bleeds and discovering their physical limits as teenagers. Hopeful when the Clotting Factor stopped the hemorrhages. Frustrated and angry when finding out the poison was in them all. Now Shelley is left behind again, and another piece of her life has faded out and gone away. She cries at the unfairness, and I know that she wonders again where the hands on her clock sit.

The folks managed to get the three of us kids *Bar* and *Bat Mitzvahed*, with big parties at the Morristown Country Club and the Holiday Inn. Relatives came in from all over Massachusetts and Atlanta and Florida, and we raked in huge piles of checks for twenty and fifty and even one hundred dollars that we would never be allowed to touch. Marty got 6 thesauruses. I got 5 pen and pencil sets.

For my *Torah* portion reading, at the innocent and easily-embarrassed age of 13, I got to explain to the audience of old people and relatives and nervous Christian schoolmates (who had never been anywhere near a synagogue) and *girls* about Jewish laws regarding women during menstruation. I had to translate a whole chapter in the Jewish Holy Books about menstrual cycles and how God had rules for them during this time of being "unclean." That's what I had to speak about up on the *bimah* in front of everyone, including gorgeous Jo-Ellen and Lynn from my class, and Mom and my sister and my grandmother, when I was 13. Pulling my pants down would have been less embarrassing. Judaism is funny.

In high school, I played the marching xylophone, a heavy wood and metal instrument which was strapped across these skinny little shoulders every Friday night in the fall while the bigger football boys threw each other around muddy little stadiums and skipped triumphant across that goal line. I was a squirrel then, jealous of all the bronco-sized football players and their big manliness and swagger and attention. How come I never got any bigger?

There was not much to me. Being in the band was all I was at that time, except for harboring that reputation as the smart-ass that all teachers probably could not stand, responding to every class question with unnecessary answers, never learning the right time to shut my own mouth. I paid for that quality many times in the afternoon after classes, having to explain myself to mad teachers and band directors, and through high school my own peers never did take me seriously. Gary was always good for a laugh, they thought, but clearly not much else. And they were mostly right.

After Sunday School one day, I was gently invited into Rabbi Matthew Derby's office at Temple Beth El. He was the pillar of the Knoxville Jewish community, a wise and thoughtful man (even to a 16-year-old) who was respected for his tolerance and understanding, here in the buckle of the Bible Belt. He probably knew I was searching for something to hang onto so that I could just get through the lousy years of adolescence, and he listened. I worried about God, and I worried that I might never have faith. I worried that I was not a good Jew. So I asked the rabbi, whom I loved and admired, who seemed to invite any question at any time.

"Rabbi Derby, if you don't believe in God, can you call yourself a Jew?"

Unlike most adults in my life, he took me seriously, which made me pay a little closer attention. His answer was certain and without hesitation.

"Of course you can be a Jew. You don't have to believe in God or even *be Jewish* to be a good Jew!" I was amazed to hear him say that, and he knew it. He could see the tiny gears in my brain working hard. "Gandhi was a good Jew!" he said with glee.

He went on, smiling, while I was riveted. "If you want to be a good Jew, then first be a good person. Being a good *person* is the trick, no matter what you believe. But that is the hardest thing, harder than anything. If you can be a good man, I would call you a good Jew." I was amazed and excited, because the trick to getting to a young man is to tell him something he *could* do. What a great teacher, Rabbi Derby. He put me in power.

By that time in your high school career, you're pretty much labeled as a geek or jock or, in my case, an annoying attention-getter, and beating that imprint is next to impossible until you move on to work or college. I didn't know that the faculty viewed me that way either, but I soon learned.

I tried out for drum major in late spring of junior year, and I didn't get it, and that about killed me. Mr. McNew, a small stocky man with a quick wit and absolute command of our huge band and orchestra, and whom I worshipped, gave the job to that goofy Chuck White. What?! This kid was way inferior to me in about a million ways! I sat in numb silence with a throbbing ache in my stomach all that night after the positions were announced, and the knot did not go away for months.

As things go, Chuck turned out to be a pretty good drum major and an even better friend, and I got a free chance to grow up a little. As they say, What doesn't kill us makes us stronger, and when the pain subsided and the scars healed, I was a bit wiser. That summer Mr. McNew made me section leader of the drummers and I relished the responsibility. I made the all-East Tennessee percussion team up in Gatlinburg that year and got to do a tom-tom solo on a record that they had made at the concert there. It was a big deal to my folks and nice payback for me.

I fell in love in the middle of my senior year, improbable as it was. A lovely and shy girl, one who had also grown up through her own kinds of adolescent angst, ventured into my camp of consciousness. Jenny was as vital as breath to me when I was 17, sweet in her pink hair-bow and Love's Baby-Soft fragrance. High school love, though, is thrilling and sad all at once. It is hard to hold, like a crazy little bird, hard to know when to let the bird fly and when to keep it warm inside your coat.

Shelley is angry now. Her eyes flash that color I do not recognize, and her voice is really a warning to run away from her, but I do not hear it. I foolishly try to make peace, to make her feel better. I have not yet learned that I must leave her alone at times like these and take that time to clean up my own life, so I pursue her further, and for that I will pay a certain price. What is wrong? I ask in a gently teasing voice, winking sensually like the lover I think I am, and she blasts away. "You don't understand! I'm losing everyone, and you think this is all funny! And now you messed up the kitchen and I have to clean it up and you still have stuff on the stairs and the laundry isn't done and you don't listen to me! You think I have to do everything around here! You're just like your father, your mother, your brother, my father, my brother, my mother....." And I am done for. I am quite hot in my shirt now, in disbelief that Shelley cannot see that I only want to help, and I finally see that it's time to walk the dog. A long walk, where I will mutter to myself about how I got into this sad situation where I am such a poor, poor boy, unappreciated as all the world. Someday, I grumble to myself, the world will know how mean she is and how nice I am.

Truthfully, I was lucky in my youth to have all the things I needed if not what I thought I wanted, and mine was a loyal and giving family. It was a shame that I could not look at all the kids at school who had to wear the same clothes every day and survive on the Hot Breakfast Program and see my own gluttony. I had things pretty good, and my parents came to every band concert and school play and awards ceremony. Not many others had that. So what if they pointed out the missed note on the xylophone or the stumbled line in the performance.

So I tried to grow up around my own self and followed those who were cooler and shunned those that were less cool, shallow boy that I was, foundering through uneventful years of high school until, hopefully, bigger things. Of course, my folks did not agree that I was an uneventful kid then. Just ask them about the time in sophomore year when I came home with bloodshot eyes, staring absently at the TV in front of everyone. One of the tuba players had invited me to ride around with him after band practice, and I had succumbed to peer pressure (that is my excuse) and puffed the frightful weed like the cool people would have done, not wanting him to think me inexperienced with the ways of pot.

I am sure that that one experiment convinced Mom and Dad that I was the drug dealer for the whole county, sure to only get worse and spend much time incarcerated and homeless as the years turned. I was so scared and shocked and guilty from their pained reactions to my experiment ("Where did we go wrong? Where did we go wrong?") that I did not even do so much as taste a beer until college. I was known as the nerd boy after that, even at Vanderbilt, drinking root beer and crème soda at the frat parties, afraid someone would tell my parents, long distance, that I had fulfilled their worst fears as an addict and unsociable vagrant.

> It is a wonderful evening at the restaurant with our friends the Cohens. The dinner is magical, thick with laughter and brotherhood and rich foods, and Shelley grabs my hand under the table and loves that hand and will not let it go and we are so connected that I know why I love her and married her and dream of her. Her eyes flash the brilliance of her depth and I catch the rays dead-on. On the drive home I foolishly make a comment, any comment, and she wheels around and debates it violently as if I am the enemy, and the momentum drains away like a broken dam. I feel betrayed and, without thinking, I tell her so, and she attacks again, knowing where to put those arrows so that I reel and struggle for breath. Why can't I be quiet? The line is drawn, as usual, as we pull the car into the cracked driveway of our home, and the distance will safely remain until a silent sleep finalizes the rift for the night. I have no understanding of things and am out of my league.

By the time I meandered my way through high school and left for Vanderbilt University over in Nashville, I had not yet found any use for myself and had no target in sight. In turn, I continued spinning my wheels and spending my parents' money, but on a more impressive scale in my first year of college.

I lied to my girlfriend Jenny about all the wonderful things I was doing when really I missed her like oxygen, but it backfired and she became jealous of all my "fun" while she was stuck at UT in Knoxville. That was one of many issues I misplayed with her. I did not know anything.

College did feel futile at first. Everyone seemed to get away with never going to class, and the boys on my floor, while never admitting to having any plan for success, seemed to make all A's and impress all the females anyway. They all always seemed to have money for pizza and eating at nice restaurants; I spent my entire year's allowance in the first month and dipped into my Bar Mitzvah money on the sly so I could keep up with them. The folks were plenty hot about my thievery when they found out. That added lots of fuel to my burgeoning reputation of irresponsibility in their eyes. Deserved, of course.

I missed Jenny ferociously and spent potentially constructive time writing her letter after letter, soon pledging my desperate love for her and telling her that I was having no fun whatsoever. She wrote me back with the same sadness, occasionally mentioning a "really nice senior boy" who was helping her to find her way around campus, or some "really friendly guy" at a frat party. That girl sure could get me going with my imagination. Wasn't she just reminding me that she was ripe for picking for some deserving guy closer to home?

This same world that had designs on her was drowning me in apathy and Thursday-to-Sunday beer parties all along the wasteland of fraternity row, where I did not drink but watched with great emptiness, trying to act as happy as everyone else seemed to be, wondering why there was not more to life than their shallow, loud escape and preparation for the next blast.

In my narrow view, the boys at Vandy who seemed to be heading in the most direction of positive force were the athletes. I got to know the scholarship football and basketball players as the administration made them live in the freshman dorm, Branscomb, with us regular boys during their first year, before moving into the football floors of the Towers across campus. These guys were huge and good-looking and always tired out, but tired with a sense of satisfaction and accomplishment that wafted all about them.

I had always read about college football players in *Sports Illustrated* and had glamorized them through my adolescence, worshipping them at UT when I was back home with my parents and the rest of the die-hard fans. And here I was living with them, watching them drink beers and have girls around (usually not Vandy girls, though, who were a bit too demure and smug and off-limits) and be cool in that casual way. I found that I wanted to *be* them, like I had wanted to be Doby Boseman, all of them, the vacuous backup quarterback and the sleek Italian-looking wide-receiver, the big dumb lineman and the puppy-dog tight-end who was not yet grown into his oversized body and role on the team. Soon they would all be football heroes after they got a couple of years of good coaching and experience. They were all who I wanted to be, smooth and directed and tired for a good reason. I was a little squirrel.

My time in the marching band at Vanderbilt lasted about two weeks, until I figured out that I was no longer the big band boy that I had been in high school. The director told me he just wanted me to move props around during the half-time shows rather than star on the xylophone. I wanted no part of that. So I gave up what had once been everything important to me. Quitting the marching band was an easy decision, since then I would have more time to goof off and wallow in self-pity.

> Shelley's father is yellow. I am driving him in my Jeep. When the kidneys and liver started malfunctioning, and the wastes would not filter out on their own, Dad sank into a jaundice from which he would be unable to escape without the ultimate price of his last breath. He and I are returning from Beaumont Hospital in Royal Oak where a gentle young doctor has inserted a big needle into Dad's abdomen and sent five liters of urine-like waste fluid jetting through a rubber tube into huge glass jars. I watched, working hard to avoid a flinch, and heard the jars fill. Dad feels a bit more relaxed now from the reduced pressure, but his eyes are not the happy lights they had been all along my courtship of his daughter; they are just yellow and fading. I try to make conversation as we pass the huge General Motors plant on 13-Mile Road, but there is little answer on the other end. This man is a real-life biblical Job: one son is dead, a wife battles depression, a beautiful daughter is going to die in her beautiful youth, and his painful legs have not worked since childhood hemophilia fused his knees. And now Dad has the look of death about his own self, a look that grows and forms, unstoppable, from deep inside. And God, he *just knows*, has not forsaken him. And he loves God back. And I feel sad and full of joy in his holy presence, my father-in-law, Eldon Bryson, as he is made to take account of his generous life and prepare for the next.

I started hanging around with the football players in their dorm rooms at night, though they were usually too tired to do anything except telephone their moms and study a little history and play bad electric guitar. Eventually, I found a bit of substance at the campus radio station where I got my own time slot, rising to become a very bad disc jockey who could only play Springsteen and The Who because I knew nothing else. Why did everyone else know more about music than me? Some of the freshman football players noticed me on the radio and got a kick out of knowing who I was. "Yo, dude, you were righteous on the radio, man." Meanwhile, I remained stunned and awestruck in their presence.

At the end of the first year, my grades stunk but I was mildly happy to have been rushed by Andy Cohen to join a nerdy Jewish fraternity, where I was the (ha-ha) star athlete during intramurals. It was true that I was, in the scheme of things, a very mediocre backyard football and basketball player at that point, but very good when compared to my frat brothers, the Jewish academicians of Alpha Epsilon Pi.

Somehow, I gained more confidence with every game, and I was thrilled that these guys counted on me athletically. So what if the other frats viewed us as the "easy win".

Late in freshman year I got enough nerve and verve to sort-of, maybe, joke to one of the star receivers, Chuck Scott, about actually trying out for the real football team. I knew that he would probably laugh at me. He did not. And I loved Chuck for telling me that I really should go ahead and do it, serious as all day. We both knew that I would be the worst player on the worst team in the Southeastern Conference, probably Division I, and perhaps in the whole of the NCAA. But it was possible, he said, that I could actually make the team since they rarely cut anyone who had some heart and worked hard.

It was time to make one choice that would shape me beyond my inauspicious past. Every thought was thick then, hard but thrilling. I would stay awake at night thinking of the importance of trying to play Division One Football with no experience whatsoever. What was I thinking? Did I want to get killed? Who does such a thing?

In the last week of school in the spring of 1982, I breathed in the bravest air I could find and walked with stony legs over to the McGugin sports building where all the offices and locker rooms were housed. I asked the first secretary inside (they were all so beautiful!) where I might find the head football coach, and she directed me upstairs with a smile that could only have been reserved for important recruits.

It all seemed so organized in that building. In the long hallway, draped with photos and accomplishments of the great Vanderbilt athletes, I asked a small gray-haired man where I might find Coach George MacIntyre. He smiled a pixie smile and told me that I was currently speaking to him. I swallowed my tongue briefly, but was able to pull it out of my throat enough to say, breathlessly, "I'm sorry to bother you sir, and I know you must be busy and I don't want to disturb you and I'm very small and have no experience, but I want to play football for you next year."

I began to list some more reasons why he should not have me on his team, but the good coach cut me off with a sparkling eye and a lovely country accent and a gentle hand on my shoulder, and he said that he would be glad to have me, that there were lots of places I could help out the team. I bet a thousand boys had heard that line from him, and 999 never showed up again. So I asked him what I needed to do. Coach Mac told me to go find Doc in the weight-room and get all my information from him, and then he was gone to a meeting and I was in the grand hallway in McGugin. Our encounter had ended, and I was still alive and not told to go home. He had taken me seriously! I staggered to the weight room in a daze, almost no breath left.

E.J. "Doc" Kreis presided like royalty, large behind his bastion of a desk in the weight room, a knowing scowl behind a walrus mustache. He was himself a monster of a man, huge, obviously able to talk the talk, walk the walk, and he was to be respected, without any doubt. He looked like a man who had killed someone and gotten away with it, smiling a criminal smile and daring you to arrest him. He could have eaten me in one bite, right then. Why in the world would this man even need a real desk? I told him that Coach Mac had sent me.

Doc looked me over with great skepticism, and his voice boomed, "Well, where the hell have you been all spring?" I looked absolutely like I would wet my pants, I am sure. And he knew it.

"Uh ...I didn't know I was supposed to ...," I began, feebly.

"Hell! You didn't know you needed to be in this weight room, gettin' yourself ready? What do you think, this is all fun? You think this is television?"

"No sir." That was the first time in my life I had just stopped and shut my mouth. My flinchy eyes remained upon this mountain of a man who could squeeze me like a pimple.

"Well, shit, let's get your name and address on the list and get you a workout schedule. You stick to this good!" he bellowed, handing me a timetable of sprinting drills and lifting techniques, most of which were in a foreign language of squats and shrugs and power-pulls. I stood there, dumb, until he commanded me to leave. "Go on, now! Get yourself ready!"

I was pleased to not be dead, so I left his domain.

The walk back to the dorms was crazy, cloudy, and buoyant. There was no turning back now. I was going to learn how to fly, to bench-press a million pounds, to push intruders away at every turn, to sweat nobly like I never had before. All five-foot-nine, one-hundred and forty-five pounds of me was going to be a football player for the

Vanderbilt University Commodores. Let the doubts of those around me begin. Damn it all, I was going to play football!

What was I going to tell my parents?

It is Yom Kippur and friends are at our table. This is the last meal before the day-long fast, and I have been careful to go easy on the spices so no one would become thirsty at services. Toying with one of our lovely flowered salad plates between courses, I drop it and it falls to the table and shatters. Shelley has such a look of disconsolation that Mom reaches out to touch her through my awkward apologies. It is just a stupid salad plate, I reason in my head, and she can always go get another one. How annoying that Shelley is so upset about such a trivial thing, especially in front of our guests. Can't she see how upset and embarrassed I am? How inconsiderate! The meal concludes and I am left with my annoyance at Shelley, apologizing all the while to her and the guests. Why is she acting this way? Will I ever understand her? Will I ever see beyond the broken plate...?

Chapter 2: Vanderbilt Football

I worked all that summer of 1982 at the Holiday Inn restaurant back in Morristown, getting up way before dawn and driving the old station wagon down Andrew Johnson Highway while most of the town slept or baked their own biscuits. We had busloads of retirees from Pennsylvania and Ohio down for the World's Fair in Knoxville, and just about all of them ate Leoma's breakfast buffet right here at the motel. It was easy work for me; just get them seated and happy while they served themselves bacon and scrambled eggs and heaven-sent biscuits that Leoma made with love. We kept the coffee flowing and the dishes bussed as we scraped quarters off the tables. They made me wear one of those big orange blouses with the big orange pockets, which did not look manly at all, like a football player should look, but I took home $40 in change about every day, which was huge.

I got off in the early afternoon, exhausted and dragging, then headed over to the Nautilus gym down the street for introductory weight lifting. It took several sessions to realize that muscles came from real effort instead of simple motion, and after a few weeks a little biceps started to show up on these skinny arms. I ran afterwards, wind sprints and speed laps on the high school track, every day. I visited the coach at my old high school and asked if I could borrow a helmet and some shoulder-pads, and though he had no idea who I was, he nicely loaned me an old set. At home, I put on the helmet and pads and, with a tentative jogging start, ran into our brick garage wall over and over, trying to imagine what it would feel like to get hit. I made sure nobody was watching as I hit the brick: Wham! Wham! Wham! The *thwap* of the equipment echoed deep inside my head. Was I doing it right? Why is it so loud inside my helmet? Was this bad for my neck?

There was no way that Mom and Dad believed that I was going to go through with this whole lunacy. Both were very quick to point out that no one was pressuring me to go out there on that field with those big men, only to get my neck broken and my leg pulled off. They said I could quit at any time, it was fine with them. It was kind of like reverse Jewish guilt, where they tried to get me *not* to do something. All of the friends in our close-knit Jewish community, who really were like family, let the folks know that I was insane. One old family friend, dear Bert Gudis, told me for *sure* that I was going to tear my knee up and be crippled for the rest of my life. When I responded, with great conviction, that I thought it might be worth all that, he snorted with all of his world knowledge and turned away for more of Mom's rice pilaf and Dad's barbecue chicken, hot off the grill. Football in East Tennessee, even amongst the Jews, was revered and holy, and that included the program at poor little Vanderbilt, which hadn't had a winning season in a decade and had been UT's doormat. Who was I to denigrate the sacred game, to desecrate my own body in that hallowed arena?

Jenny wanted nothing to do with this football thing, and she let me know how angry she was that I would want to spend time away from her just to go run and lift weights and waste my time. We drifted away from each other as I got deeper into my workouts, and this brought up a little melancholy and a lot of guilt. I finally realized that if she did not want to support my silly idea, then I was going to have to go it alone. It was easy to see how she could have become offended by my lack of attentions and my selfish goals, but it was time to let go, and she had to do the same with me. Soon it was August and things were moving fast.

Even though I was a sophomore in the fall of 1982, I was allowed to come to the freshman football camp a week earlier than the rest of the varsity since I was new to the game. Coach Mac acted surprised and pleased to see me at pre-season camp registration (while I was sure he had no idea who I was), and Doc Kries (who I believe *did* remember) greeted me gruffly, with a bit of a scowly smile. I loved Doc instantly, as did anyone who ever met this mammoth of a man, and I wanted to do nothing but please him from the start. The other coaches did not care a bit who or what I was; they had not recruited me and knew nothing about my lack of abilities. I realized later that they needed to show off the scholarship kids they had recruited, and walk-ons like me were expendable and insignificant and often in the way.

I walked into camp with the idea that I would do whatever it took to stay on the team, and that I would not care how low I was placed on the depth chart. I would let everyone know that I was there to learn and help in any way, and no one was to worry about me being disappointed. I soon realized that the other walk-ons had been football stars at their own high schools just a year earlier, while I had played the xylophone at halftime.

They had us go to team and position meetings and get to know other football players, some of them absolutely huge and muscularly defined while others were just big goofy kids. They were all just like I was, nervous and excited and ready to earn a spot somewhere doing something, though many of them thought they would be stars by the time the season started.

Since I had actually been there for a year and they were all true freshmen, I was able to show some of them around campus, and they were grateful. All size and ego aside, they were scared little freshmen, unsure of what they were doing there so far from home. And the returning varsity players would be there in five days, ready to knock some heads.

Many of the new freshmen were humble and kind, like Will Wolford, who was easily the most likable and earnest of all the freshmen. Obviously, Will was also an amazing athlete. He was 6 foot 6 and 280 pounds and could dunk a basketball flat-footed. He would eventually start on the line as a true freshman, hold that position for four years, make All-America, and later become the first million-dollar offensive lineman in the NFL with Buffalo and Indianapolis and Pittsburgh. He was probably Vanderbilt's best football player ever, though linemen rarely earn that type of distinction. I got to eat chicken and French fries with Will over at the training table in his first week of big-time college football, and he was tickled that I was trying this game out for the first time, all 150 pounds of me. I'm proud that I knew him when he was just starting out, though I doubt he remembers much about me now as he is busy running the Louisville arena football team.

The receivers coach gave us all playbooks at our first position meeting. I had never seen one before, and it showed. When Coach Flip went over defensive coverage, I had absolutely no concept of what he was saying about Cover One and Man Under and Zone, and my head was spinning with this new terminology. I later would find that the other freshmen were just as scared and confused, afraid they would be called on by the coach and look dumb too. At the end of the first meeting, Coach Flip kept me behind. He looked right into my eyes and said gently, "Now, Gary, if you find that this isn't for you after a few days, you make sure that you get this book back to me."

I told him 'yessir' and right then knew that there was now no way I would quit. He lasted until the end of that season and then moved into a desk job in the athletic department. I lasted all four years on the field. Coach Flip, who eventually treated me quite well, was Gene DeFillippo. He became the Athletic Director at Boston College, and he's a good man who remembered me twenty years later.

In front of the equipment cage, I took whatever padding the manager, Bill, put on me, and that included two pairs of cleats, one for artificial turf and one for grass, that would be mine forever, no matter what. They let you keep the shoes in college sports! I got a gold helmet and eventually made it fit by adjusting the chinstraps. I hoped I was doing it right. The temporary white athletic tape across the forehead of my helmet said "GERSON". In my locker basket was a mesh bag with skin-tight grey shorts, a half grey T-shirt, socks, and a jock-strap that were to be washed after every practice in a washable mesh bag. I had never worn a jock strap before and didn't know that your butt hangs out, uncovered. How strange.

I shaped a mouth-guard in a pot of hot water in the training room and sucked all the air out of it, pressing it against the roof of my mouth with my tongue to make it fit firm against my teeth. I was nervous that someone would know I had never done all of this before and made sure to watch others before I tried anything. Many of them were as unsure as me, though I didn't know it then. There were shoulder pads (too big; I had to trade them in later, embarrassed) and leg and girdle pads, which fit into little slots in the uniform practice pants. For the rest of my life, I would have that bad dream where the game was starting and I could not fit all the pads into their proper places, frantically trying to make them go in, and I would always wake up in a panic. How many other football players have had that dream, years after their last game?

I was not a very good receiver, but I did not totally stink. Coach Flip was patient enough to teach all of us the correct pass routes, and I listened hard and learned where to put my feet and hands and head on every step, becoming a bit more confident every day. There were so many details for running and catching a ball! I loved, absolutely loved, being out on that field in the stadium, skipping over the lined plastic grass, seeming to jump high and run fast with the other guys, like when you're a little kid and get that new pair of sneakers that make you fly.

Sometimes the artificial turf would grab your rubber cleat as you casually walked across the field, and you would stumble awkwardly. The veterans called that the "turf-monster" and the freshmen learned that the turf-monster could bite. I got lots of turf burns on my elbows and knees from falling and skidding on the fake grass that first week, and they stung in the shower when the water hit, as if someone were rubbing the wound with sandpaper as the skin contracted. There was always the shrill sound of guys sucking in wind when the water suddenly hit their burns after practice. I learned to tape my elbows.

Other walk-ons, once great starts at their old high schools, quit and went home, frustrated because the coaches could not see how "wonderful" they were. My assigned roommate left after the second day; he had come in thinking he was going to beat out Jimmy Arnold, the All-America punter who had a 46-yard average. My roommate was punting about 30 yards. See ya'! After 5 days, I was still there, nothing to lose and already able to run a decent pass route.

When the rest of the varsity returned after my week's introduction to the game, my old friends from the year before were absolutely astounded to see me out on the practice field. "Gers!!!! What is UP! You playin' BALL???"

You could see it on their faces, their eyes all big and shocked. And I will tell you that from that first day they treated me like one of them, every man on the varsity respecting me for being out there to sweat and ache alongside them. How amazing to be instantly bonded with men whom I had held so highly, to be one of them, to be allowed to learn and drill with them. Of course, everyone knew that I threatened no one else's playing time, and that probably helped in the realm of male acceptance.

We ran pass-routes over and over and over. Soon I learned that, while painfully slow, I could make a few head-fakes and get open when playing against the good defensive backs. Sometimes that would make the other receivers shout out my name in delight, seemingly impressed when I made a decent catch or got the defender turned-around and stumbly. It was hard to tell if they were making fun of me or not, but it didn't matter. Getting a slap on the back or a high-five from a teammate became my only goal, and I actually got to catch some passes from Whit Taylor, the second-highest-rated passer in the country (behind the great John Elway of Stanford) that year, every day in practice. Whit was the best quarterback in Vanderbilt history, some say, though Jay Cutler in 2005 was pretty darned good. And Whit was the same size as me, though a little thicker with well-earned muscle. When he first spoke to me, I was so thrilled I almost couldn't talk, like a young teenage girl being spoken to by a rock star. One of his linebacker friends used to call out to him whenever he completed a great pass, in falsetto, "Oh, Whit honey, kiss my baby!" The whole team would crack up.

> At one of the first *Aid for AIDS* walkathons in Ann Arbor, Shelley is asked to be the keynote speaker, and I go along, clueless about anything having to do with gay people. It is 1993. Shelley stirs the group with stories of her brother Patrick, how lovely he had been, and she swears that he has not died in vain. Some people cry a little. Men are holding hands. After the speech, we sell T-shirts at a table as the walkers return triumphant. A disc jockey starts playing upbeat music and the air is joyful and full of sunshine. Men approach our table in pairs to comment on the design on the shirt, and they hug Shelley and thank her and shake my hand and look me in the eye and I look back. It is important that I look back. I must smile and be confident. A smallish muscular man, shirtless, begins dancing near the speakers, twirling in utter happiness and freedom in tight red jogging pants, and, in my heart, I dance too. He seems absolutely above all of us, in celebration of his mere presence amongst so many who are loving and caring enough to give up a glorious Saturday to come together. I am so happy that he is happy that my eyes water a bit, and I have that same feeling that I had felt once, so long before, when I had made the team.

As time went on and September arrived, it started to sink in that I had not been dismissed yet. Coach Mac, while busy with other important matters of running the team, seemed to like me, and the rest of the team adopted me as sort of a pet, a curiosity. My parents continued to worry, but there came a fabulous satisfaction when the school year began and the harsh pre-season practices ended, where my parents could tell their friends that I was healthy and an honest-to-goodness member of the football team. The smart Jewish boys at the Alpha Epsilon Pi house teased me ceaselessly about becoming the jock amongst them, and I could tell they were really happy to have me hanging around the frat, a sort-of real football player.

After a while, when the depth chart got established and I was in place in the far basement, I got moved over to the scout team with the other bottom dwellers to help teach the defense what could be expected from each upcoming opponent's offense. I took this role very seriously and worked as hard as I could each practice. Once I got to be Willie Gault, the world-class sprinter from Tennessee, and I was assigned an orange jersey with #80 on it. That's probably where the comparisons stopped, but I wore it with pride as the varsity boys pounded me.

One day, I was told to run a post-corner pattern against our first defense, which meant that I was supposed to run a long route, first looking over my inside shoulder to fake the defender and then suddenly turning to the outside. As I came out of my final turn, the ball was in the air and coming over my outside shoulder. I jumped higher than I ever had before and made a one-handed snatch, flipping over in mid-air and landing on my shoulder and head just in-bounds, ball in my grasp. The entire first offensive team and coaching staff, across the field, had just taken a water break at that moment and happened to be looking my way, and they let out a shriek of delight at my catch. I trotted back to the scout team quarterback and looked so cool as I casually flipped him the ball and rejoined the huddle, slapped and shrouded in praise by my teammates. Moments like those became my Saturdays. I belonged out there, if only for brief moments, on the occasional Wednesday.

As the season began, it became clear that this Vanderbilt team was special. Doc had made the players strong and fast with his demanding off-season strength program. Our offense turned out to be quite innovative, relying on a short passing attack in place of an inside rushing game, especially after our star running back, Ernie Goolsby, had gone down for the season in the opener at Memphis State. Our offensive coordinator, Watson Brown, who had been a former star quarterback at Vanderbilt just a few years earlier, was the true leader of the team, getting extra yards and touchdowns out of men much smaller than the ones you would find at Tennessee and Michigan and Notre Dame. After an early-season loss to Alabama, our season started to take shape.

Highly ranked Florida came to Nashville on a perfect night, and our bend-but-don't-break defense held them in place for much of the game, even though the great James Jones of the Gators (and later the NFL Detroit Lions) had over 200 yards rushing. One play on offense let us know we were blessed for the season. In the fourth quarter, Whit Taylor threw a ball that bounced off tight end Jim Popp's shoulder and right into the ready hands of receiver Phil Roach. Phil sprinted for the end zone some forty yards downfield, sure to score a touchdown. Somehow he was tackled and stripped of the ball just short of the goal line, and the football bounced free into the end zone. Lineman Rob Monaco, who had obediently pursued the play all the way downfield like all really good linemen should, pounced on the loose ball for a touchdown, and we won 38-31. Forty-two thousand loyal fans went crazy, and it was obvious that this team was going to be different from every other Vanderbilt team in recent memory.

We lost "between the hedges" down at Georgia after leading into the fourth quarter; had we won that game we would have been Southeastern Conference Champions and gone to the Sugar Bowl! Against Mississippi, linebacker Joe Staley came out of nowhere and intercepted a pass to preserve a narrow victory. Some people said that was the most important play of the year for the Commodores. With every dramatic win, a possible Bowl invitation loomed closer. People around the country were starting to talk about us. Gamblers in Las Vegas won a lot of money betting on Vanderbilt that year!

Surprisingly, I got to suit up against Virginia Tech in the middle of the season since they were non-conference. We destroyed them. Leading 45-0 in the final minutes, I realized that my teammates were starting to chant my name with big smiles on their faces. "Gerson! Gerson! Gerson!"

Holy Cow! Were they going to put me in? What would I do? I only knew a few of the plays! Coach Mac called me up beside him on the sideline! Oh no!

"Gerse," he said with his pixie grin and sad dog eyes, "I'd love to put you in, but I just didn't have a chance to check your eligibility yet, so I can't do it. You understand?"

He could see how shaken and relieved I was. "Coach, I'm so glad, 'cause if you put me in, my heart would probably come right out of my jersey."

That quote made the Monday *Tennesseean* in an article about how this Vandy squad was made of real team players, from superstar quarterback Whit Taylor all the way down to little Gary Gerson. Some people might have been offended by the opposite comparison to Whit, but I was thrilled, and so were all of my friends. My parents got sent copies of the paper from acquaintances all over the state, and they were just bursting with pride.

After that game, we all went into the locker room and listened to Coach Mac. He told us with great excitement that we had been invited to play in the Hall-of-Fame Bowl in Birmingham, Alabama, on New Year's Eve! All of the coaches were teary-eyed and hugging each other and jumping around, since most of them had really worked quite hard to shape our group of young men. It was the first winning season in 10 years for Vanderbilt. I was so proud of my team, and I found out that even the walk-ons like me would get to go with them to Birmingham!

There were a whole bunch of important looking men wearing suits in the locker room that day after the game, smiling and shaking hands with the players. One man, wearing a sticker on his lapel that said "Hall of Fame Bowl", came up to me and offered sincere congratulations. I thanked him and asked if he was on the Bowl committee, and he said, "No, son, I'm the Chancellor of Vanderbilt". It was Joe B. Wyatt, whom I had not recognized. Whoops. Guess I should have paid attention to the campus newspaper more often.

On the way out the door after showering, Doc handed me an envelope. Noticing my confusion, he told me with a gruff smile that it was meal money, allowed by the NCAA. Inside was $10. I was getting paid for all this too! I showed the $10 bill to my folks outside the stadium with great pride at what I had "earned". Dad wryly reminded me that another $10,990 and I could repay that year's tuition loan. Funny man, that Dad.

We beat Tennessee in the rain to end the season, and the newspaper picture of Whit Taylor with the ball held over his head as he crossed the goal-line with the winning touchdown on a gutsy quarterback keep was symbolic and satisfying. Leave it to Watson Brown to call a simple option play on the goal line… what a genius. Our final regular-season record was 8-3, the best in decades for starving Vandy fans.

A girl in Shelley's sixth grade science class stays after school to talk to her beautiful teacher, my wife. This girl's father happens to be the caretaker at that very cemetery where Shelley's brother and father are buried, and the girl lives on the grounds. ("Imagine", says Shelley to me, with great joy, "Being 11 years old and living at a cemetery!") The girl had invited a friend over that weekend, another student from Shelley's class, and together they had gone out to the Bryson gravesites and cleaned off the area and placed flowers at the headstones. Shelley had tears in her eyes all ready to spill, she tells me, and she hugged the girl mercilessly. While Shell cannot go into that cemetery, for she just is not able to look at the plot purchased for her years earlier, empty beside Patrick, she feels a blessing that Dad's and Pat's places are being loved by someone who lives right there next to them.

My parents had been season-ticket holders at the University of Tennessee for some twenty-five years, and even they had skeptically become Vanderbilt Commodore fans, especially after the inevitable victory over UT. And they were going to see their son on the sidelines of a bowl game in just a few weeks! Dad was a huge guy who could have played football at Penn if not for his bad neck, and all across the state his furniture customers asked about his son who had walked-on at Vandy. I believe that Dad was about as proud as a father could be when he talked about me to all those store owners. Whenever someone asked my parents if they got free tickets to the Vanderbilt games, they took great amusement in saying, "Free, hell! These tickets cost $10,000 each!"

While Coach Mac was a really nice person, and I really did not know much about the way a college program ran, it became clearer to me as the season flowed others were really in charge of the individual parts of the team. Doc was the person all the players looked to for direction, especially in the weight room, and his presence was felt every day in practice as he led stretches and shouted sparse praise and did a lot of butt-chewing. Coach Watson Brown was the brains and spirit behind our offensive success, and the individual defensive coaches were respected for getting much effort from an unspectacular and undersized corps of defenders. Coach Mac always lectured to us for a long five minutes before each game about how we would respond if we won the coin toss. Few listened to him since all the starters were thinking about their own responsibilities. Still, Coach Mac would sometimes go on and on about the sun position and wind and stuff like that while the big boys got more and more stagnant. He was the head coach, so he could say what he wanted, but it was interesting the way he lectured about not much. Hey, we were headed to a bowl game, and he was a Coach of the Year and the toast of Nashville. What did I know?

I figured out that if I drove to Birmingham from my grandmother's condo in Ft. Lauderdale, I could sell the airplane ticket that had been provided by the bowl committee and "legally" put a few dollars in my pocket. So I had the nerve to beg a ride to Birmingham from Allama Matthews, the tight end, and big cornerback Leonard Coleman, the interception king, two All-Americas who lived in Florida. Allama reluctantly said yes, probably thinking I would be an annoying little bug, but only if I drove part of the way while he slept. It was a deal. Of course, I had never driven stick shift before, but did he really need to know that?

In an interesting sidelight, there had been some early plan that we were going to play Stanford in the bowl game. What a great match up: the best academic teams from the South and the West, the best quarterbacks in Whit Taylor and Stanford's John Elway, and innovative offensive schemes to satisfy every fan and football connoisseur. That plan was buried when California beat Stanford in their season finale by returning a kickoff all the way for a touchdown while pitching the ball five times and running over a trombone player in the end-zone. That became one of the most famous football plays of all times, and it kept Stanford out of our bowl game. We would play against the Air Force, a tough team that ran the option, instead.

I spent Christmas with my family at my grandmother's condo in Florida, proud to be out on the beach with my new body, which had gotten some decent muscles from all that running and lifting. I loved going to the beach just so I could show off a little, no longer a little squirrel inside my shirt. More of a bigger squirrel.

Allama picked me up near the interstate in Ft. Lauderdale, and we continued on to Boynton Beach for Leonard. When we got there, I saw that Leonard, who would be in the NFL in a few years, lived in a tiny little house and had a little boy a few years old. This was a shocking thing to me, the naïve kid, that a college student could have a child that had obviously been fathered in high school. How awful and embarrassing for him! Mean Leonard, who scowled at me all during practice and never hesitated to bury his helmet between my shoulder blades when I tried to catch the ball, was kissing his little boy over and over as he said good-bye. It was a moment of confusion to me, compounded by mean and stoic Leonard living in the housing projects of Boynton Beach and loving his little boy so much. I knew nothing.

We decided to drive overnight and reach Alabama in the morning, and I got behind the wheel of Allama's Celica about midnight, hoping they wouldn't notice that my gear-shifting skills amounted to grinding hamburger. As they slept, I cruised down Interstate 10 near Tallahassee, happy to be safely in fifth gear and focusing on not falling asleep. I did not notice that the car I passed at 80 mph had blue lights on top. The Florida state policeman was kind to me as I nervously explained that the two sleeping giants in this car were Vanderbilt stars on the way to a bowl game, and he let me go, unimpressed, as he warned me to turn off my brights if I decided to pass another car on this road. Allama awoke just as we were free and driving away, and I told him to go back to sleep, everything was all right, except for my racing heart and dry mouth and the thought that I almost got a ticket in Allama's car.

We stopped near the Alabama border at 3 AM to see Allama's relatives, and we woke up the whole household on a dirt road just to say hello. I felt quite sheepish as a realized I was the only white person in this tiny, crowded house in the middle of the night. The two littlest children stared at me with their mouths open, and an easily-smiling man, perhaps their father, sat in a pair of shorts on the arm of an easy chair, gently stroking the head and face of a sleeping infant on his lap. Nobody really said anything to anybody but it was understood that the dropping-in was accepted and appreciated. After refusing a cold drink and some food, we continued on. Our visit there was soon only a dream, a world I would not know. And I would never begrudge the money these two men would earn in the NFL.

That week in Birmingham was like magic. We had easy practices, we had great hotel rooms, and the food was outstanding. After every meal, we received another envelope with fifteen or twenty dollars inside for "meal expenses." Over the whole week I pocketed about $125 while spending nothing on food. I supposed this was the only way the school and the Bowl could "pay" an athlete for all of his work while staying inside the NCAA's monetary rules. All of us college boys, especially those with kids at home in the housing projects, were not about to complain.

We went to a banquet thrown by the Birmingham Vanderbilt alumni (boy, were they ready to have a party for their long-suffering heroes), to fancy restaurants, and to a nightclub along with the Air Force team. The Bowl Committee had arranged a hypnotist for our entertainment, and my teammates literally pushed me up on stage as a "volunteer" from the audience. The hypnotist guy made me feel like, for some reason, I really wanted to do a striptease in front of everyone, spinning my jacket around and throwing it into the audience while undoing my shirt. I believe the audience was howling, but it never really became clear to me, like I was in a fog. How do those hypnotists do it? He stopped me just before I took off my pants, to the screams of my teammates. I would've done it.

In the lockers before the game, the coaches were walking in circles, looking up with tears in their eyes. They had just learned that our offensive coordinator, Coach Brown, had accepted the head-coaching job at the University of Cincinnati, a great loss for our team. That meant the breakup of an exceptional coaching staff that had brought our tiny school a great season, a bowl invitation, and a rare win against the Big Orange. The seniors got together, and before we took the field one of them went to the front of the locker room area and got all our attention. He announced that the seniors wanted to dedicate the bowl game to Coach Brown for his leadership and innovation through this great season. It was an uncommon and touching gesture. And then something curious happened.

Coach MacIntyre interrupted the seniors and spoke out to all of us, "No, no, you want to win this game for yourselves. We don't want to go making this into a dedication to any one person. This is all for *you*, not Coach Brown."

The room was a bit stunned. Coach Mac had taken a very sincere and gracious gesture and turned it around in front of all of us. Perhaps Coach Mac meant to give us, the players, praise for the fine season, but no one really took it that way as we looked around the room for some validation from our confused leaders. Shortly afterwards, we took the field, a little confused and certainly disappointed that the dedication was not allowed to stand. Oh well, on to the field we went for stretches in a carnival atmosphere. We were feeling too good to care about much anyway.

And so the game began. I stood on the sidelines while 75,000 people cheered us on in an amazingly full stadium. In the third quarter, Norman Jordan scored another touchdown on a pass from Whit Taylor as we were appearing to dominate our opponent. On the sideline after the play, I heard Norman say to his old and dear buddy Whit with a knowing smile, "We're just showin' off now!" Little did he know.

The audience, as well as our defense and the rest of the team, were stunned when the Air Force quarterback turned a crucial third-down sneak play into a very long touchdown run. That put the Force up for good, and they won by eight points, Vandy unable to catch up. There was not much sadness, really, as the game seemed anticlimactic compared to the season as a whole, especially when held against the Tennessee win, but it still stung a bit. A loss is always a loss.

Whit Taylor was saluted as player of the game, despite the score, having thrown for over 500 yards in a truly remarkable performance. This overshadowed, unfairly, the twenty (!) receptions by Norman Jordan, the tiny, dedicated running back who had been the X-factor in Coach Brown's offense this whole season, fighting back from second-team status in the early going. These two players had been friends and teammates forever, and it was the last game Norman would play in pads. Whit got drafted into the USFL and was a backup with the Michigan Panthers (Bobby Hebert was the first-stringer, and he was really good), came back to coaching at Vandy for my senior year, and then played a bit more in the Arena Football League. Everyone admired those two and their quiet leadership and how far they had taken little Vanderbilt. Norman soon became a stockbroker and made a lot of money and did fine color commentary for the 'Dores. Playing on the same team as them, and Will and Leonard and Allama and Joe, was a crazy honor for this little walk-on who spent the whole season in amazement and awe at this company.

So we all went home, but not before Mom took all kinds of photos of me and my teammates, with me looking embarrassed the whole time. What a year it had been, the best year in Vanderbilt football in forever, and I had been told by Whit and Norman and others worthy of respect that I had been a key part of our success. But looking back over the past several years it all came at a price, as football always does. I learned this for sure: you never play football for free. You may pay for it when you are sixteen, forty, or seventy. But you pay.

All through the season, I had been getting beat up on a daily basis. There was the helmet underneath my shoulder pads that knocked everything around my right deltoid out of place, my shoulder aching nonstop for the next several years. I had smashed every one of my fingers at some point, and there was practically no skin on my knees and elbows from the unforgiving artificial turf. Looking back at all the scabs and stingers and ice baths, there was no doubt that I had regularly gotten the shit kicked out of me by huge men, by the field, and by my own lack of preparation.

But I had not quit. I had never thought of quitting. And I had gotten stronger and faster and smarter. In the weight room, I was no longer a beginner, and I finally had some arms with a little meat on them. On the field, I had gotten a tiny bit of respect from men who were All-America and going to the NFL. It was worth every bit of pain. How do you explain this to someone who had never played football?

> I sit at my computer and type out the student reports, due every quarter. My tension is obvious. Shelley walks into the office and sees me deep in process and thought. She begins to talk to me, and I am unable to focus on her words; this is all due tomorrow and I have to plow ahead. So she stops and glides over in that way that she has, standing behind my chair. I feel her there, warm and lovely, but I continue typing. I get goose bumps from her presence, though she has not touched me yet, and I fight to not notice her. Her hands rise up and grab my knotted muscles between shoulder and neck, squeezing them, melting them. She does not have to, and I do not ask her to, and I am probably still mad at her for some trivial thing from before, down in the darkness of resentment. But she works out the kinks and she giggles, as I have to bow my forehead to the keyboard in ecstasy. She has surprised me once again with a rare, lovely, loving gesture. It is so nice to be kneaded.

Back in Morristown after the bowl game, I relaxed for the rest of winter break and saw some high school friends, and I even got invited to a party at the house of a really cool guy from my class. Back in high school I never got invited to parties, except by the thespians and the band members, most of whom participated in both as a nerd perfecta. I put on a tight shirt (actually, all of my shirts were tighter now, but this one particularly so around the neck and biceps) and went on over to his house, confident and glowing. At the party with all the cool people swirling around, loud music and cool people making me dizzy, I kept my arms folded so my meatiness would stand out a bit more. I was truly surprised when yet another cool guy came up and asked about football at Vanderbilt. I explained my year and he eagerly drank in every word I said, then he told me that had proven him wrong: "Gary, I never thought you'd do anything big with your life, not on this scale."

Now that might have been taken as an insult to some people, but I thought it was the greatest thing anyone had ever said to me, one nineteen-year-old to another. I ate it up.

Back at Vandy after Christmas, the second semester of that year was filled with weight lifting, football meetings, fraternity parties that I was invited to but never went, and attempts to blow off school in some fog of discontent. I still didn't know what I was doing there, and finding balance between my football efforts and academic progress was elusive. However, in one moment of enlightenment, I took a second geology class from a great teacher, Dr. Molly Miller. She vividly described the formation of Earth, dinosaurs, fossils, carbon dating, and other events that made my heart beat a little faster, stuff I had loved since I was a little boy. She was giving answers to questions I had never even known how to ask. I became friends with Bob Illes, a working-class third-string tight-end from Cleveland, and he persuaded me to join him and major in geology. We had spent a lot of time together on the meat squad, and he was a good guy, straightforward and smart, who busted his butt in the classroom and during study hall.

I had a decent spring practice session out on the Astroturf. The better receivers had some injuries, so I got a lot of practice time with the first and second team, and I gained a lot of confidence. Coach Sherman, the new receivers coach who had been my scout-team assistant, started to count on me quite a bit, and I caught a lot of passes against the first team. Coach Sherman emphasized, "Gerse, I'm gonna get the ball to you, so you be ready. I mean it, now!"

I heard most of what he was saying, though part of me couldn't believe it. The gap between me and the good ones started narrowing, my arms and neck and legs got big, and it started to become clear that I could play a little bit of ball. Even though I still had much to learn, I was in love with this game of football. Vanderbilt football. The guys who beat Tennessee.

Chapter 3: Infatuation and Football

I hadn't heard from her in a year. And then one day, after the old season was buried and work on the next one had begun, the Jenny that I had kept in that closet in my heart invited me up to Butler University for her sorority formal. My old girlfriend had transferred to the Indianapolis school for her sophomore year, perhaps hoping to start afresh as a grown-up, away from our youth trappings. I showered quickly after one of the spring practices, jumped into the old station wagon (10 miles to the gallon) and flew up the interstate towards Indianapolis. Got stopped for speeding and sat through the officer's lecture with my teeth clenched, getting hotter and later by the minute, wishing he would get my spanking over with and let me go already. "You do know you were going over the speed limit, don't you?"

What do you say to that, I mean really? "Yes sir."

She greeted me with her shy smile and my heart went all crazy with that familiar feeling, great hope and infatuation bubbling up, out of control. How could I ever have lost my love for her, my dreams of that sweet face?   We went off to the Holiday Inn Holidome and danced and talked with her friends and their dates, the Butler guys impressed that I was a "real" Division I football player. I was Jenny's long-lost boyfriend, the jock, and that was cool. She was prettier than I remembered, blossoming in some interesting way, and I was strong and confident, different. The evening passed in a blur. We kissed and snuggled together all night, and I left the next day believing that poor Jenny had been starved for me. My head and heart were full.

So now I had to ruin it.

When I got back to Vanderbilt, I wrote Jenny a letter. I was going to be the noble guy, giving her a chance to see if I was really what she wanted. After thanking her for the wonderful weekend, I told her that I would be dating other people (even though I had no intention to) and that she should also. The letter insulted her, and I was too dumb to see why.

A week later I got her response, in a letter all hot and mean. She told me that she was actively dating other men, had met a "great guy" while partying with her friends at Purdue, and was not the studious and reserved girl I had thought she was. I was stunned. It hurt to think that she might like some guy as much as me, might let him kiss her, might open her heart to him. My head reeled and my chest tightened.

I immediately called her. "Did you really mean it? Do you really have another boyfriend?"

"Wouldn't you like to know? You're off playing football so what do you care?"

She was cold and distant, hinting at affairs with some other boy, just leading me nose first into a jealous abyss, one that I probably deserved. My heart thickened as it hammered inside my chest. The conversation ended abruptly, and I was sickened to think that I had lost my sweet and pure Jenny. And it was all my fault.

I agonized over Jenny for the next several weeks, calling her in tears to find out if she was still looking at others. She seemed delighted to tell me that, yes, too bad, she was. By the end of the school year, I was pleading with her to come back to me, to be my innocent little girlfriend once more. I was a sad case, chasing things that did not exist, hoping for things that were not, and blind and deaf to the difference.

I tried to focus on school, but slacked off on my work, failed my history class and was placed on academic probation. I had to petition to return in the fall, and this meant taking the dreaded summer classes. What an idiot I was.

In summer school my concentration somehow returned, and I was able to push Jenny out of my mind. Some switch got flipped on (was it because I was now 20?). I learned how to study, and I finally started going to every class, which is the first rule of college success. My second American history instructor was fantastic, a guest lecturer from Tennessee Tech who effortlessly spun colorful tales of the Civil War and Roosevelt's New Deal as if they were romantic stories. I got all my grades up high enough to come off probation by the end of the summer, barely, with two A's and a B. The whole thing was embarrassing, but my folks were very supportive, even though I had refused to show them my report card that had the F stamped across it.

I spent every summer afternoon over at McGugin, lifting weights under Doc's glare and catching footballs with the other receivers and the quarterbacks. I put on more weight and learned how to catch the ball with my fingers instead of my chest, and we all worked on form and technique every chance we got (I just watched the good ones and did what they did, exaggerating every move and spin). Most enjoyably, I played pick-up basketball every day with members of the Lady Commodores basketball team. This made me faster and stronger and gave me great wind in my lungs, running hard for hours.

I got to be fast friends with those amazing and elegant ladies, finding ways to work on sprints and coordination up and down the court during the pick-up games. The women seemed to like playing ball with me, probably because I always hustled on defense at all times, unlike the other males out there whose egos would not allow them to appear to work too hard against "girls". That was no problem for me. There was not a lot of ego there to get in the way.

Over the summer, Jenny transferred back to University of Tennessee over in Knoxville, and then immediately transferred again over to David Lipscomb University in Nashville, so my pathetic pleading had seemed to have worked. It was obvious that she had moved in order to stay close to me, playing for my approval, trying to regain that joy of our youth together, but we still never really talked about why she was doing what she was doing.

She must have been disappointed that I was going on with my plans to continue football, especially after whining like such a sad little boy all the previous spring, and then her transferring closer and all. I expected more from her than she had to give, I had no idea what she expected from me, and the dance continued. I alternated between deep undying love for her and confusion at her disapproval of me trying to play a game that probably seemed pointless, me in way over my head.

When all the players returned for my second pre-season camp in August, things were different from my first year. I was faster and more efficient when I ran, I had lots of energy, and I caught everything that came anywhere near me. My teammates seemed fascinated by my progress and my big arms ("Gerson on the *juice!*" they joked), and the coaches also seemed astonished that I was beating the defensive backs. I felt strong in some new way. Then again, when you start at zero, any improvement is obvious.

While I still held little expectation for playing time that season, it was apparent that I was going to have to be considered for something, somewhere, perhaps on one of the special teams, perhaps as the third wide receiver or flanker. As the season opener started getting closer and closer, and I seemed to be eating up the defensive unit on the scout team, I felt like I owned the field. I grabbed every ball, even when it was thrown short or behind me, and the coaches starting learning my name and noticing me on the grass. All you really need is one defensive coach to start yelling at his d-backs to verify your effect as a scout-team receiver: "Hey, how can you let Gerson get open?   Get your head in it!"

This was getting interesting!

And then one Monday just before the Maryland opener, as I caught a swing pass and turned upfield on the last play of a light practice day, I hit a wall. The great free safety, Manuel Young, whom I loved for his brave performance on every down, grabbed my jersey after the catch, no harm intended. My cleated foot was planted firmly in the grass, and the shoe stayed stuck while my body spun. The loud pop was the base of my tibia cracking, and I actually felt the blood, free of its bony channels, rush in to fill up my lower leg. That was some serious pain, and it came quick.

The thing I will remember most as the team jogged off the field as practice ended, many of them oblivious to my crumpled heap over on the sideline, was the defensive coach, Kurt van Valkanburgh standing over me. While I had not been directly under his jurisdiction, I had been responsible as a scout-teamer for trying to make his defensive backs better. He had seen my improvements from the very beginning, and he was a respected coach. He just looked at me sadly, his head gently shaking, a furrow on his brow. The expression on his face seemed to speak for him, as if he were saying, "Gerse, after all your hard work..." Then they carted me off.

I had to watch my team flounder for the rest of the season, trying to yell encouragement from the sidelines without getting in the way, but I felt like I was annoying everyone. The cast stayed on for seven weeks, and when it came off we were just finishing a very disappointing 2-9 season. Mine had been the first of a dozen injuries to our star players, including that same Manuel Young, who had broken *his* ankle in the Maryland opening game, five days after breaking mine. Another *Tennesseean* article preceded the final game at Tennessee referring to the "Gerson

Curse," coined by the beat reporter Jimmy Davy. It was kind of cute, referring to our many injured players and me being the first one to go down.

After the injury, I started going to classes religiously and actually earned some respectable grades. I really liked the professors in the geology department, especially the paleontologist Len Alberstadt and the mineralogist Arthur Reesman, and I started working harder to show them that I was capable. My buddy Bob and I continued taking all the classes necessary for satisfying the geology major, and we became good friends, me the goofy, artsy, wise guy, and Bob the straight, blue-collar hard-working student-athlete. We started spending evenings and nights in the geology lab, studying fossils and minerals and thin-sections of igneous and metamorphic rock, frantically attempting to interpret complicated phase-diagrams and somehow understand the very basic laws of thermodynamics and crystal growth. We worked our butts off (him harder than me), quizzed each other nightly, and our grades rose. The professors starting calling us by our first names and seemed amused by our Mutt-and-Jeff partnership.

Every midnight after studying was done, Bob and I watched "Three's Company" reruns on his tiny television in the room he shared with Pat Kalnas, another underused football player. Sometimes they had a beer or two or three or four. At those times, Bob often had tobacco spittle or the remnants of a Wendy's Frosty streaming down his chin. We laughed as he spoke with great reverence of the comic skills of John Ritter on television as Jack Tripper. I told Bob he was an idiot for liking that dumb show, which always made him furious, which made me laugh at him more as he drooled all over his dirty T-shirt. Bob would say in a fake stutter, "Wha- wha- what are you talking about? R-r-r-ritter should get the Emmy this year!"

I also made friends with an extremely kind defensive lineman who had just returned to the team after a year's leave. Karl Jordan had a huge smile and a massive chest, so tight and cut it looked like two brown leather pillows were strapped across his ribcage. He was a solid and chiseled man, and he first approached me in the weight room when I needed a spotter on the bench press, the cast still on my leg. He gave me a lift-off and kept my arms in-line during my repetitions. Karl did not speak until I was finished, an accepted sign of respect, even though the weight I was managing up over my chest was negligible for someone like him.

"You the Gerse," he smiled at me, his slight lisp instantly endearing, his tone conspiratorial. "I heard about you."

He talked as if I was famous, with a wink in his voice. I liked him immediately, this huge lineman impressed by some tiny backup receiver like me. Karl had missed the bowl game during his year off, but he was working to get back on the team now. He seemed like a guy who had paid his dues, and everybody respected him.

KJ moved in right around the corner from me on the football floor, and we spent many late nights talking about our dreams and loves. He always kept an air of mystery about himself, not wanting to reveal too much but letting me know I was welcome in his world. We were an unusual pair, a giant black man who looked unbelievably mean, and a small Jewish receiver, goofy and naive, but we accepted that our paths were meant to cross. He teased me about my home-town honey, insisting I was just "whipped" by her, and I prodded him about his sexual conquests, imagining him to be master of that realm while he insisted he was not. At that time I had thought every good-looking football player was incredibly and effortlessly sexually active with dozens of pretty girls every night. Except me, of course. He just laughed and laughed when I talked about that kind of stuff. "Gerse, you a trip."

Yeah, yeah, I might be a trip, KJ, but give me some pointers so I can get some girls, willya?

When I went back to football that spring after the ankle healed, Jenny and I drifted apart once more in a semi-agonizing silence. Dealing with her was not much fun as she sulked about all the attention I gave football, and I played the martyr for her not understanding. What a lousy dance it was. And then we were not dancing anymore.

Following the dismal season, one year after that great Bowl Game, Doc made it his job to lay down the law and get us going in some positive direction. He organized form-running workouts at 6 in the morning all through the winter and spring, and he made sure that the senior leaders would chastise anyone who was late or skipped any session. He dictated, "Any member of each unit who is late will mean the seniors will work it off. Too bad for them."

This tactic worked, and our shared misery brought us closer and gave us all a sense of direction, one unit with common goals. The seniors carried us through the early morning agony and made damn sure we were there on time.

We all had to wake up at 5:30 and, in the mean January cold, trudge over to the track together. God, it seemed like a long way with dark and frost looming all around. The linemen were told to push Doc's jeep over so he could sit where it was warm and watch, and I guarantee that the linemen hated doing it. We jumped and bounced and sprinted and practiced every type of loaded direction-change Doc could think of, one day on the track and one day in the frosty field, and it was brutal on everybody. There was moaning and puking and gasping for breath. We loved it, cursing.

I did respectable work with the big boys in the early morning, considering I was just coming off a pretty bad injury, and the springs in my legs started to come back some. The best part of the whole deal was that we had huge breakfasts after every session, even the walk-ons. The brothers who ran McConnell Catering, huge Vandy fans, came over and made a big deal out of all of us, thrusting huge plates of eggs and bacon and sweet rolls at us until we were stuffed. This made going to 8 AM classes not so unbearable, but by 9:00 I had to drag my sad body back to my room for a nap, feeling drugged from lack of sleep and hard work, my legs all quivery. It was like I had never really been tired before. *This* was tired!

I was able to continue my lifting and basketball program in those summer months before my senior year, my third season on the team, and I got closer with some of the lady basketball players. Karen Booker was this beautiful forward on the team, a starter, and I stuck to her passionately when I had to cover her during a pick-up scrimmage. That was probably my first respectful relationship with a female my own age, where my expectations were real and my affections level. I often wished I had started a romantic relationship with that lovely woman, though she stood several inches taller than me and was a star, but I was too chicken to even think of it. She had the most beautiful eyes, though her hands were curiously moist and cold, which we laughed about. Once we held hands and watched TV together in her room, but it never went further. Dummy.

Karen ended up being an MVP for the Lady Commodores, then a coach and a pro in Japan. I think of her sometimes, having written her a couple of letters right after college, and today I wonder if she ever remembers me. She was so nice and so lovely.

Our football team remained close through the summer, everyone working out together and eating at the same time. The athletic department found it economical to hire the wonderful McConnell family again instead of opening up the training table, and they brought in a real southern supper to the McGugin Center each evening for the athletes. Without breaking any NCAA rules, I made an arrangement with Charlie McConnell to help him set up the buffet and pour sweet tea and lemonade for the athletes in exchange for supper each night. That fried chicken was worth every ounce of work I gave, and I strangely enjoyed the extra humility I gained by serving my teammates and cleaning up after them. They kidded me, but my friends knew I was working hard for my green beans and apple pie, and for my team, and that was worth something.

My third season on the team started with not much to write about. I had not improved as dramatically as I had in the previous fall, and a step of my quickness was gone from the injury to my poor ankle, which was still puffy and tender and rigid. A crop of talented freshmen was brought in, and a couple of promising new receivers pushed me back to the bottom of the list again. Any distant thoughts of me becoming a "producer" on this year's team evaporated quickly, and I resigned myself to contributing, once again, on the scout team. There, at least, I could be a leader in some respectable way.

So I did my best, and I really loved the guys who were out there with me, fighting to stay alive versus the first defense. John Bell Whitesell was a country boy, a walk-on like me who had little thought of actually taking the field as a running back, though he was strong enough to be a member of the kick-return team as a "reward" for his efforts.

On the scout team, John Bell was hilarious as he acted overly polite, a big grin spreading across his face, seeming to be so pleased to see us all once again as we returned to the scout quarterback after each play. He would say, enthusiastically, "After you! No, I insist!" when joining the huddle, and "Why, thank you very much!" if complimented by one of us after a good run. We'd hoot and holler at that, though breathless.

John Bell, Bob Illes, Pat Kalnas, and I ended up forming a "supper club," going to some hole-in-the-wall near campus every Tuesday night for all-you-can-eat spaghetti on paper plates from a friendly Chaldean named Said. John Bell, in his overdone country accent, pronounced the owner's name "Sah-yeeeeed," which Said loved. We spent those evenings trying to out-polite each other, rushing to open doors and hand out napkins. Those guys were quite large, so onlookers must have thought we were crazy, but the key to it all was remaining overly-sincere and gracious to the point of nausea. "After you! No, after you! I insist!" Other customers would chuckle.

One of our highlights was the time Said let us try his water pipe, filled with a sweet tobacco. John Bell let another wide smile smear his face next to the spots of spaghetti sauce as he exclaimed, "Shweet, Sah-yeeeed!" while the white smoke dribbled out of the corners of his mouth. We rolled on the floor for an hour. John Bell later became a lawyer, which I still find hilarious, but I bet he works his butt off for his clients. God, I loved playing ball with that guy.

When that third year got under way, Doc had us good and ready. We charged out of the gates and opened the season with four consecutive wins, including a stunning upset of Alabama in Tuscaloosa, engineered by quarterback Kurt Page and gruff offensive coordinator Lynn Amedee, who had no idea that I existed. While the great Alabama coach Bear Bryant had recently retired, they say that this game was the one that put him in his grave. We were 4-0 and in the top twenty in the country after 'Bama, and Coach Mac was the toast of the national sports scene once again.

While it was understood by the team that Doc had gotten us into this attitude of winning, the press and community was giving Coach Mac credit for our success. More and more, Doc, company man that he was in his loyalty to the coach, moved to the background so Coach Mac could have his glory. As Doc moved away from us and

Coach Mac tried to lean in as "motivator," things began to slip away. Doc had pushed us to win, and Coach Mac was urging us not to lose.

Tulane slunk into Nashville with a record of 0-4 and soundly thrashed us on every down of the game. One of their defensive backs took to taunting our sidelines mercilessly with trash talk as the final minutes ticked away. He humiliated us by running back and forth, just out of reach, taunting, "Y'all ain't nothin'! Y'all ain't shit!" The season was over, our confidence spent.

We barely contested Tennessee and the season ended in great disappointment with a 5-6 record after such a great start. Coach Mac remained as coach due to past "success," but it was clear that he was not the one to lead us to another bowl game. The season of great promise disappeared. Somewhere, our season of potential had been squandered and a stack of confidence misplaced. Then would come the winter of greatest shame for all of Vanderbilt sports.

A couple of weeks after the football season finished, word got back to the dorms that Doc was in trouble. Since everyone in the athletic community worshipped him, we all tried to rally to his side, but he had made himself quite unavailable. The word around town was "steroids," and this was as serious as college sports could get in the middle of the 1980's. There were a lot of rumors, and it took a while for the smoke to clear and the truth to wind out. The story unfolded and it had been a tangled web waiting to snag somebody, Doc being the sacrifice to society for our evils.

Here's the way we think it unfolded. A track star at Clemson University had died. The autopsy had shown phenylbutezone, a performance-enhancing drug often used on horses, in his bloodstream. The prescription bottle found in his college room had been traced back to a Nashville pharmacist, who happened to be a friend of Doc's, a guy who worked out with us in the Vanderbilt weight room. And it was learned that Doc had somehow been involved in getting this prescription through that druggist for another friend at Clemson, who gave it to the dead track star. It might have been minor involvement, a reference or something, but Doc's name was out there. Lots of inquiries were made into that pharmacist's records, and there were many unexplained orders of anabolic steroids. More questions were asked and the flames got hotter. Local newsmen swarmed in to get this story of national and societal importance. *Steroids.* What a word.

The athletes all talked to each other in closed rooms, in whispers, trying to find ways to stay out of trouble and keep Doc safe. I had a flashback to earlier days in the weight room hearing Doc tell a couple of athletes that steroids were terrible, that they would ruin you, that they were bad for your health. "You don't want to be doin' that shit, y'hear?"

But it became clear that somehow, in a roundabout way, some athletes had learned where to get some "safe" steroids, from Doc's buddy the druggist. Did Doc have anything to do with this? That was unclear. I want to think not, but I will never know that answer.

In my heart I knew that Doc had had only the interests of the athletes on his mind. We all knew that a football player who wanted steroids would get them no matter what. And if that athlete bought his steroids from an illegal seller on the black market, who knows what nasty substances would actually be in those vials, injected into those strong thighs? Young men hoping for miraculous strength and recovery could end up poisoning themselves. The only answer to that problem was the purchase of steroids from a "safe" dealer. Not taking steroids, for some of these men, was not an option.

Everyone knew that Doc would never hurt anyone associated with Vanderbilt. He had gotten us so far. Most of the press pointed fingers at several of the athletes, blaming them for lots of evil and wrongdoing, saying that using steroids was cheating. But I knew these guys, and they were not cheaters. I had seen them work their asses off every day.

While I had been naive enough to accept the inside jokes and talk about steroid use, all of us were also deeply aware of the reasons why a kid would inject. If you weighed 280 pounds and could bench-press 400 pounds, and the guy across the line from you out on the grassy field weighed 290 and could bench-press 450, which one would have been more likely to win the battles on every down? Which one, in his own mind, stood the better chance of getting the extremely elusive NFL contract? If those two were on the same team, which one would get to start? That was the line of thinking of the steroid user. Anabolic steroids may not have actually made someone a better football player, but the added confidence of extra weight and the illusion of extra strength could work wonders on the young athlete's psyche. The laws of physics, especially those involving inertia and momentum with increased mass, did not lie. And, of course, the athlete on performance-enhancing drugs might be able to recover faster as well, quickly ready for the next day's battle in the weight room and on the field.

Jimmy Davy of the *Tennesseean* was the fellow who broke the story, and the sight of him at McGugin Center started making people anxious and angry. This nice fellow who had covered our games and practices, and had earlier written a couple of articles that included me, was now seen as a rat, rooting through all the trash at Vanderbilt. He was soon taken off the beat for his own safety, and none of us ever saw him again. He probably felt lucky that an over-reacting football player did not try to hurt him, so passionate was everyone when these matters surrounding Doc came to light. Lots of strong young men were very mad and frustrated then, and they would have fought lions and crocodiles for Doc, no doubt. I wonder to this day if Mr. Davy has any regrets as to what happened to our team.

The athletic director, Roy Kramer, was a former football coach and was highly respected by everyone in the community and in the NCAA. He called a meeting of the football team, and we were silent and wide-eyed as he entered the room. He was grave, serious, and focused. Mr. Kramer had the voice of a leader, and many of us in the room thought that he would have been a great coach for our team right then, like he had once been up at Central Michigan.

Mr. Kramer spoke in a very stern voice about our conflict. It was the first time in my three years on the team that I heard someone address steroid usage with any seriousness. He said, point blank, "I will give this team one week. At the end of this week we will begin frequent and random urine tests, and anyone who has even a tiny amount of anabolic steroids in his system will be told to leave this school and forfeit his scholarship."

And then he let us have it with some more unexpected information. "We have a list of the student-athletes at this school who have been involved in the purchase of steroids. If you come and speak to me today, in my office, I will make sure that you are protected from prosecution by the law. But you will be admitting guilt. You will be called an 'unindicted co-conspirator.' In no way will you be punished for this admission."

We looked around the room at each other with wide eyes as he continued. "Men, it is time for us to come clean in every sense of the word."

This was serious! The room was silent and uneasy, and someone asked about Doc. Mr. Kramer told us that Doc was on a leave of absence, and it was too early to tell what would happen next with him, but we all knew that there was little hope that he would be back. We were requested to speak to no reporters of any type, as that might serve to hurt Doc. There were a lot of scared kids in that room at that moment, frightened for themselves and mourning our beloved Doc. Mr. Kramer was tender for just a moment as he said, "We all love Doc. I love Doc. But our words can only hurt him as they will for sure be used against him. Please be careful what you say, especially to the media. It is better to say nothing."

When the list of unindicted co-conspirators was published in the newspaper, it was a shocking number. About half the team was on that list, including some names of kids I would never, ever have suspected. I felt like such an idiot for not knowing about all these guys, but I also felt terribly sorry for them. I could only imagine the humiliation of what it was like for them to have to tell their parents about what they had done. In fact, my parents even asked me if I had been involved in any of this, seeing as I had become stronger and faster since my first days on the team. They had no idea that my growth was insignificant compared to most of those who had injected. Shoot, I could barely bench press 185 pounds on my finest lift. Compared to some full-tank linemen who were well over 400 pounds on the bench, my needle was at zero.

Over the next week, you could see lots of linemen and linebackers "deflate" as their steroid-enhanced water retention had been stopped out of fear of dismissal. These guys instantly got smaller and lost their muscular definition; it was amazing to see the transformations. Coach MacIntyre made himself accessible during all of this, but it was also clear that he was not to be held responsible for any of our possible wrongdoings. Basically, he had stated to the press and administration that he had had no idea that there was any steroid use on the team, and the allegations had shocked him. In a way, this gave us all the appearance of Coach Mac leaving Doc to twist in the wind, alone, even though we all knew that he loved Doc like a brother.

I had another memory of the previous summer, when one of the defensive ends showed up to start his lifting program in July. He was tall and considerably skinny then. A week or two later, he was obviously much bigger and I heard Coach Mac in the weight room exclaim in mock innocence with a wink, upon seeing his bigger athlete, "Hey, who blew you up?" I think he knew.

Doc was put on hold for the whole of winter and spring, and Coach Mac tried to build some team spirit by attempting to emulate Doc's spring program from the previous year. The assistant coaches took turns getting us up at 6 AM for form running, but they had no idea how to motivate and correct our form as we ran. The seniors were frustrated but continued to try to lead by example. I was one of them, though there was a limit to the number of teammates who took me seriously.   Doc would have made them listen to me. He would have held me up as a senior who deserved respect, like he had done for all seniors. But he was gone.

I was on schedule to graduate that May, but, knowing I had one full season of eligibility remaining, and still being completely and totally dedicated to our team, I applied to graduate school in order to play that one final season. I somehow got into the Vanderbilt Owen School of Business, thinking that I might become a sports agent or work for some sports firm after receiving an MBA. However, just as the next school year was starting, I realized that I did not want to wear a suit and argue about numbers for the rest of my life. So, I went to Dr. Reesman, my old advisor in the geology department, and he arranged for me to transfer into the masters program in geology. I realized then that geology had been a wonderful part of my young life, and I was quite happy to be back on familiar turf.

In May a letter from Jenny, congratulating me on graduating, surprised me. She had transferred, once again, back to Butler, her fifth move. The letter made my heart pound, especially since she told me that she had heard a lecturer at school who reminded her of me in that the speaker had some really deep and meaningful thoughts about life. Wow! That meant that she had some appreciation for my depth (ha!) and thought that I was something special! That letter started me thinking about her again, slowly at first, and then constantly. And these thoughts eventually snowballed into the belief that Jenny had searched the world and had realized that I was magnificent. My doomsday ego had returned for a final round.

To my parents' chagrin, I decided to forego graduation ceremonies and drive up the east coast of the United States and across half of Canada with my friend Bob. We had done all of our studies together, and we were going to look at geological formations and sleep in tents like the academic vagabonds we imagined ourselves to be.

Bob had finished the year with an overall GPA of 3.51 and had been named Academic All-America; I was extremely proud of him, and a lot of his work ethic had rubbed off on me, causing my own GPA to rise every semester. Once thought to be a washout as a football player, Bob had also surprised a lot of people by seeing considerable action at tight end during his final season, subbing for starter Jim Popp, an eventual draft choice of the Chicago Bears.

The coaches had kept trying to put other players in at tight end, but they all made mistakes or dropped the ball or became too unreliable in other ways, and Bob always knew where he was supposed to be and played hard every down. So he got playing time, and earned every second, and I was proud of him for that as well, for not quitting like so many others would have done. After three-plus seasons of being kicked around by the coaches, he finally became a significant team-member on Saturdays. He had one more year of eligibility, but after his graduation he silently told the coaches to shove it by taking his diploma and running off to grad school. Smart boy.

Our trip up the coast was a lot of fun, though we were horribly unprepared for the cold and rain and raccoons all along the way. Bob's tent was a rickety old thing that leaked and fell in the wind, and Bob snored like a jackhammer. I often had to sleep with my head outside just to get away from his buzz saw tonsils, even though it was cold as hell.

We drove all the way to Nova Scotia and I fell in love with that whole area, especially the giant granite outcrops at Peggy's Cove outside of Halifax. One night, we decided to drop in on a local bingo game, and I somehow won the final jackpot, which was an unbelievable $200 Canadian. We slept in a real hotel that night and ate the expensive local delicacy of scallops and lobster, sleeping like millionaires. Bob laughed and laughed when I got that final number, the locals grumbling.

Unfortunately, I was unable to keep my focus away from Jenny all during this great trip, and I bored Bob many times with sighs and dreamy talk of "what ifs" along the way. When I got back to Morristown after dropping Bob off in Cleveland, I gave Jenny a call, and we agreed to meet at my house. I was so nervous I could not think, as my imagination had led me to believe that this was the same innocent Jenny that I had always loved.

The night was warm and lovely. We went to a movie and then took a walk and talked about where we were each going in our lives. She seemed happy for me in all my pursuits, and we kissed. It all felt so natural and good, and it appeared that she actually appreciated me going back for that one last year of football as a graduate student. Meanwhile, she was to be back up at Butler finishing her final year, just a five-hour drive up the interstate. After that date, we both went back to school, visions of her angelic face and pouty lips firmly planted in the front of my brain. She had worn Love's Baby Soft, clearly for me.

In my final August football camp, I tried to get the coaches to notice me. Dreams of catching a real pass in a real game still remained, though I was willing to be a hard worker back on the scout squad. There was always the chance that I could earn a spot on one of the specialty teams, so I volunteered for every scout squad just so the coaches would see me. I rushed up the middle against the first punt squad, and Jeff Holt hit me so hard my shoulder popped and turned blue, but I kept coming back for more. I ruptured my bursa on my right elbow and it swelled up like a purple grapefruit, and I tore all kinds of ligaments in my constantly swollen fingers, but I stayed. I tried to be a real leader out on the scout team, chewing out the clumsy freshmen when they did not move as quickly or give as good of a picture to our defense as they could have.

One day in the middle of the season, one of the freshman linemen missed an assignment, and I chewed him out a little. He shrugged. On the very next play, he made the same mistake. I pulled him aside and told him that he was not helping the team with his poor attitude. He barked at me, "You ain't my coach, so shut up."

I was incensed that someone would talk to a senior that way, especially me, so I told him to get back in the huddle or make me shut up. He pushed me hard, and I came back and shoved him surprisingly far back, seeing as he was almost twice my size. As he came at me, preparing to grab at my facemask, I flicked my foot up into his groin, scoring a direct hit on his poor gonads. He stopped in his tracks, stunned, and dropped to one knee. At that exact moment, I felt my entire football career at Vanderbilt slip quickly away. A teammate *never* kicked a teammate in the crotch; that just was not done in football. And I felt everyone, the coaches, the players, my friends, all move one step back from me in disgust. I had screwed up in a big way, and there was nothing I could do to take it back.

As the next few weeks went by, my teammates stopped joking with me, and I was no longer the cute little walk-on. Because we were in the middle of a horrible 3-7-1 season, no one had been in the mood for dealing with discontent amongst the ranks, and the coaches were quite impatient with me. They stopped calling on me to jump into the extra scout team drills, and I felt like I had been secretly blackballed. And deservedly so.

The only thing I could do was go talk to Coach MacIntyre. I had thought that he liked me, and he would help me figure out how to get back in good graces. Time was running out for playing in a real game.

I knocked on Coach Mac's office door for the first time since joining the team, and he cheerfully invited me in to sit on his couch. "What can I do for you, Gerse?" he asked with that smile on his face.

"Well, coach," I started, unsure of myself, "I've been working real hard so far this year, and it's getting down to the last few games, and I was hoping I could get to play a little in the real games..."

A surprised and delighted expression came across him, as if I had asked him for a million dollars. "Why, Gerse, I can't do that to you," he said in a protective voice. "Now where would you think you could play?" he asked in seeming disbelief.

His response to my request sounded as if I was not really a football player, after all this time, and it knocked the wind out of me. I had to reach deep for enough breath to continue. "Coach," I started to plead, "I don't want to play all the time, just maybe on one of the special teams. Like punt rush. I've been working on that with the scout team..."

There was a sharper edge to Coach Mac's voice as he inquired, "Scout team? That's not real football, come on now, son. And whose place would you take on the punt rush? Son, that's rough out there with the real players. It ain't a game, it's a war."

I answered that I could be the outside man, like Kermit Sykes, or...

He cut me off, almost angrily, "Now Gerse, you ain't nowhere near as good as Kermit, and you ain't gonna take his place out there."

I was starting to choke up out of frustration, realizing that my chances were running out. I could hardly speak. "Well, what about somewhere else? Maybe on kickoff?"

He was stern now. "Gerse, you ain't big enough or fast enough, and that's that." Then, gently, as if it was decent of him to feel for me, he added, " I'm afraid you might get hurt out there..."

My face was hot, and I felt tears coming. After all those injuries on the practice field, the broken leg, the ruptured bursa, the grinding shoulder, the stunned and swollen fingers, the 6 AM wake-ups, he was daring to tell me that he feared for my safety! As I started to argue further, not ready to accept that I would never get to play on a Saturday, Coach Mac stood up and ushered me out of his room, telling me that he was busy, go on, go eat some supper. I stumbled out with no air left in my lungs.

I held up my head until I reached the practice field in the back yard of McGugin, and then, alone, I wept with big wracking sobs. I felt all of my love for the game and the team drifting from my bones, and it hurt me unlike any other hurt. All that work, all that unselfishness, had gone unrecognized by those in charge. Yes, I had screwed up a couple of times, but I had given everything I had for the team, including my "girlfriend," my health, my precious time, and my heart. And it did not matter to anyone, not even Coach Mac. In fairness, his job was in question at that point, and it was obvious to anyone else that I was the least of his worries as his final season was coming to a close.

After I walked away from the practice field with two varsity footballs I had found under one of the tarps, I found that I needed to think, so I did not go to practice for a couple of days. Very few players, and no coaches, called me to find out where I was, confirming that nagging feeling of unimportance inside me, fostering my sense of martyrdom. KJ came by to check on me a few times, but I ignored him, so he left me to my thoughts. By that time he was just trying to hang on to what was left of his last season.

Soon I realized that I wanted to "hurt" the team and coaches by not showing up. But I also realized that I sorely missed the daily games against the first defense, and that I was being a petty little quitter. So I went back.

I was sort of welcomed back by some of my friends on the team, and it felt natural to go out and catch passes against our best defense, getting them ready for the next game. The work was always there, and I stayed and finished out the season.

At the last home game against Virginia Tech, my fraternity brothers had arranged a surprise for me, much to the delight of my teammates and the embarrassment of myself. First, there was a poster in the corner of the end zone that read "GERSON #23 FOR HEISMAN". The guys on the team couldn't get over that and kept laughing up until kickoff.

As the game got under way, some of the players pointed to the student section across the field. My frat brothers had smuggled in a bunch of large cards, no easy feat since hand-posters were banned at Vanderbilt, which read "GERSON 23" on one side and "HEISMAN" on the other. There was one letter or number per card, and they kept flipping the cards back and forth in unison; it was hilarious. They were not done.

After half-time, KJ came over to me and told me to look up in the air. Sure enough, there was an airplane hauling around a banner that read "GERSON FOR HEISMAN". This was unbelievable, and the crowd loved it. My fraternity brothers, who had no idea of my frustrations and sadness, who imagined I had been content to hold the coach's headset wires during the games, had, in those simple gestures, offered some strange validation, and I loved them. I didn't get to play, but nobody cared. Bruce Smith was an All-America defensive end at Virginia Tech, and he killed us.

Our last game of the season was at Tennessee, and before the game Coach Mac cautiously approached me with a kind look on his face. He asked, "Are you all right now, Gerse?"

I said that I was, with a look of slight confusion.

Coach Mac then surprised me by saying, "You're not going to throw any more footballs at me, are you?"

I had absolutely no idea what he was asking me, or why. I must have looked tremendously confused, and I told him that I did not understand what he was asking.

He said that he knew it was me who threw that football at him before the Georgia game a few weeks earlier, and that he understood why I was upset with him. I was absolutely horrified, and I told him that he was mistaken, but he clearly did not believe me. Then he rose to give his pre-game speech about kickoff strategy, leaving me to my bewilderment.

As we entered the field and moved to the sidelines, I grabbed Coach Mac and made him look me in the eyes. I said, with a great pain in my voice, "Coach, I would never throw anything at you. I love you."

I meant it. He had, indeed, given me the chance to be a part of something great, and it had been my own fault that my expectations had gotten so high. I did not want Coach Mac to think that I would ever hurt him or the team. I had no idea who had thrown a football at him, but it was not something I was capable of doing. He turned back to the important matters of running the game, and I went to hold the wires of the headset of another coach so no one would trip over them. It had been decided that I was not going to play in this last game.

Tennessee beat us by many points, and everybody got to play, except me. My career at Vanderbilt was over with the final gun, and I sprinted straight for the locker room through a sea of orange-and-white confetti dropping from the upper decks. I showered quickly, and when the rest of the team entered I was already getting dressed and packing my travel bag. As Coach Mac was completing his final speech to tired, grumpy college boys, I rudely walked out of the room, leaving my uniform and pads in a pile on the floor while he spoke. I doubted that anyone noticed.

I joined my folks and Jenny right outside the stadium and declined to answer any questions about the game all the way back to Morristown, trying to hide in the friendly folds of the hills as we wound through the familiar farmland. It was all over. There would be no catches, there would be no varsity letter, and there would be no cheering for me, the way it had happened in my dreams for the previous four years.

I asked Jenny to marry me. I did it because I thought I was going to lose her again, and because I thought that she loved me. We told our parents over the Thanksgiving break, and they seemed delighted, though a little hesitant.

When my folks asked me how I would support my young bride, I told them that I would quit school and get a job doing something in Indianapolis, where Jenny was happy and still in school. They thought this was an incredibly stupid idea and told me that I was backing out of a deal I had made with them to get through grad school. I felt horrible when they said that.

My folks were also unhappy with every suggestion I made about the wedding, and they stopped talking to Jenny altogether. She started to ignore them likewise, and communication was at a standstill. None of us had the ability to behave as an adult and keep the lines open, so all of us started to drift away from each other. I was in the middle, pulled between the great love of my life and loyalty to my parents. The strain increased through the Christmas holidays, and Jenny and I returned to my pitiful apartment in Nashville with the New Year of 1986. I tried to cook a hamburger dinner in my little toaster/oven, and it didn't work right, and Jenny started crying. I vowed to her that I would never be dependent on my parents again, and I was ready to face the world along with my loyal new wife, and our strength would see us both through.

I was wrong. Jenny grew more sullen and withdrawn each day, and she left earlier than planned to head up to Indianapolis. I let her go, believing a couple of days to cool off was a good idea.

Not only did I never see Jenny again, I never even had another conversation with her. She returned to Butler and immediately forgot about me. She dumped me coldly, refusing to tell me that she was no longer mine. I could not get a hold of her on the phone, and eventually I found out from one of her housemates that she was back with an old boyfriend, *staying overnight* with him less than a week after leaving me. I was numb. Had this entire romance been a lie?

At first I tried to be a gentleman, making an attempt to understand and forgive. I wrote Jenny notes saying not to worry, that I would be okay, playing the martyr role very well. But then the anger came, and I locked myself into a lab room up on the geology floor and threw heavy rocks against the wall, trying to shatter them as explosively as possible. When I finally did get Jenny on the phone, a month after I had last seen her, I could not control my voice as I screamed and screamed at her, trying to hurt her with my words flung long-distance. She remained silent, and hung up before I was finished.

There was a part of me that went crazy then, completely out of control. I had invested in so many things, and I had lost all of them. I had been very foolish. The three things that had been so precious to me were now gone: football, my family, and Jenny. It seemed there was nothing left. All of a sudden, the anger went to a dull ache, and then I felt nothing at all.

It took a long time for the numbness to wear off. In a stroke of luck, the geology department at Vanderbilt offered me a graduate assistantship. This would pay for all of my tuition and a significant stipend in exchange for teaching a couple of labs each week. This was a true blessing. Also, a delightful grad student named Tula offered me a room in the home she had been renting. This turned out to be the best relationship I had ever had with a woman in that it was strictly platonic and highly respectful. We knew our boundaries and enjoyed each other's company immensely. Tula was wonderful and helped restore my faith in women. We ate supper together and talked about how the day went.

I had a small operation to repair a torn ligament in my hand, and it was almost refreshing to feel something, even quite a bit of pain. I cried a lot in the operating room, and the tears on my face were welcome, serving to wake me from my self-pity.

When all was done, for the first time in my life, I was self-sufficient, free, and able to make my own decisions without worrying about how they would affect others. This was an amazing feeling. It became a relief, finally, to be done with football and Jenny and the approval of my parents.

I also found out that I was a natural at teaching my lab classes. It was a great challenge to be able to put complex theories and thoughts into understandable terms, to build an explanation bit by bit so it could be comprehended at any level. I loved being able to paint pictures in my students' heads.

At the career placement center, I looked up teaching jobs and found one that started right after that spring semester. It paid a tiny salary and came with no guarantees, far off in rural Connecticut. I sent an application right away and was soon offered a position. The journey would continue.

Chapter 4: Africa

With a sense of finality, I loaded everything I had into the trunk of my Vandy-gold Mazda 626, which my parents had bought me when I was a sophomore. (I was in a snotty mood then and refused to thank them, angry that I had to give back the old station wagon I had come to love. I wasn't going to give my folks the satisfaction of feeling appreciated.) When I hit the road this time, I planned to abandon everything I could shed from my past, to head for Connecticut, to start something fresh and new. I had walked away from a scholarship in geology after only one year of grad school, so my parents thought I was a dropout, but it was time to move, now, with no excuses and no baggage from the past. This liberation made me drunk and giddy with power. I was truly on my own, in a car with good mileage, paid for by my parents with no recognition from me.

Nature's Classroom was based at a YMCA-camp up in northeast Connecticut, just south of Great Barrington and the Massachusetts border. The "school" was facilitated by a bunch of people like me who were, it seemed, searching for something deeper in life. Many of them were there to teach kids about living with respect for nature, of course. But most, like me, were there for refueling, unable at that time to deal with the oppressive crush of responsibility and rent and food bills and grades. It was like we were in an adult "time-out" from the real world. I quickly felt that I fit in nicely.

I tossed my backpack on a bed in an open dormitory structure, which had once been a barn, my "space" separated from the others by a sheet hung over the rafters. The teachers were lounging about, sleeping, picking at a guitar, enjoying the day off. I acted like I was unpacking, but I was really drinking in my independence and the feel of the place. Soon I would be accepted, but there were some tests to pass.

I was stunned to find there were angry women there, crazed with the opportunity to tell me how wrong I was to be a man. These were not like conservative Vanderbilt sorority girls, for sure, not vacuously primping and planning for the next party date. Most of theses women were quick to verbally whip me if I said anything remotely sexist, so I learned to be careful when I said anything at all in their presence. Several of these same women also let it be known that they were available, effective immediately. I thought that tough Barb, who celebrated her monthly period like it was Mardi Gras, was going to bite my head off one moment, then smother me with ferocious kisses the next. I was a bit scared, and probably thrilled, by her and her tough buddies. Soon enough, though, they all became amazing friends when they realized I was harmless.

Ben was a former worker at a Ford plant in the Midwest who had been laid off. He had lost all his possessions that he had bought on credit, and he was miraculously recovering from some intestinal cancer that was supposed to have killed him a year earlier, so he said. While bitter about the loss of his possessions, he was learning to live in peace. Ben was also a fabulous "Indian guide" who knew a good bit about homeopathic medicine. Once he treated me for a migraine by having me chew rosemary seed as he gently rubbed my neck with a hot towel. It was a nice try.

Jim was a former teacher from Minnesota, recently divorced. He was a neat-freak, ironing even the colorful bandannas that he wore around his neck each day. Jim was always, amazingly, involved romantically with one of the young female teachers from each of the visiting schools. In between visits, however, he was constantly sullen and hiding out from his other ghosts.

There was this one woman, Susan, who would not leave me alone. She would take any opportunity to hug me and kiss my cheek and rub my shoulders, and all of this was quite creepy and very embarrassing. But I did not know how to tell her to leave me alone without hurting her feelings, so I just put up with it all, gently pushing her away and making excuses when she got too close. There was no way to make her stop doing this, and I did not know that I *could* press the issue in the days before sexual harassment. So I spent a lot of each day avoiding Susan while she told just about everybody what a great lover she thought I would be. She was yucky.

Each week at *Nature's Classroom*, we would receive a busload of 12-year-old kids from Hartford or New York City, most of whom had never seen a bunch of trees all in the same place at one time. We would take the kids out in small groups and play community-based games and do activities that showed the connected aspects of all nature. There was a lakeshore to explore, a beaver-dam colony in the woods, a mountain to hike, and streams to jump over, as well as lots and lots of trees and boulders to hug and rub and sit on. Every day was filled with pure oxygen and energy.

We would dress up in period costumes and pretend we were the original pioneers who settled the area. Once I dressed up as Charles Darwin and tried to explain "my" basic theories of evolution, all in a ridiculous Scotch brogue. Ben taught me how to have the kids hide at night, "the way Indians used to do it," as another group passed us on a trail, oblivious to our presence. If the other group all got past us without noticing us, we were the winners, but the kids were not allowed to scream out in glee; they had to keep their pride inside so they didn't make the other group feel bad. This was called "bouldering," since you were to keep as still as a boulder while everyone walked obliviously past and the kids loved it. We told them it was a game the noble Native Americans used to play, and like the real Braves, we would always take pride in our restraint, never taunting our "victims" after they passed.

I really learned how to teach kids during that session, how to keep their attention and when to let them run free to discover their little world. I found that teaching was what I should do, and the *NC* administrators offered plenty of praise and encouragement. It was thrilling to be counted on and deemed responsible by my peers. I made good friends, though I wasn't very good at being a hippie. Together we really worked hard to make a difference in each child's life, and we were usually dead by Friday when they went home.

There was another fellow there my age who had also studied geology, and we started to hang out together. Stuart Dalton had graduated from Brown and had been at *Nature's Classroom* for a full year, and I found that he was hilarious and inventive at all times, a great teacher. He was the only guy there, I figured, who wasn't hiding from anything. Stuart also wanted to drink deeply from the world, and he had given lots of thoughts towards moving on and doing exciting things in far-off places, recognizing no boundaries. I latched onto him, realizing that he was someone I wanted to be like, thoughtful and responsible. He had a girlfriend who just hung all over him, and he was so good-natured about her and everything else that I could see why she would like him.

Stuart had made plans to go on an archaeological dig with a Canadian university, up in the Bliss Islands off the coast of southern New Brunswick, just north of Maine. For some reason, he flattered my by asking if I would like to go along and do the "dig" with him for six weeks after this session of Nature's Classroom. Of course, I said yes. Together, we left this place behind, along with pieces of ourselves scattered all about the trees and boulders. My short time there had been so wonderful.

The Canadian crew from St. Mary's University up in Halifax was a friendly group, totally laid back in all manners, tolerant of everything, and heavily dependent on beer. These people were greatly pleased to have us Americans along, and the little island on which we were to be encamped was stunning in its starkness. It was the site of an old fishing weir and a dumping ground for Micmac Indians some few thousand years earlier.

Stuart and I were hard workers, but he was particularly thorough and efficient, so he was given some choice jobs around the site. A Canadian fellow my age, but seemingly much younger in his mannerisms and responsibilities, took a real liking to me, especially after he found out that I had been a football player at a major American school (ha!). I showed Colin how to catch and throw a football I had brought along, which thrilled him since he had been a passionate rugby player, and I gave him a taste of my Red Man chewing tobacco. While I had not been a frequent chewer, I had stuck this pack in my car some months earlier and for some reason had brought it out to the islands. Colin was hilarious in his first attempts to spit, making that funny sound like you might hear on an old movie where geezers are spitting into a bucket. You could tell that the flavor was not as nice as he thought since he always seemed to have a wince on his face while chewing.

Colin also showed me how to play rugby, at which he was quite adept for his small size. On an off day at the dig, he took me to a local high school field where I played my first rugby game and scored a couple of majors (the equivalent of touchdowns); what a blast that was, using some of my football skills to run down the ball and dive into the end-zone. What a great sport!

I developed crushes on each of the girls who were working at the dig. None of them seemed to care that much for me, except for one young lady from Washington, DC, though I was never quite sure. That is, up until one night when we went for an innocent walk around the island after supper. We cut through some of the growth and ended up on the other side of the barren island, marveling at the sheer beauty of this place, but when we turned to go back, we noticed that it was too dark to find our way through the woods. We tried anyway and took some wrong turn. Soon we ended up in an unfamiliar place, on a rocky cliff where the walking was slippery and the waves were breaking some twenty feet below. We were a right bit scared. It had gotten very dark, and no one was responding to our yells, our voices lost amongst the crashing water.

As the hours went by, and we had decided to stay in that one place, hoping that someone with a flashlight might come looking for us, the temperature dropped steadily. In an effort to keep warm, as we had both been a bit sweaty and were now chilled, we huddled together on a patch of moss in order to share body heat. For some reason, we also shared a kiss, then another, and we became quite passionate. This was a weird situation, my strangest ever with a girl, making out when soon we might be hypothermic.

We eventually stopped kissing and started shivering, her quite violently, so I worked hard to keep her warm, having her lie on top of me as I rubbed her vigorously. Whatever arousal there had been evaporated in real concern. We each slept a little bit, shivering through a very long night, trying to share body heat. Luckily, it was not too long until the sun started to rise, and we found the trail in the breaking morning light and stumbled into the campsite where everyone else was sleepily eating breakfast, as if nothing had happened. When we explained that we had been lost all night, they all looked at each other and winked and jabbed elbows into each other's ribs. They all thought we had sneaked off to be alone with each other! Even Stuart seemed incredulous at my "story"! This girl and I continued to be sort-of romantically entwined for the duration of the dig, though we really had nothing in common, and it did not take long after that for us to drift apart. I did visit her in her rich Washington suburb once, several months after the dig, where her parents were quite unimpressed with me, and, by then, so was she.

Stuart had been planning his next move and writing letters, and he had made phone calls every time we came back to the mainland on the weekends. He managed, though I could not figure out how, to get me a spot with him on another dig, this time in Nairobi, Kenya, with the National Museum! Stuart had somehow gotten in contact with a French archaeologist, Helene Roche, and arranged to help her and her team in excavating a tool and trash pit for some ancestor of humanity that lived 250,000 years earlier. What a great opportunity for us both!

I figured that I had saved enough money to get to Nairobi and other locations if I lived cheaply and slept in tents or hostels. The pitiful little salary from Nature's Classroom had gone unspent for 9 weeks, and I had stipend money left from Vanderbilt in an account down in Nashville. Plus, there was the extra thousand I had been able to recover from the extremely nice jeweler who had refunded Jenny's engagement ring costs after she had finally returned it. I felt like a truly rich man, on my way to see the world with nothing to tie me down, with a good friend at my side, looking out for each other.

Stuart and I had elaborate plans: we would do the dig for the six week duration, and then we would take another six weeks to tour that fabulous country, doing safaris and hiking and climbing Mt. Kenya. After that, we would somehow cross the Indian Ocean, land in Bombay, weave our way up to Nepal, and do a long trek through the Himalayas. This was going to be great. His girlfriend was going to meet us in Katmandu and walk the trek with us.

Off we went, though my parents could not understand how I could just pick up and leave all of my life behind. It was hard for them to comprehend that I was rehearsing a detachment I had only read about in religious studies classes some months earlier, that I had full designs on clearing out my insides and becoming a renunciate, a *sanyassin*. Stuart and I were going to be like that character in *The Razor's Edge*, embracing things as they flowed towards us in the stream of life and then letting them go as if we had no real need for anything but the clothes on our backs. It was our plan, and we were young enough to let it happen and comfortably naive enough to think that everything would fall into place.

The French team in the tiny village of Isenya, south of Nairobi, seemed to think Stuart and I were wonderful Americans, and we worked hard to learn French table manners and be model citizens on their turf. Once again, Stuart was an ideal field archaeologist, patient and thorough, and I did a lot of manual labor in the hot sun, enjoying the direct equatorial rays and savoring the feeling of returning strength from such vigorous physical workouts as hauling buckets of sand and moving machinery with the African workers. Stuart and I fell into a nice routine, waking in our two-man tent to the sound of hot water being poured into a washbasin by a local worker outside, eating amazing meals prepared by enthusiastic Kenyan cooks, happy for their tiny pay. A great benefit of our experience was relaxing at the long table under the lovely flowering pepper tree while the black starlings stared, through circular and bright yellow eyes, at our beckoning crumbs.

We worked at the dig in the morning and late afternoon. It was necessary to assume a five-minute break every afternoon at around 2 o'clock to scramble a tarp over our site to protect the dig from the dust devils that would fly down the dry riverbed, the tiny tornadoes throwing sand and pebbles into our faces. The hot African sun on the wide dry plains made for these daily whirlwinds, and I saw brave children throwing rocks at and dancing around the dust devils as these small cyclones swept slowly across the playing fields at the local school nearby. The children always ended up crying from the pebbles thrown into their heads by the swirling funnel of wind. Stuart and I shook our heads and laughed.

We found several ancient and crude stone tools every day at the dig site, mapping out the finds with our compasses and levels so the data would all be accurate and publishable. Stuart found some intriguing obsidian axes that revised some of the theories of the area, and I was able to unearth a ram-like horn-core as well as a tooth from an ancient elephant, *Elephantis rikii*, that completely re-dated the dig site by some forty thousand years. The French people went crazy over that tooth, and they celebrated and made me feel like a hero for digging it up.

One day, after a particularly grueling session of hauling sand buckets, I awoke with a pulled muscle along my rib cage that completely incapacitated me. Every breath was a chore, walking was agony, and a laugh or cough was a physical impossibility from the sharp pain that enveloped my torso. I could do nothing but sit straight upright all day, helping the tall Maasai women sort the dirt for tiny mammal bones while they whispered to each other in their musical language and laughed at me. They mischievously taught me to say a few words in Maasai and laughed at me more when I tried them.

Stuart missed having an English conversation partner down at the dig site, so he made every effort to catch up under the pepper tree at supper when he came back.

Unfortunately, he had a great sense of humor, and I fought hard to keep from laughing at his silly observations, which only made the task more difficult, as anyone who has tried *not* to laugh would know. I was able to keep control just enough to breathe, for a while, and my ribs really hurt!

And then we overheard one of the French team, speaking to a British worker, asking about a scientist who just happened to be named MacMurray. Immediately, Stuart looked at me, and I looked at him, knowing that we both were envisioning Fred MacMurray of the television show *My Three Sons*. It was too late to save myself, because Stuart was also a master of impressions, and he immediately threw out the voice of William Demarest as gruff Uncle Charlie, saying, "Steve, what am I gonna do with these boys....".

I had to laugh, but I couldn't, and I started to implode. I went into spasms where my rib muscles contracted involuntarily, trying so hard not to laugh. My gyrations made Stuart crack up completely, and I had to force myself to awkwardly rise from the table in convulsions, grasping at my poor sides and slinking off into the night to keep from bursting. The poor French team must have thought I was insane or going off somewhere to die, and I did not return for at least a half-hour, continuing to fight the urge to laugh on my own in the bushes. Stuart did not apologize, the bastard, and I cursed him to his face while he giggled some more when I finally returned, exhausted, to our tent.

On days off from the dig, several of us younger workers would take one of the rented cars and go driving off to one of the game parks, where we would get out and walk in the shadows of giraffes and ostriches, though not too close! One rest day we went exploring a cave in some hills, and I went off by myself for a ways to see if there was another cave on the other side of a small rise. I encountered a pile of dung near some matted grass on the side of the rounded hill and remarked to myself that it was much bigger than dog scat.

Thinking for a couple of seconds about that, I suddenly realized that it was probably the droppings of something that would not hesitate to eat me at that exact moment. I looked around quickly while my bowels tightened. Cursing myself for wandering off from the group while in the true wilds of deadly Africa, I cautiously ran to the group waiting for me at the car, trembling and looking over each shoulder the whole way back. What idiot goes walking around by himself in the grasslands of a wide-open African game park!

We stopped at a small village store, which was another simple mud hut with an open window and shelf, on the way back to the site, and I bought a small packet of candy. Noticing that it was slightly wet, I shrugged and ate it anyway. The next morning, I did not feel so well, and I returned to the tent to nap after lunch. I did not wake up to go back to the dig in the afternoon, and Stuart let me stay there sleeping. But when I had the groggy urge to go to the "bathroom" (a pit toilet around the side of a hill) a little later, I found that my head was spinning and my legs would not work. I had to stop and rest about ten times on the short journey to the toilet because each leg felt like it weighed a ton. The fever in my body was undeniable. After an eternity, I half-crawled back to the tent and started sobbing during moments of consciousness, occasionally drifting into sleep or stupor. Stuart returned from the dig after what seemed days. I made him realize that I was very sick, and Helene, the director of the dig, put her cool hand on my flaming forehead. They drove me to the hospital in Nairobi in their little rented truck.

The waiting room was a strange place. The same people kept asking the same questions over and over, and I told Stuart several times that I needed help because, in my feverish delirium, I thought I was turning into a werewolf, or perhaps a lion. It seemed that Stuart laughed absurdly or paid no attention or floated to the ceiling, but it was clear when my mind would allow that he was quite worried about me. After an eternity, I finally got to a hospital room of my own and went to sleep. Stuart made sure I was safe and returned to the site. Had I not been so sick, this would have been a great experience, time in a Nairobi hospital. It took a while for my mind to come around.

For the next three days I was treated like royalty. The Indian and Kenyan nurses were as beautiful as fashion models, bringing me fresh exotic juices every few hours and making me comfortable in my immaculate bed. Starlings and sparrows sang in the flowering tree outside my window, and the doctors treated me like a returning war hero. I drew the line when one of the nurses told me to undress completely, that she was going to bathe me; I insisted that I would wash my own self, thank you! When

I got the hospital bill after the three days of treatment, it amazingly amounted to only about $80 US. I should have stayed longer!

I was eventually allowed to return to the dig after allowing my intestines to clear themselves out, though it was never certain what my ailment had been. The doctor had suggested malaria but it probably was more like some intestinal infection; I never found out for sure. The symptoms returned twice more while I was in Africa, but neither time was as severe. Stuart and I served our term on the dig and bade farewell to the French. Our journey continued, though we were headed for some unexpected turns.

All during the dig, Stuart and I had become voracious readers, digesting several books each week and anxious to trade for more on the weekends in Nairobi. We particularly enjoyed the Somerset Maugham novels about people who had given up conventional life to paint or go off to study religion in Tibet, each character finding an inner peace after dramatic turmoil. Maugham's writing was captivating, and we were able to find humor in his British spelling of certain words. A jovial greeting of "Hulloa!" exactly as it was spelled in a couple of his books, intrigued us. How was that word to be pronounced? Stuart and I enthusiastically greeted each other with that word, in a forced British accent, for the next several months.

I also read books on religion and peacefulness within a person's soul, still dreaming of finding myself quiet on a mountainside in the Himalayas, and I ached to go there. Kenya was indeed a beautiful country, and the people were absolutely lovely and so friendly to us, but it was clearly a politically unstable place, where I felt guilty about my "wealth" and could not quiet my still-raging mind. Thoughts were still coming fast and furious about Jenny, football, and the parents who, after I had tried to prove how dedicated and directed I could be for five years at Vanderbilt, had yet to think of me as a responsible adult. I felt myself to be the martyr, and I needed even more distance from the past, though I was already halfway around the world. While my self-pity had not been the right way to go, the prescription of separation was proving itself to be correct. I was still withdrawing in order to reload for future battles of real life.

Soon, Stuart and I bickered and had moments of silence between us. Yet we continued on towards Mt. Kenya, along with two girls we had met along the way, one from California with big legs and another from Australia who did not say much. We weren't lovers or anything, but we men did feel like the protectors of these "frail" creatures. We were all horribly unprepared for a trek up to 17,000 feet, but that did not stop us from trying it anyway. From a very small store we bought the last loaf of bread, a chunk missing due to a mouse's ambition, along with a couple of chocolate bars, two potatoes, a packet of soup, some hard-boiled eggs, and a sheath of spaghetti noodles. I had on good hiking boots and a few layers of clothing, topped with an ill-advised blue-jean jacket. My backpack contained my water bottle and a thin Blue Kazoo sleeping bag from North Face, good to 20 degrees Fahrenheit. I had already lost my hat, and most of my toiletries had been stolen by local boys while away from my tent on the dig.

The climb up was pleasantly gradual through the rain forest zone, though we had to stop continuously to listen for the crunching leaves of rhinos or elephants. We were pretty sure we were going to be charged by something that wanted to trample or gore us. Little Sykes monkeys threw branches at us and cautiously tried to grab our backpacks or steal our food when we stopped for rest breaks. Up we went, into the more barren zones, where radial succulent plants lined our paths and the view above became more and more impressive. Through the U-shaped glacial valley I trudged, most of the others far ahead of me as the effects of less oxygen slowed me. A tiny yellow bird flitted around my head and occasionally rested on the metal frame of my backpack, fearless and cheerful.

We arrived at the little visitors' hut in the middle of the second day, cold and exhausted, with the dark rocky spires of Mt.Kenya knifing through their glacial shrouds just in front of us. It was good to be young and stupid, breathless in the arms of a great mountain, exhausted, cold, and exhilarated.

Stuart went with the girls up to Point Lenana, one of the obvious volcanic necks that jutted up next to a wide swath of ice, but I was too tired to go up any higher, and I needed to be by myself. So I walked around at 16,000 feet, peering into the amazing ice cave at the base of the Point, as close to the equator as one could get and still be touching fields of glacial ice. I wandered around the lobelia plants and fallen rock blocks, and once I came around a corner and startled a huge owl, as big as a golden retriever. He had been trying to root out a hyrax, an unusual rabbit-like rodent with genetic ties to the elephant (!), from its hiding place in the rocks. The owl immediately abandoned his prey and swooped upwards towards my face. I did a furious duck-and-cover, feeling the owl's feathers brush over my back as it lunged and then fled over the ice-wedged boulders. My heart was high up in my throat, and my blue-jean jacket had white scratches across it from the owl's talons.

Stuart and the girls returned around dusk, exhilarated by their intense climb, and we shivered in the tiny resting lodge, begging the Kenyan guides who actually lived there to build us a fire. We were able to boil a pan of water and cook the spaghetti and soup mix together, and with the fried potatoes and an onion I borrowed it from the grumpy guides when they were not looking, it was a glorious meal. We sucked life out of that pot, and it kept us warm until the next morning when we began our retreat.

It was obvious that we were getting cranky, having seen each other through a stressful ordeal up the mountain, but the trip down was unusually uncomfortable for me. For some reason, I did not want to be with anyone there, and at the same time I felt like they did not care that much about being with me. Real or perceived (or paranoid) feelings aside, I decided on the way down that I needed to leave them. And I did not care if Stuart would be left alone, to fend for himself, to find his own way to Nepal and beyond. I had to tell him as soon as possible, so he could prepare himself and I could get going.

At the flowery hostel at the base of the mountain, I bought enough supplies to make a stew of soup mix, noodles, beef (found hanging inside a screened area at the local store, not refrigerated), and eggs. Everyone was still grumpy as I started to talk to Stuart. I explained that I needed to be alone, that it was not his fault, and that I was tired of Africa and longed for the sacred and holy lands of India and Nepal. Everything I said was like a lame excuse, and he probably felt horribly offended that I no longer wanted to travel with him. The girl from California tried to tell me that I was "not giving Africa a chance", not appreciating the beauty of the place, but nothing could be further from my mind. I needed to be alone, truly alone, and I needed to leave as soon as possible. I told Stuart that I would get in touch with him at the American Express office in Katmandu, and we would meet again in that holy city. The next morning I loaded up and hiked away from the most beautiful spot in Africa, the green fields awestruck by the majestic Mt. Kenya, alone, Stuart not speaking to me.

I returned to Nairobi and suddenly decided to head to the coast of Kenya after all, delaying my trip to Asia. I got on an overnight train, sharing a second-class berth with two Kenyan businessmen on their way to the Indian Ocean shore. The train shook and rattled all night, and I ate fruit and biscuits and read Maugham under the dim light next to my heaving bed.

The dirty and wonderful coastal city of Mombasa greeted me with a burst of humidity and exuberant clatter as I hiked towards the marketplace in search of neat things. There was a room in a cheap but clean hotel, and I maneuvered the blackened city in wonder, smartly avoiding dark enclosed areas where thieves and pickpockets lay in wait. I bought huge pamplemouses (plump grapefruit) and oranges in the city market, making the dour traders laugh with my attempts at bargaining. At night, I walked the city streets against the advice of all tour books, easily the only *mzungu,* the only white guy, in the entire city. People stared and always smiled at me as I mingled in the crowded streets, a festival in the air every night, me chewing on skewered sticks of gristly beef and fresh flat bread that cost a nickel. The smells and sounds of this big nasty city reminded me constantly of how happy I was to be "out there".

I stayed there for two weeks, loving the dirtiness and the friendly shopkeepers, listening to them when they told me which parts of the city to avoid. Soon I came across a curious group of high school boys who invited me to join them in a soccer game. They laughed uproariously as I tried to head the soccer ball and bounce it off my chest, missing completely each time, while they were so adept. These boys were Muslim, and they treated me with kindness and fascination. I went with them around town and ate with them in little restaurants while old men in fezzes stared at me. I loved them so much for embracing me, and some even invited me into their home for a movie (*Rambo*, no less) on their shaky and primitive VCR.

I thought about trying to stay there with them for a few weeks, perhaps renting a room in a Muslim house. But then one older, scruffy guy tried to make a point of my Jewish-ness. He had a glazed look in his eye from chewing *mirrah*, an herb that had some drug-like effect, and he questioned me harshly one day: "Where are your parents from? Grandparents? Russia? Sounds Jewish to me."

I lied to him, telling him that my family was Catholic. I did so because I thought that he might kill me. It was time to leave. Good instincts.

So I moved on up the coast, taking a bus to Malindi, where I checked in at the youth hostel on the beach, a paradise with sun and sand and happy young people like myself. No sooner did I start to relax than I met a young lady from New Zealand who invited me to go on a strange adventure with her. She had heard about a few people who had taken a bus inland to the jungle and had hired some local tribesmen to take them down the Tana River, all the way to the Indian Ocean, in a dugout canoe. Bravely, she asked if I wanted to go, since she did not think a woman could do that alone, and I said sure. Why not?

We took a bus to some remote village where the German missionary who seemed to run the town was quite annoyed by our presence, especially since we were not married to each other. I explained that we had just met, which made him more annoyed. But word quickly got out what we wanted, and soon we were greeted some tribesmen who offered to take us downstream for a few dollars, though they spoke very little English and indicated they had not done this before. So we set off with backpacks and water bottles in this dugout canoe down the Tana River. Crazy.

The girl turned out to be quite thoughtless. She drank all of her purified water immediately and had no iodine to purify more. Then she wanted some of mine, and I gently insisted that we conserve it, since we had no idea if my iodine pills would clean up the river water, which no doubt had germs as big as hamsters swimming around in it. This incensed her, and she strangely chewed me out for my "selfishness". I'm sure the two guys paddling the canoe thought that that was hilarious, the "lovers" having a fight. A few moments later this same angry girl asked nicely if she could put her feet in my lap while she napped in the sun. Weird.

Down the river, we occasionally saw hippos rise at random from the river bottom, reminding us that they could pop up under the canoe anytime they chose, and that made our guides visibly nervous. They were also nervous because huge crocodiles slid into the water every fifty feet or so as we rowed downstream, anticipating one of us falling overboard to become a fine meal of rare white meat. On we cautiously rowed while the Kiwi Girl whined and complained and slept and I asked myself what I was doing this close to death on the Tana River in the middle of wild Africa with a New Zealand brat.

We stopped at a small village along the river to spend that night, and the only people who spoke English were the two local teachers, who made us a meal of baked cornmeal. When we asked, they also boiled water for us to drink, though they could not understand why we just didn't drink out of the river. Try explaining the concept of germs to someone who has never even heard of a microscope; they thought we were nuts. It was obvious the people in the village had never seen *mzungu* before, and here were two of them, one with bright white hair and the other a smiling goofy-looking boy not much older than the village hunters. The children wanted to touch our hair. They were so lovely in their curiosity, constant smiles on clean dark faces.

At sundown the men took me to the banks of the Tana River to bathe. They thought that I was afraid of crocodiles since I didn't go in very far, so they tried to reassure me with winks that no one had yet been eaten there. The men didn't know that I had once read about a type of germ or fish or something that would swim right into your urethra and painfully infect your entire being, so I got into the water only up to mid-thigh. To the delight of the other naked, muscular, unashamed men, one fellow asked me in halting English if I was afraid a fish would "bite off my penis". I was incredibly embarrassed and couldn't make eye contact with anyone as the other men giggled at my red face.

On we went the next morning, the river becoming menacingly wider and the current harder to row against. In fact, the tide was coming in, so the last few hundred feet took hours as we toyed with capsizing. Finally we pulled into the village at the end of the Tana River, on the Indian Ocean. We paid our guides and I thanked them, though the Kiwi was anxious to move on to her next village, so she didn't bother to thank the brave men in her hurry to find a bus. In the village we went our separate ways, me sipping sodas and reading on a bench while she took photos of the town square and looked at maps. Village children came over to stare at me as I wrote in my journal, and one of them drew a picture of a jungle bird for me. Eventually, the girl and I got on the same bus for Lamu, a lovely town farther north, but we were intentionally seated far apart, her in the front and me in the back.

Just outside the city limits, the bus suddenly stopped and huge uniformed men with machine guns boarded. I got my passport ready since I figured it was just some sort of third-world security check. But they took the stunned Kiwi girl by the arms and pulled her off the bus, and the driver threw her bag into the dirt and sped off. I was stunned and very worried for her, so I persuaded the driver to slow down a little to let me off the bus also. I walked to the now-visible army base nearby and tried to make friends with the very gruff guards and soldiers at several desks doing paperwork. Such magnificent looking men, tall and strong in their fatigues, clearly the best Kenya had to offer for defense of their reasonably stable country.

After much friendly banter and attempts to show that I was harmless, the guards let me visit the Kiwi, alone and in a sparse cell, and she was overjoyed to see me. She had been crying and had no idea I had even gotten off the bus. I really felt sorry for her, behind bars and scared out of her mind, not knowing what was around the corner for her.

I went back to the guards, and found out that the area we had been in had been classified as a high security zone, since it was near an army base and an uprising had been warming up with some Ethiopian refugees at a nearby village. Her looking at maps and taking photos had been suspicious, and villagers had "told" on her. That made sense to me. After a while I convinced the guards that she meant no harm, and perhaps the word of an earnest American made a difference.

The Kiwi was quite relieved, though she stayed upset for a long time as we once again waited in the village, and she eventually got on a different bus headed back to Mombasa, and probably on back to Nairobi. The New Zealander had had enough of this rugged area for a while. I headed further up the coast, still in wonder at this magnificent country, no grudges held.

In the tiny resort town of Lamu, I discovered a lazy paradise, with the local chant of *poli, poli* everywhere. *Slowly, slowly*, the locals said with easy smiles, offering sweet drinks and relaxed conversation. I found a hotel with a cheap and colorful room overlooking the Indian Ocean, warm breezes moving the bright drapery over the clay windowsills. I ventured outside for a walk in the ocean air and found myself at the local playing field where a huge soccer match was being played, on sand! The crowd was howling at the raucous game. One young man would kick a pile of sand and fake the other team into thinking the sand was actually the ball while really taking the ball another direction, and it was such a neat offensive trick that I found myself laughing along with the locals.

That night I sat in a patio restaurant by the beach and sipped juice drinks and talked to everyone, Germans and British, and local men who wanted me to go fishing with them for a "small fee." The next day I met a friendly group of Dutch women who invited me along on a boat trip aboard this crazy fishing boat called a *dhow*. It looked like it was made of scrap, kind of like a Chinese *junk*, and might fall apart if it tried to turn quickly. How exciting!

One of the women, Anna, was attractive in an interesting way, quiet and shy, but with wonder behind her wire-rimmed glasses and kind eyes. I talked to her and she acted as if a man had never spoken to her before, though she was eight years older than my age of 22. I ended up holding her hand on the boat, soaking in equatorial salt wind under the huge white moon. She seemed to be in heaven, and I was flattered. The next day, the same group of women asked me to join them in their last week driving back across Africa. I accepted.

We took off and headed for the Ngong Hills, where the author Karen Blixen had lived, where they had filmed "Out of Africa". It was romantic, and Anna and I kissed at the waterfall. We shared a tent that night, and the other women thought that that was charming and cute. Anna was very open and free with her sexuality, and we had a wonderful night. Until, of course, my sickness came back and my fever raced to 103 degrees, and I started shivering. Then it started to rain, and the tent was leaking. Anna got out and started to fix the tent, totally naked. She was a lovely woman. Even though I was delirious with fever, it touched me that she wanted to take care of me, something I would never have been able to ask of Jenny back in our days.

We enjoyed a week of safaris and rides across the plains, looking at elephants and lions and eating great camp food. The Dutch are brilliant at cooking in pots on top of small stoves, and we ate like royalty. They told me of the somber beauty of their own country and were respectful of my status as American. I told them of my love for new cultures and American football. Somehow they knew there was a football team in Amsterdam, American football, and that these teams were hiring Americans to coach and play for them. The idea intrigued me, so I stored it in my head for later.

I had a plane ticket for India, and the Dutch had to return to their own country, where Anna was an instructor of nurses in a hospital. I bade them a tearful goodbye and promised to come to visit as soon as I could. Anna was very sad and tugged at my heart with her quiet sobbing. I told her I would come, and she believed me.

I soon got on a plane for Bombay. The chapter on Africa was closed, and my romantic vision of Asia and peace and happiness and the Himalayas awaited. But first, the swarming, sweaty charm of India called.

Chapter 5: Mountains and Flatlands: Himalaya and Holland

I ndia. The mere word conjures up images of steamy heat and shallow brown rivers and cattle. People upon people upon people. And something that is sacred about India which transcends the crowds and mud and confusion. You feel it the moment you step off the plane, some holiness that Westerners might not "get."

Arriving by Air Kenya in Bombay (now it's called Mumbai) after an equally steamy and packed flight over the Indian Ocean, I joyously breathed in the moist, fertile air. A few rupees found me a cab and a little hotel room in a busy section of town. Walking outside, children besieged me, begging for coins and putting their hands in my pockets while I tried to fend them off, laughingly at first and then annoyed and a bit scared that they would take anything not attached. When they finally left me alone, I bought a collection of quartz crystals from a street vendor which was stolen out of my backpack within the hour.

The first evening there, I sat in a restaurant where I had no idea what to order from the strange menu. The kind manager spoke English and offered to bring me a good meal, about which he was quite right. It was very spicy Indian food, but I ate it all and enjoyed it immensely, my first real restaurant meal in weeks. A man sitting near me showed me how to eat the pungent dishes, some picked up with fingers and some with a spoon, and some scraped onto tasty flat bread to be carried to your mouth. At the end, the manager gave me some seeds to chew to freshen my breath and "aid in my digestion," which I dutifully undertook. I tasted those acrid seeds for hours and slept well in that city that night, the sound of idle and dying chatter from the humid street rising to my window upstairs.

In a note left hopefully at the Nairobi airport, Stuart had said that he would meet me in Bombay, but he never surfaced, so I decided to head up to Nepal myself. After a day of walking the bustling streets and mailing a package of souvenirs home to my parents in Tennessee, I went to the train station and found a million people waiting in a thousand lines to buy train tickets. I got in one queue, and kind people quickly urged me to the front of one line, smiling, smiling at the dumb westerner, their heads shaking and bobbing with delight at my confusion. "Please, please, go to the front! Go!"

I got information on the next day's schedule, buying my ticket from a tiny, impatient man behind the caged window. I would have to take two different trains to get to the Nepal border, then a bus into Katmandu. The trip would take three days.

I put the second-class ticket into my passport pouch and went out again into the nighttime streets of Bombay. There was a carnival in the park near my hotel, with slow rides and carousels, the sellers of festival toys and treats all around. Families walked arm in arm, proud fathers watching their happy children. In a small wooden stall, a worker squeezed long stalks of sugar cane with a mechanical press, the juices running down a wooden chute into a waiting glass. Families were happily sipping the pure sugar juice, sharing the container, and my mouth watered. The glasses were returned and rinsed out in a tub of water. I bought some of this delicious sugar cane juice for a nickel, one rupee. The man at the press presented it to the westerner with great flourish. It was magnificent and refreshing.

With my first swallow the clock started: it would take 36 hours for the germs to gestate and revolt against my insides.

The taxi that took me to the station early the next morning was scarcely as big as a golf cart, the hyper driver constantly hooting his horn along with every other vehicle as we sped the crowded street. I soon got on the train with several men in my compartment. My berth was folded on the top, and I opened it and put my backpack on it. I climbed up over the indifferent men, then settled in with a book and waited for the train to really get going. When it finally did, we never got above 15 miles per hour, which was probably good since the whole contraption rattled and shook so much. On we chugged to the northern border. The men in my car ignored me, proper in their second-class status and certainly not willing to make a big deal about the Westerner above. The scenery of rice fields and ramshackle farm buildings went by, punctuated by stops in small village train stations where children sold tangerines and juice and biscuits for pennies, even at two in the morning. I drifted off to sleep and woke often, the train always coming to a stop for more passengers, three here, five there, many holding chickens or bags of vegetables.

The next day as we trudged and clattered along, I felt a little sick, a little feverish. I bought a few Indian sodas, trying to settle my stomach, and I slept a lot. I had to change trains after a day, and my new compartment was filled with about twenty people who were shocked to see a Caucasian like me sitting with them. My berth was out of reach because five sleepy people were sitting on it and I couldn't bring myself to ask them to move, so I sat in a corner on my backpack and watched and daydreamed in the beginnings of delirium.

My illness intensified, and I finally had to ask the people on my bed to move so I could lie down, and they did with smiles, quickly, no problem. Then I tried to sleep. I hallucinated that there were people staring at me, right up in my face, and I couldn't seem to wake up. I was getting very sick and scared, alone now, remembering how bad it had gotten in Nairobi, soon unable to tell what time it was and what was reality as I drifted in and out of lucidity.

I spaced fitfully between sleep and stupor that night, continuing to hallucinate through a dull nausea, my stomach starting to gurgle and roll. More people were in my cabin, maybe twenty-five, and I had some paranoid feeling that they all wanted something from me, even my own oxygen, as they seemed to close in around my spinning, burning head. The cramping in my belly intensified and I continued to fear the throng of people in my compartment, so I grabbed my bag and staggered off the train at the next stop, in some tiny city, out of my head with fever. It may have been after midnight, but I was not sure.

At the small train station, I found a driver of a bicycle-rickshaw, asleep in his passenger seat, and I persuaded him to take me to a hotel. I lapsed in and out of consciousness in the rattling buggy as he grumpily peddled. It was 3 a.m. when I looked at my watch, or was it? After what seemed like hours, the rickshaw driver brought me back to the train station and somehow let me know that there were no hotels open. I became angry at his lack of effort and demanded that he take me to a hotel right that minute. He reluctantly took me back out on his rickshaw and found a hotel in the small, darkened downtown of this unknown city. I managed to sign my name, and the sleepy clerk led me to a dark room with a bed and my own pit toilet, a hole in the floor, reasonably clean, thank goodness. The cramps overtook me, and my intestines finally went crazy. I was sick in a big way, vomiting and diarrhea, all the time, absurdly thankful that there was my own meager toilet nearby and that I had my own quiet place to lie down in between explosions. I was able to fall asleep on the bed for an hour at a time, a punctuated equilibrium.

The next 72 hours were a blur as I slept and moaned and emptied myself of the vile things inside. I felt weak and dehydrated but managed to crawl down to the now-bustling street below to buy orange sodas from a vendor, which was all I had swallowed for three days. By the time the fever started to dissipate, my pants were conspicuously baggy and I had no energy at all. My mouth tasted of the spices from that Bombay restaurant, and it made me nauseous to even think of eating Indian food again. That feeling has lasted 20 years; today I can't even smell those spices without getting that taste of illness.

The only book I had with me there was a copy of *Zen and the Art of Motorcycle Maintenance*, which occupied my weary mind throughout the ordeal, whenever I had moments of lucidity. I would read for fifteen minutes and sleep for an hour. I was thankful for the distraction of that book, which was like a detective story of a man in search of meaning. That was what I was doing, after all: searching for something in some strange place, not knowing what I would find. There was even a peculiar joy in being sick and alone in such a strange place. I was never scared there, for some reason, and thankful for that particular peace.

I walked hopefully to a small restaurant on my last night there and ordered some soup and bread, as non-spicy as possible. A young customer sitting next to me asked if I was from America, and I said yes. He was smiling, and his questions and opinions of Americans were undoubtedly from movies he had watched. He asked me, shockingly blunt and almost comical in his thick Indian accent, "Do you like to fuck? I love to fuck. American women like to fuck, don't they?"

Stunned and embarrassed, I smiled and shrugged and turned away to my food. I didn't know whether to laugh or tell him to leave me alone, so I did neither. He had obviously watched too many blue movies about America. Was that what everyone thought about us, that we all had carefree sex all the time? And by the way, how come that never happened to me?

I got back on the train the next day and headed up to Nepal. We arrived, finally, at the Nepali border, where I was to get on a bus for Katmandu. Several others were making the same journey as I, and we were taken to a cheap hotel to wash up and rest for an hour or so. After passing through the armed checkpoint, where I was required to purchase a permit to enter Nepal, I found myself in the land where I had hoped to find some little-known secrets of being.

When my bus landed in Katmandu, I found it to be a sprawling city, shrouded in unspoken mystery. The buildings were older than time, it seemed, with ornate woodwork and sweet, smiling children looking out from every window. There were temples on each street as well as great piles of trash. Dogs roamed the streets, small and cute, picking at the garbage. The hint of the Himalayas was everywhere on the horizon, a sense of pure greatness. I went to the American Express office and was thankful to find a letter from Stuart with directions to his hotel. It had been two months since I had left him.

Stuart was overjoyed to see me, and I was honestly relieved to be with him. He had already explored the city and wanted to show me everything: the Monkey Temple, the sacred funeral pyre where they burned bodies by the river, the old city, the shops and marketplace. He took me to great restaurants with Asian and Western food, and there were hippies and young people like us everywhere. But the city was distinctly under the influence of something greater than the presence of all of us, something very powerful and full of history and stories and royalty and God. It was hard to remember ever being so happy.

We basked in the city for a week, me regaining all my lost strength and pounds from the sickness, Stuart waiting for his Cathy to arrive from the states. By some strange chance, we ran into two wonderful people from our teaching days at *Nature's Classroom*, Steve and Barb, who were now a couple. Steve, who we sometimes called "Laszlo" for no other reason than that he looked like he should be a "Laszlo", tall and handsome, had to be one of the coolest guys in the world. Nothing ever bothered him and life amused him, and he always laughed at my stupid jokes and made me feel like I was brilliant, even when I was annoying. Barb had once been the angry feminist but now had a great sense of humor about it. You still had to watch what you said to her, and she let you know, though in less-pushy way now, when you were out of line and being sexist. I was very careful, and I loved them both.

When Cathy arrived to Stuart's great joy, we headed by bus up to Pokhara, a smaller city in the Annapurna range, to begin our major trek. We feasted on water-buffalo steaks for a buck at some fashionable restaurant where more hippies hung out, washing it down with banana-yogurt *lassis* and Coke. We got some maps and hitched a ride to the trailhead for five rupees on a massive dump truck loaded with soil, taking a rocky road that was not really passable by any lesser vehicle.

We were going to trek the Annapurna Loop, a 350 kilometer hike around that significant range of the Himalayas. This circuit would include a gradual climb up to Thorung La, a mountain pass at 17,000 feet that was actually a saddle between two huge peaks, and then down the other side. Our journey was going to take three weeks, and we were all beside ourselves with excitement. I chattered like a stoned chipmunk, spewing nervous, annoying comments while Laszlo laughed uproariously and everyone else smiled along. I was drunk with joy.

We all hiked together for the first day, but conversation started to get old and we all became a bit irritable, the euphoria wearing off with the physical strain. I felt like the fifth wheel, the only one without a partner. The athletic Barb and Steve wanted to hike faster so they went on ahead by a good margin, and Stuart and Cathy decided to stay and linger at one village that they had enjoyed, so I hiked between the two couples, by myself, knowing that there were friends a days or two on either side of me. My trek became most peaceful.

The tiny villages were spaced every few miles apart, so I would move through one or two every day. The trail had used to be a trade route to Tibet, but it had closed when Chinese troops had taken over the Tibetan border, so now it was just a chain of small farming villages, partially sustained by the trekking business that had developed in the 70's. The people there grew rice and made yak-butter tea and were tolerant of us strange foreigners since we were a major part of the economy now. It cost fifteen cents to spread your sleeping bag out on one of their straw-filled mattresses up in the loft, and meals cost the same amount again. You could point to items on the shelf that you wanted to eat, eggs and ramen noodles and biscuits and fried potatoes. I once had a package of German biscuits that had to have been on that shelf for ten years.

The amount of elevation you had climbed could be gauged by the cost of the Coca-Cola. Since every case and crate had to have been hauled in by porters, hung from their heads by thick straps down their backs, the higher the elevation meant the higher the cost. Coke cost about a rupee, or a nickel, in Pokhara; it cost five rupees if you went another 2000 feet higher; and it was forty rupees in the little shop before the Thorung La at the highest point of the journey. Theories of the Economics of Supply and Demand were illustrated in pure form! Had I learned that in Rendigs Fels' economics class at Vanderbilt?

Every day I arose at dawn for a cup of tea, a fried egg, and some toasted flat breads, or *chapattis*, with jam. The main room of each dwelling was always filled with smoke from the stove, which burned dried yak dung as fuel, and your clothes quickly smelled the same way.

These mountain people counted on the yak for *all* their staples: meat, wool for clothing, milk and butter for the creation of tea, dung for burning, bones for fertilizer, labor for turning the corn-grinding wheel. These long-haired cattle were fierce-looking, and we often had to remember that they were only glorified cows when we passed them free-roaming the trail.

In one farmhouse there was a young woman who wanted to show me how she ground corn for her family, so she motioned me to come into a side room off the main house. I sat on a stool while she mashed and mashed with a stone pestle, looking up to smile at me occasionally. She had the typical lovely dark skin of the Nepali woman, bright teeth and eyes and beautiful long black hair that she obviously oiled and kept nice.

She stopped what she was doing and gave me a big smile as she took a handful of corn and tossed it into a heated pan, looking around conspiratorially, and she toasted it over the open fire in the small room. Popcorn! It popped just a small bit, enough to open the kernels a little and make them chewable, but it was so delicious and different! We smiled and nibbled and I watched her grind more corn. She was about 17 or 18, and I think she just wanted some company. It must have been a lonely life for her up there at that age, not married yet, unsure of where she would be in the years to come. I was completely charmed, and a little scared that her father would find me in that room with her and cut my head off.

While hiking the trail the next day, I came across another lovely Nepali woman sitting on a rock as I came around a corner. She was soaking in the sun after having washed her long black hair, and she was combing it and rubbing oil in it with her eyes closed. She was luxuriating like a cat on a warm rock, all stretched out, and she was the most beautiful woman I had ever seen. I approached and she acted as if I wasn't there, but I couldn't avoid her since she was so close to the path. A huge waterfall ran in the distance behind her, framing her beauty. She finally opened her eyes, nodding slightly and saying "Namas-te", the traditional Nepali greeting and salutation. I was in love.

"Namas-te" meant something like "I honor all the inherently good qualities you possess..." and I said it with great reverence to everyone I met. They always smiled and returned the greeting. The beautiful girl by the waterfall did not smile at all. She was too beautiful to be bothered with niceties, I thought. I stupidly asked if I could take her picture, pointing to the small camera I had pulled out of my pocket. She shook her head no, annoyed. I moved along, feeling like an idiot for imposing on her peace. It was the last time I asked a Nepali if I could take a photo.

Gradually I made my way to higher elevations, to Tal, the city by the mountain lake, and to Tatopani, which means "hot water." The bath I took in the hot springs there was my first in two weeks, in a shallow rock pool just along the snow line of the Himalayas. The dirt fell away as if I had never bathed before. The mountain peaks were in full view now, monstrous and imposing, and I felt small next to them, perhaps finding some perspective. I was incredibly happy. My head seemed to have cleared, and my pace had been good up the mountains, legs strong once again.

In Menang, at 10,000 feet, I had to remain a couple of days to acclimatize. I was feeling light-headed from the lack of oxygen. The city was at the same height as the clouds and there was the unmistakable chill of winter coming. No other westerners were there, and the children stared at me and said their greetings before hiding behind pillars or fountains, shyly avoiding the strange-looking white one. I ate potato stew and bartered with an old Tibetan man for cheap gemstones, convinced that my geological background qualified me as a gemologist. From a Chinese refugee, I bought a bronze Tibetan tea set for my parents, which I carefully wrapped and loaded into my backpack. Prayer flags, white cloth hung from strings everywhere, cast blessings into the air with each breeze, and they gave the village a festive look.

When my breath came easier, I was able to move along. The next two days would be hard. I slept in a tiny village that was at 12,000 feet, and I was supposed to make one more stop at the base of Thorung La at 14,000 feet since it would be a very tough climb up and over. However, since I had left that previous village before dawn, I decided to skip the last stop at the base and continue on over the big pass that same day. After all, that allowed me many hours to get from 14,000 feet to 17,000 feet and back down to the little tea lodge on the other side at 15,000 feet. I could make it; I was Superman. The natives at that last little rest stop at the base begged me to stay with them one more night and start afresh early the next day, but I refused, ready to tackle the high mountain pass.

Soon there was a steeper slope made of cobble-sized debris from ice-wedged rock outcrops. Leading up to the mountain peaks, I passed several lobate glaciers, hearing their pendulous limbs suddenly crack and rumble off in the distance. While there had always been a breeze, there was no wind sound as there were no plants or leaves to blow, and the only person or living thing for miles and miles was *me*. I crossed a shallow frozen river and squinted in the bright sun at the peaks around me, going up and up. The lack of oxygen was much more noticeable now, me taking two steps and then stopping to catch my breath, over and over. Two steps; stop. Two steps; stop. I briefly thought about turning back, but I didn't want to backtrack and waste all that time, so on I went, two steps at a time, stop, and breathe. The day went on; the hours passed. The sun moved across the clear, thin sky, towards a rocky peak, though I did not notice it so much.

The rock debris was soon as big as briefcases scattered about, not moving when I walked on the thick pieces, and the trail was now marked by small piles of rock instead of a worn groove through dirt like down at lower elevations. Around every corner I thought I would find the pass, the *La*, but all there was only more path up. I looked at my watch: 4:30, then 5:00, then 6:00. Time was slipping by. Twilight arrived and moved through, faster than me, and I finally reached what appeared to be the top of the pass just as sunlight ran out. I was exhausted and still had to descend at least 2000 feet of steep, rocky terrain to the nearest lodge. I stumbled a few times. As darkness closed in, my tiny flashlight was obviously not going to suffice, and I fell down a slight incline that I never saw, landing on my backpack. That was it; I could not see the trail marks in the distance, and I did not want to fall and break my leg or get lost in this vast, wild, open place, so I decided to stop. The temperature was dropping rapidly.

I found a flat rock on which I lay my thin foam pad, and I got out my friendly, but nearly useless, sleeping bag and spread it across the rock. I set my backpack as a wind-stop against the breeze coming off the mountains and settled in for an uncertain night. I did not take off my clothes in hope of keeping in some body heat, and I made a big mistake by keeping my boots on, tightly laced. I stopped feeling my feet after a couple of hours, but did not think much of it since they were tucked safely away in the recesses of my Blue Kazoo.

It was 8:00 p.m. when I had gotten into my bag, and the temperature kept falling. I tried to stay snuggled inside for warmth, but then I found I wasn't getting enough oxygen, so I had to stick my face out and breathe rapidly, then tuck myself back in and draw the string tight. Time was unmoving. I checked my watch frequently: 9:00, 10:00, 10:30, 11:00...on and on, the night becoming colder with each slowly passing hour. Eventually stars appeared which meant there would not yet be snow, thank goodness. I guessed the temperature was well below freezing, and dropping. I alternated between shivering and gasping for breath, and this kept me awake, the crack and crash of glaciers occasionally punctuating the stillness, far off in the cold distance.

There were peaks to either side of me, 25,000 feet high, and I was nestled between in the saddle of the wide mountain pass, a speck in this great range. I thought I might drift off to sleep but was jolted repeatedly by my fear and that occasional grinding slip of glacier off in the distance. There were no leaves rustling or crickets chirping or wind whistling through anything. Just me and the mountains and the stars and the light breeze trying to suck my heat away from me. I looked at my watch: midnight. No sleep would come tonight. Five more hours until the hint of sun.

I heard a sound on the side of one of the mountains, but how far away was it? Could it be the grind of footsteps? It was a distant crunching sound, rhythmic, like the footsteps of a human. Not a yak; definitely two legs. Perhaps it was another hiker, foolish like me, on a mountain in the middle of the night. The crunching got a little louder. I was at the low point of the pass, so whoever it was would have to walk by me to get over to the other side... but wait, why were these footsteps coming from the tall mountain beside me instead of the valley below? And I know that I didn't make a sound when I walked because the rock debris was too big for me to move with my 175-pound body. Maybe this was an animal... but, no, it had that two-step rhythm. Crunch, crunch, crunch, ... he or she or *it* was getting closer to my little spot on the flat rock, not stopping to breathe, not struggling with the debris or the cold or the lack of air.

I was on a little shelf before the trail dropped off again, so I knew that the traveler would have to rise up before reaching me. He would not see me until he got right up next to me, climbing that last bit of debris before the highest point of the trail. Crunch, crunch, crunch: a nice pace, I thought... but wait again, I remembered that I had to take several breaths every two steps... how could this....thing... set that kind of pace, if he was human? I started to hyperventilate inside my bag and had to stick my head out again to get some air again. Fear was creeping up on me too, and I wondered if this was some crazy nightmare. Not so. I was awake.

It was now just below me, climbing up that last bit of rock, perhaps 100 feet left to ascend, and it was clearly not on a trail. I heard some breathing, like an overweight man grunting through his nose while focusing on his walk. I had a Swiss army knife in my pocket and got it out, flipping the ice-pick blade open, bracing with a need for defense. My muscles tensed and I started to breathe faster, all while trying to keep quiet. Closer it came, crunch, crunch, crunch! It was just below me now, coming up. Was it going to step on me? Had my knife blade locked? Was I hallucinating?

Just before it showed itself as it rose up so close, just below the level of my own rock, I meekly opened my mouth. "Who is it?" I asked. It stopped. A small rock slipped and rolled down the slope nearby. For a split second, there was no sound at all. Then, with a shrill grunt of surprise, it ran back from where it came. Ran! Crunch-crunch-crunch-crunch! It stumbled a little but maintained a very quick pace, its sounds fading around the side of the mountain saddle, disappearing into the starry night through the rocky debris.

Oh my God! What was it! I really started to hyperventilate now, trembling and freezing all at once. It took me another hour to calm down enough to put my knife away. No way! Could that have been...? No, it was not possible. Not.... the Yeti. The abominable snowman? No way.

I had heard stories; we all had, of the beast that was a distant link to humans, living a hidden life in the Himalayan folds. Rarely seen, its scream occasionally heard, its footsteps and some obscure swath of fur or some bone fragment the only clue to its existence. Could I have heard that thing next to me, the Yeti? Who could I ask? Who would believe me? God was I cold!

The night moved slowly, 2:00, 3:00, 4:00, and there was no way I was going to go to sleep. I shivered and fought for breath over and over. Finally, finally: the stars dimmed as the first rays of sunlight streaked the night sky. I was so relieved, dizzy, totally fatigued, and my feet were numb up to my knees and had been for the last five hours. I figured, though, that I could just walk it off and the feeling would return. I climbed out of the bag and packed it up and rolled up the pad to put it away. I was dehydrated from cold, but when I went to drink some water from the plastic bottle I had put in the bottom of my sleeping bag, it was frozen. My feet ached as if asleep, like sand was in them, but I was not worried yet. These toes were now useless lumps and I could barely keep my balance.

I opened a pack of biscuits from my pack, and they had frost on them. Everything I owned was stiff with cold. I got my backpack on and saw a nearby rock pile that showed I was still exactly on the trail. The first bit of sun touched the tip of the tallest mountain and light started to cross the saddle where I shakily stood. Small piles of rocks marked the trail down to the valley below, still very far from any human dwelling or evidence. I was remotely glad I had stayed there for the night because the slope was steep and jagged, and I could have easily fallen and gotten hurt bad. I started down, pausing to take a photo of the mountains around the morning sun and me. I was very sleepy, almost drugged, as I prepared to leave my nest.

As I checked the camera in my pocket, I wondered again about my visitor. What if I had waited just a bit longer to speak, until it had shown its head as it rose up from the rock below? Could I have taken a picture? What if I had taken a picture of the Yeti? I could have been famous, I dreamed...

My legs were not working right as I fought my way down the steep rocky slope. I knew I had to descend at least 2000 feet, and my legs were strong enough to bear that, but my feet stayed numb as I stumbled often. My toes felt like beanbags, just sort of flopping around in a weird sort of way inside my boots. What would it look like when I took off my shoes and socks? I worried all the way down the mountain trail that my toes would be black.

After four hours of descent, now mid-morning, I saw a small tea lodge in the distance, at the point where the trail leveled off to a more reasonable slope. When I finally reached it, two women were sweeping the stone steps in front and building a fire for their tea. They looked up, obviously surprised to see a Westerner stumbling down the mountain trail at that time of day. They spoke in Nepalese, and I think they were asking me what in Hell I was doing up there during the night. They made tea for me as fast as they could, and I drank five cups before feeling warmed up and not so thirsty. In some hesitant desperation, I took off my boots and socks and found my toes to be pasty white, but not black like I feared. I inspected them closely and found them to be quite cold to the touch. I put them by the fire to warm, but I couldn't feel the heat at all and worried that I might burn them, so I put my socks and boots back on. I paid for my tea and left for the village nearby, wondering if I should have mentioned the word *Yeti* to the women.

I found a very nice little lodge below the mountain pass, in a village where an ancient monastery lay crumbling to dust. I got a nice room with sunlight streaming in and decided to rest here for a few days. The manager was a teenage Nepali man who wore jeans and a British T-shirt and spoke very good English. He had lived in England for a while and seemed streetwise, though he was clearly comfortable among the country people who lived and worked nearby. This hotel was also a little farm, with goats and chickens milling around the lovely yard, surrounded by a low stone wall.

The next day, though my feet were starting to ache more, I walked about the village and went into the crumbling monastery. I could tell that the building would fall at any minute, but I ignored the crude warning signs. In some rubble at one of the inner rooms, I saw a little leather strap sticking out. I dug a little in the loose sand and found that it was a purse-like container filled with herbs of some sort, like a medicine man's kit. I found two more buried nearby. I put them in my pocket and took them home, not knowing anything about them. Customs could have had a field day with that had they searched me later, the young American with the bags full of strange herbs...

Back at the hotel, lying in a chair in the yard, I enjoyed the sun. The Nepali manager and two country workers were preparing the area for something, spreading a cloth on the ground and bringing out tools and pans of water. I asked what they were doing, and the manager told me that they were going to make sausage, and said with a generous smile, "Would you like to watch?"

Sure, I told him, and they led a goat right into the backyard area where I had been laying. They tied him up to a small tree over the blanket, and the manager took his very sharp knife and slit the goat from neck to mid-chest. Before the goat could move or bleat or anything, the manager opened the goat's chest, reached in, and pulled out what I think was the goat's heart. The goat suddenly became glassy-eyed and fell straight down. That was the first time I had ever seen anything killed in front of my own eyes, and I was stunned at how unreal this scene was.

The workers methodically took the goat apart, setting the innards off to the side where they were chopped up into a chunky pile on a tree stump cutting board. The meat was set into another blanket and hauled into the kitchen for curing and storage and distribution, I figured. The young hotel manager took the intestines and uncoiled them, squeezing out the stuff onto the grass for the birds to pick through. The head went into a basket and was covered. I had to look away many times until I got used to the carnage, which eventually became fascinating.

When the intestines were cleared and tied off, the manager starting stuffing the chopped organs into the long intestinal tube and pushed the mass on through to the tied end. Eventually the intestine was full and was brought into the kitchen. I followed and saw them put the whole thing into a pot full of boiling water and spices. In a few minutes, they pulled the long curled thing out of the pot, now nicely browned, and divided it and started eating it, fresh and hot and steamy. The manager smiled and generously offered me some. I tried to eat a piece but just could not bring myself to put it in my mouth. It smelled good, but I think the look of mild horror was still on my face, and the Nepali men laughed good-naturedly and said things about me in their lovely language, shaking their heads and smiling.

I figured my feet would warm up, but they never really did. In fact, I did not feel my toes again for a couple of months, and there was an aching throughout them that was deep and annoying, but I was thankful they were still mine.   The Nepali winter was coming, and I figured it would be best to move on back to Katmandu and then, eventually, to Europe. I left a note at the little hotel for Stuart and Cathy, and set out on the trail. I was rested and happy again, and my legs were strong and firm from all the climbing and walking, everything I needed in my backpack.

All along the journey, the thing that kept entering my mind, which I kept dreaming about, was that I still loved football and wanted to play more. Even while trekking the Himalaya, I kept picturing myself catching a short pass across the middle and turning up-field at just the right time, making the defenders miss, finding the sideline and following it to the end zone, linebackers diving helplessly at my ankles. For some unknown reason, all the pain and humiliation and mistrust of the past faded when I realized how much football had meant to me. I had more business left on the gridiron, I figured, and I was only 22.

In Katmandu I pulled the folded envelope out of my pack that had Anna's number in Amsterdam on it. I went to the post office to call her, and it was a complicated and long process with operators and payments to a man behind a counter, but it was worth it because she was thrilled to hear from me. I asked if I could come stay with her, and she wept with joy. Maybe she was more excited about the prospects than I was, since I wanted to explore the possibilities of football more than the lure of relationships. I bought the ticket that day for the Netherlands on KLM.

I found a small Dutch-English language guide in Katmandu, and I studied it while sipping tea in smoky restaurants. The pronunciation guide was excellent, and I practiced all the numbers and basic phrases. *Nederlands* seemed a lot like English, and certain words fit really well with our own language. For example, "*shtuff-sucker*" meant vacuum cleaner, which was totally logical to me. The "g" in Dutch was to be pronounced like the Hebrew "ch", in the back of the throat. I got the counting and greetings down pat.

I bid Nepal a sad and grateful farewell, leaving a note explaining everything for my friends at the American Express office. I vowed to return to the Himalayas someday. I am sad that they have had so much unrest there since my departure.

Anna met me at the modern Schipol Airport with flowers and more tears. She seemed frailer than I remembered her in Africa, different, but still pretty. I was happy to see her too, anxious to get on with the next phase of my life. Was there football here? Anna was excited to tell me that she had called the Amsterdam Rams of the Netherlands American Football Federation. The Rams and the Crusaders were two Amsterdam teams in the league, and very competitive. So the Rams coach-player-founder, Ronald Eggar, was very excited to meet an American college player.

Anna lived in the suburb of Reigersbos, which meant "Heron Woods" and was just a short train ride from Amsterdam. Like much of Holland, this area had been reclaimed from soggy wetlands by draining and damming the area. Earthen dikes and canals, adding to the charm of the country, were everywhere, ready to fight back the rush of water. It was an engineering marvel, this country that had once been under the Suider Sea. The people were resolute and proud of their forebears' ingenuity. Housing was in great demand, since Holland allowed in many immigrants without hesitation, but Anna, being a teacher, had a great modern apartment. I moved my backpack in and she welcomed me home.

I called Ronald of the Rams and he invited me to an indoor throw-around in a local gym, giving me instructions to the building with very good English. Almost everyone in Holland knew English; their schools made them learn so that they wouldn't be limited to Dutch in an English-speaking world. At the gym, I showed up with tennis shoes and shorts and wrist tape and supposed I looked like the experienced athlete. Everyone else there was in jeans or nice sweat-suits. They ranged from 15 to 40, most of them 30-ish laborers who had seen American football on local cable specials and just wanted to hit someone. They had mostly learned about the game from highlights and movies, and watching them try to catch the ball and cover receivers made me realize that few of them understood the intricacies of the game. I nodded greetings to some of them, and stretched in the corner. Ronald came over, a thick man with obvious strength. Unlike some of the others, he obviously knew what a weight-room was for.

I tossed the ball with some of the younger boys, and they quickly saw that I knew how to catch a ball. The leather felt good. My eyes and hands knew where to go, and the throws were easy, familiar. After a while, we started running some crude pass routes, under Ronald's direction.

My routes were crisp and linear, unlike the circular and gradual routes of the beginners. The ball stuck to my hands like it was part of me, and I tucked and turned up-field each time in a familiar motion. I had the advantage of growing up with a football in the backyard and having learned the game from some of the best in the country. The Dutch were all just now learning. I liked where I was right then.

When sides were chosen for a loose pick-up game, I was the first taken. It was incredible to be wanted for the first time in my football career. I caught several passes from the young quarterback and he seemed thrilled to throw to me. One boy named Ivan, whose mother had moved to Holland from the Dutch colony of Surinam, came up and smiled a charismatic smile and told me he loved football. He asked me if I would teach him how to play, and it was obvious that he was hungry to learn. I was flattered, as he was already a pretty darned good football player.

Ivan and I became inseparable. He was 15 and a tremendous athlete, lithe and graceful and the only other person who seemed to know how to really catch a ball. He idolized Gary Clark of the Redskins, who was the perfect NFL receiver at that time. Ivan studied and emulated Clark's moves from the TV highlights as well as he could, and Ivan was good at it. As we talked, I found out that he lived in a housing unit just a block away from Anna in Reigersbos, along with three other young men from the team. Ivan was the star of the Second Division Rams, a younger group of players, the Rams' "minor-league" team.

Ronald liked what he saw and invited me to join the Rams, and I was thrilled. So what if it was a bunch of guys putting on shiny uniforms without understanding the game. So what if some of them were thugs who just wanted to smack somebody in the head. I was going to play. And to top it off, Ronald asked me to help coach the second division team, with all those nice young players. I would get to play alongside them, too, if I wanted, since there were no Americans on that team yet. Each Federation team was allowed two players from outside Holland.

Anna was excited for me, since she wanted me to be happy and stay with her, and I felt appreciated for the first time in a long while. She knew nothing of football but was eager to learn, and I found her to be an interesting woman. I found her quirks cute, such as the way she always dressed in clothing better suited for a man, flat and baggy, like the Annie Hall look in a way. She seemed pretty smart but never wanted to seem smarter than those she was around. And she always let me know that she wanted me to be happy, that she would do anything for me. I felt that I loved her, and I knew she loved me. Perhaps there was in imbalance of love offered, but it did not seem to matter at that time. I was still healing and needed some attention of that kind.

When the weather got better, the team played a pickup game in a local park in complete pads. I had had my parents send me my cleats from Vanderbilt, and the team loaned me a set of equipment, though everyone else was expected to buy his own. We looked like a glorified gang of thugs and many curious people gathered around to watch us slide around in the mud in the middle of Amsterdam. Players were just hitting each other everywhere on the field, regardless of where the ball was. I stayed far to the outside and ran pass routes and stalk-blocked the man covering me, who couldn't get around no matter what he did. It felt wonderful.

We went to a sleepover football camp for three days in some city outside of Amsterdam. The team had hired an American coach and two other player/coaches from the local American Air Force base, none of whom had ever coached before. In fact, the head coach was just a good old southern boy from Alabama who drank beer and told people to block harder and run faster. He knew nothing of the game or how to coach it, but he had gotten the job by sounding knowledgeable. I took the younger boys off to a separate practice field and taught them the basics of stance and start and form running. They wanted to learn. I had to chew them out a little to get them focused, and they responded by working harder. All young men want direction and to be told to stop screwing around. How did I get to be a coach? Wow.

My kids got better, and we figured out which plays would serve us best, nothing fancy. The boys who lived near Anna became the nucleus of the team since we practiced plays in the yard near their home every day. Ruud was the quarterback, a tough kid who threw surprisingly well for a newcomer, and his brother Emil was a decent running back who did as he was told and ran hard. Ivan was the receiver, and I was the flanker. Other guys, some flabby and out-of-shape, became the blockers and backups, and we had enough people to play every position. These were nice young men, respectful and appreciative of the American who "knew" so much.

When we first started our practices as a whole team back at the Rams' practice facility, the players were jogging or walking around casually, stretching whichever way they felt like, and not looking good doing any of it. I pulled them together, looked them over with the sternest face I could muster, and told them that this was not the way to play winning football. They listened, eyes wide. It became clear what a serious attitude could do for a group of young men.

I explained what I expected of them, and they starting working. Our drills and stretching became rhythmic and regular, and practices began to flow easily. We ran the same play over and over until it worked flawlessly, and it was obvious that we were starting to care for each other; the boys started to help each other learn the plays and use good form. If a play worked, the man with the ball was expected to come offer thanks to his linemen, which the big lugs loved. By the time we had a first scrimmage in spring, under typically-overcast *Nederlands* skies, we could move the ball and take it away from the opponent.

Ivan was a great receiver and we played off each other well. I often set screens for him and him for me, and we blocked downfield like pros. Our big men stood strong and made holes for the running backs, and our power sweep to the right side was devastating to defenses as Emil ran as fast as he could with the ball. His brother Ruud became a confident quarterback, throwing very well under pressure and never straying from his protective blockers, who worked very hard to keep defenders off him.

I caught a couple of balls and faked out some defenders, and Ivan caught pass after pass, often making his defenders look silly. In one game, Ruud hurt his shoulder and I had to step in at quarterback, which was silly since I had never even practiced that position, but we did okay and completed a good few passes. After our first victory, I was allowed to present the game ball, which I gave, with great flourish, to the entire offensive line. They went crazy, throwing soda and beer all over and shrieking with delight. What fun to be able to help make these young men so confident and proud.

Anna was still hoping I was happy, but her constant attention began to wear on me. I felt guilty for being there with her when I did not return her affections readily, and it became a bit smothering in her modest apartment. Little things she did began to bother me, and I magnified them in my restless brain. She was such a nice woman, but the luster had worn off quickly.

I caught several more passes and guided our team to a win or two, but my unhappiness with Anna was starting to make me a bit depressed. While I liked trying to learn Dutch and shopping and cooking and being in this delightful country, I was getting itchy to move on to a more relevant phase in my life. At least I had football working out for me.

In our fifth game, I caught a pass and turned up-field. I was knocked out of bounds by a defender and landed on my right shoulder, full-force. It stung a little, but I ran back to the huddle, proud of the big yardage gain I had just made. On the next play, I was supposed to block a defensive back, but when I lifted my arms, only the left one went up. My right shoulder seared like it had a sudden gunshot wound and I realized I was in trouble. I pulled myself out for the rest of the game.

That night it was so sore I could not sleep, so Anna took me to a hospital for evaluation. The x-ray revealed nothing, though I told the doctor that he was not scanning far enough up on my shoulder; he had been focusing on my A-C joint, the one that connects the clavicle to the top of the shoulder. The Dutch call it the "*klavier-sleutel*", or piano-key, since it can be pushed down like the hammer of a piano. Made sense. My clavicle ached endlessly, and I had to rig up my own sling since the doctor told me there was nothing wrong with my throbbing shoulder.

I was careful and rehabilitated my wing as well as I could, remembering the care given at Vanderbilt to my numerous injuries, and I eventually came back to play one more game some weeks later. My heart wasn't in it though, and I started planning to go back to the United States. Anna was devastated that I was not going to stay, and I was horrified and guilt-ridden at the thought that I might have misled this sweet girl. She sobbed for days, fighting to keep some pride but failing miserably, trying to convince me she was worthwhile. Ivan's mother let me move in with them for a few days while I made arrangements.

The team was saddened that I was going to leave, especially the young men who had risen from such a basic level. They presented me with a team jersey and flag, which touched me deeply. My young friend Ivan had had no other male figure in his life, and I felt really lousy that I would be leaving him since we had spent nearly every day together since I had arrived. I honestly loved that kid. I tried to think of ways that I could get him to come with me, but there was no chance.

I got on a plane in the middle of summer, meeting my brother in Atlanta so I wouldn't have to make my parents see me on such short notice. There was much to be done. I wanted to be a teacher and a coach. Surely some school would want someone like me, a guy who would work hard and always remain loyal. I would go back to school to learn how to do it, maybe get a Masters in Education.

As another aside, when I had a shoulder operation two years later to remove some torn cartilage and smooth some bone, the doctor asked, "When did you break your collarbone?" The x-ray revealed that I had indeed, a couple of years earlier, broken my collarbone high up. It was clear as day, the doctor said, and the bone had knitted well.

Chapter 6: Cranbrook

Back in the states, there was no money left, and I was torn between going back to school to get my teaching degree or finding a job for a while, maybe in Nashville. I got my brother to take me from Atlanta back to East Tennessee to see my parents, and I was going to have to ask my folks for some cash, that was clear. Phooey.

We had been virtually out of touch for a year. Anna had found their number and called them in tears to ask about me as soon as I had left Holland, further confusing them. What did they think of a son who had dumped a poor girl overseas, dropped out of a masters program at Vanderbilt, and circled the globe in search of self while living out of a backpack? It was obvious they were proud of the European football thing though, since they had mistakenly thought it had been like the NFL and had told all their friends. I felt more at peace than I had in a long time.

I saw my car, the cute golden Mazda they had bought for me a lifetime ago. It had been parked for a year in their driveway, on a slope, so there was a divot in the brake pad where the shoe had been stuck for that whole time. It felt good to drive again, since I hadn't done so in over a year, though every time I slowed down I could feel the divot rhythmically grinding away in the brake.

I borrowed a few hundred dollars from my folks and headed to Nashville, knowing I could crash at the Alpha Epsilon Pi house. I was a bit more of a celebrity now, and it felt good to be treated so royally by the awestruck younger brothers. I visited my old professors, who offered me more scholarship money to come finish the masters degree I had started a couple of years earlier, but I turned it down, perhaps foolishly. It seemed time to prepare for teaching, since that was what I really wanted to do. So I headed over to the career planning office again, and I asked about education colleges while looking for teaching jobs.

My buddy Andy Cohen, who had been my big brother at ΑΕΠ and had encouraged me entirely in my football journeys (he had been an all-state tight end and punter in high school), called me up and invited me to join him and his wife, Sheila, for a little vacation up in Michigan. Andy had started working for a buddy's father in the steel business, and Sheila had gotten a teaching job at a high school called Cranbrook. They were housemasters in a dorm there also.

I remembered Andy telling me about Cranbrook years earlier, since he had once been a star there, and he had gushed that it was more beautiful than Vanderbilt or any school in Nashville. I hadn't believed him. How could a high school be all that?

When I got to Bloomfield Hills, one of the wealthiest villages in the nation, I passed all kinds of country clubs and wide sprawling estates. There were the homes of entertainers and pro athletes and fast-food magnates, Aretha Franklin and Piston basketball star Isaiah Thomas and Mike Ilitch of Little Caesars Pizza who owned the hockey Red Wings and the baseball Tigers. There were massive green lawns and wealth everywhere, and nestled in the middle of all of this was a magnificent 340-acre spread, its stony walls enclosing the rolling hills of the Cranbrook Educational Community.

Inside the Cranbrook compound was a science museum, an art museum, a prestigious academy where one could earn a masters degree in fine arts, and the schools. Not only were the buildings architecturally unique, but they also followed a wonderful formula of mixing structure and symmetry with the whimsical freedom of the artisans who created them: a brick pulled out here, an ornate sculpture there. Ivy and trees and students swarmed in and amongst the brick and stone and steel.

Eliel Saarinen had designed this place at the request of the Booth family back in the 1920's. The Booths were newspaper magnates who had purchased the old farm-site, with orchards all around, at a time when it cost near nothing; now the land was priceless. Saarinen's architecture was deemed genius, as Booth had allowed him to use any and all materials that he demanded, and the school had gained renown as one of the best in the country.

There were originally two campuses for the high school, though they had since been theoretically merged into one big upper school. The boys' campus of Cranbrook was modeled after the old Cranbrook Kent school in England, with slate roofs and ivy-covered brick and an old Eastern boarding-school feel. And across the man-made lake stood Kingswood, the girls' campus, Saarinen's jewel, ornate and spectacular. Strong lines of texture and art-deco motif set it apart from any structure ever built, thin wavy sandstone pillars holding up magnificent green copper roofing. It took my breath away the first time I saw any of it, literally. A statue by Carl Milles or Marshall Fredericks could be found anywhere on the property, and a lyrical Eero Saarinen window frame or lovely Loja Saarinen woven tapestry was around every corner inside the buildings. Sight lines and vistas abounded, intentionally, as the senior Saarinen was a genius at layout. Cranbrook was now a national historic site, and people came from all over the world just to walk around the campus. It was easy to see why, and I was quite smitten.

Andy and Sheila showed me around with pride, and I was astonished and in love, all at once. Being in charge of the Cranbrook dorm meant they actually got to live there inside this gem! It was early August, so there were few teachers around and no students, and it all seemed idyllic. God, I was envious of them, living and working right here at the most beautiful place in the world.

Sheila introduced me to several administrators at Cranbrook, including the new head of the Upper School. Arlyce Seibert, a confident woman who wore poufy scarves, mentioned to me that there was a partial opening as geology and Earth science instructor since the previous teacher had recently taken a similar job out east. She asked if I would like to apply for the job, since Sheila was in high esteem there and had recommended me. I really couldn't believe it. Didn't I need a teaching certification to teach? They told me that I needed to work towards one, but that I did not need certification immediately at a private school. I was more than qualified, they said!

Arlyce had me interview with each of the deans of academics, student life, and boarding. For a 23-year-old, having a Vanderbilt background mixed with international archeological and athletic experience must have impressed them. Maybe I had them all fooled...

Arlyce called me in and offered me a part-time job as science teacher and assistant football coach, and she told me I could move into a small two-room apartment on the top floor of the dormitory. Money, a job, and a home, all at once! She then mentioned that it was too bad I didn't have a religion background because there was a part-time opening in the religious studies department as well. I was excited to tell her that, at Vanderbilt, I had chosen a minor in religious studies. Plus, I rushed to explain, I had gotten first-hand experience with Buddhism in Nepal, Hinduism in India, and

Islam in Africa, not to mention growing up Jewish in the Bible Belt! Did that qualify me to teach teenagers about the world's religions? Her eyes lit up as she revised my contract to read "full-time". We were talking serious money here, some $17,000 a year!

Andy and Sheila were ecstatic, and I could not believe my great fortune. I screamed the news over the phone to Mom and Dad, who were overjoyed that their second son was finally going to get to work. I was instantly a teacher and coach!

Football pre-season started right away, so I had to meet the coach quickly. Dave Schuele was one of those old blood-and-guts, three-yards-and-a-cloud-of-dust coaches, all crew cut and clipboard and whistle and tight black football shorts. He spoke slowly and simply, each word brought out with great effort, then repeated: "What we ...*have*... to do, ...coach,..... is make ....uh.....football players. We have to make football *players*." The man was a living, breathing football cliché, and I loved him. He asked me to put together some of my best passing plays and coordinate our air game, which thrilled me, since I still remembered our wonderful passing offense at Vanderbilt. Of course, he neglected to tell me that his teams only ran the ball, throwing only when absolutely necessary. Dave liked to run the option, pure and simple, and only bad things happened when the ball was in the air, according to his long-held beliefs.

The option is a fascinating offense at the high school level. It can be a great equalizer against bigger teams, especially when you have a quarterback who knows what he's doing. The idea is for the quarterback to put the ball into the first runner's stomach, sometimes giving it to the runner and sometimes faking the give, depending on what the defense does. Then, if the quarterback decides to keep the ball instead of giving it to the first man, he has the option of running with it or pitching it to a third runner. When it is executed well, the defense is left scrambling and guessing and can become very frustrated trying to find the ball. The triple option, they call it. How fun!

We had a marvelous quarterback named John Edman, smart as a whip and quick as a whippet, and amazingly sound of character. He was such a good person that all I wanted, even though I was 6 years older and practically into adulthood, was for him to think highly of me. So I worked with him a lot and taught him where I wanted him to look and throw on the chance that the coach could be talked into a passing play.

We threw and threw and threw after practice, and he had a crisp arm, just like Whit Taylor at Vanderbilt. He was darned good, and Coach Schuele knew it too. I never had to tell John twice how to execute each part of the play. He corrected himself, figuring out where the mistakes were and adjusting them without a spoken word from me. Coaching him was an honor. Kids like that make guys like me look good.

In the classroom once school started, I worked my butt off. In Earth Science, I was going to make sure these kids learned about the rock cycle and crystals and clouds. In my senior religion class, I had each student do a project on some branch of religious studies. One of the kids in that first class of mine was a true soccer star, soon to be world famous. Alexi Lalas was a pretty good student, but who could have predicted that he would be on the U.S. World Cup soccer team and make the Olympics and become the most recognized American soccer player in the world? I don't know if he got much out of my class, but I sure like telling soccer fans I once taught him. I doubt he remembers one thing about me.

I guess I did a reasonable job in that first year because they not only offered me a contract for the next year but they also made me a house advisor in the sophomore dorm. Now I was in charge of 25 boys, each fifteen years old, some from Detroit and Pontiac, some from Saudi Arabia and Europe, others from Korea and Hong Kong. What an amazing place Cranbrook was, and they were giving me more responsibility, even though I was only 24.

Paychecks piled up on my desk since I never needed to leave campus. I got up early each day and prepped for lab classes and taught, then ran over to sports practice and the weight room and then to my other responsibilities in the dorm at night, a quick stop for meals in between. The school asked me to coach the fencing team, which I knew absolutely nothing about. "That's ok," said the athletic director. "The kids'll teach *you* how to fence."

The fencers were a little nerdy and bookish and artsy, but I took these poor kids out and had them running the stadium steps like football players. They loved me barking at them. It gave them something to whine about with pride, how hard mean Mr. Gerson had made them work just for fencing. I loved being around these kids, who were totally different from football players in their dramatic flair and thespian senses of humor, and they did indeed teach me to fence. I ended up competing with them in several tournaments, since the competitions were open to anyone, and I got to use my foil against fencers from University of Michigan and Wayne State and Oakland University. The college kids all loved to fence against the students from Cranbrook, who were pretty darned good, despite their coach. Several fencers had gone on from Cranbrook to become All-America fencers in college, and there were even some Olympians, though that was before my time. Ann Marsh used to come over from Roeper school to scrimmage with us since they didn't have their own team, and she eventually got a medal in the Olympics for foil. I tell people I coached her too, though she could have sliced me up on the practice track had she chosen to.

At the end of the summer, I was again working with John at quarterback, and we were pleasantly surprised when a magnificent athlete named Ivan Boyd decided to come out for the team as a receiver. I had never seen a young man so talented in the ability to catch a football and move upfield after the catch. Ivan had just gotten over knee surgery and was not expected to even try out for our team, but on the first day of pre-season he left us all with our mouths agape. On one long pass downfield from John's strong arm, Ivan actually overran the ball. In stride, he reached behind himself and caught the ball with one hand behind his back, striding into the end-zone as nonchalantly as an afternoon jog. I had never seen anyone at any level of football do that.

Coach Schuele let me put more of the passing offense into our game plan since we had more talent than before. Ivan had made a believer out of the Coach, snatching the ball off his shoestrings or leaping high into the air to make a one-handed grab in the corner of the end-zone. John had been a good quarterback, but Ivan made John a superior one, and we had a fairly successful 6-3 season with very small players and no defense. Coach was not a very innovative guy, but he always put in many hours and tried to teach the kids an honorable game. I certainly did not want all the responsibilities his job demanded, and I was content to work with receivers and quarterbacks, especially the two we had that year.

I was extremely proud when Ivan was signed to the last football scholarship that Boston College offered in the spring of 1989. In fact, his recruitment was based solely on a shoddy highlight film that one of the volunteer coaches put together, barely showcasing Ivan's exceptional talents from that season. In 1993, Ivan's final college year, on national television, against Notre Dame no less, Ivan caught two amazing touchdown passes and helped to set up the game-winning field goal with a short, clutch reception right up the middle of the field. I was watching the game in the dormitory office, and I got so excited with my yelling that kids were running for cover. This was perhaps one of the greatest college football upsets in history, and I felt like I had caught the touchdown passes myself. I even called the *Detroit News* twice, telling them to make sure they put the name "Cranbrook" beside Ivan's name, though they ignored me.

Sadly, when Ivan and John Edman graduated, the next few teams suffered greatly and Coach Schuele retired as coach.

In the science building, I shared an office with Randy Tufts who was an extremely kind and gentle teacher. He was fifteen years older than me and offered suggestions on how to deal with a whiny boy or disruptive girl or whatever, but not in a pushy way. When I eventually started listening to him, teaching became much easier and less stressful. Randy certainly knew all the tricks, and he became a good and trusted friend, like he was my older brother showing me the way.

In fact, I breathlessly admired all of the teachers at our school. By then I was only teaching freshman science, along with one senior geology elective class. Our department was remarkable. Frank Norton was a genius physics teacher who intimidated the hell out of me. Bob Greene, his huge black beard hiding a perpetually kind face, was a quiet and thoughtful environmental-science instructor who never spoke without considering each word carefully. Russ Conner had taught science for 25 years and knew just about everything (and wasn't afraid to prove it), and Ed Vandam was a doctor of chemistry who never got tired of thrilling kids with balanced equations and puffs of smoke. Sue Spencer was the department head, clucking about us like a mother hen, making sure forms got turned in and labs got cleaned up. All I wanted was for them to think that I was earning my keep. The whole faculty was such: good people who were great teachers, who cared utterly about our students. And they welcomed me into their fold, which made me feel that I, too, was doing important work.

My days were filled with kids and classes and preparation for everything, and I hung out with the Cohens at night. Andy and Sheila and I played basketball three or four nights a week in the Cranbrook Gym. Since Sheila was the girls' basketball coach, she could always get us in and find us a ball. And, of course, even though her knees were totally shot from too many surgeries when she was a high school and college star, her jump shot and defense were still incredible. Andy was just a goon with his big square body, always bullying me to the basket and shoving me around; I usually tried to get on his team so I wouldn't have to cover him on defense and get beaten up.

We played with some old friends of Andy's from his Cranbrook days, guys who were now lawyers and businessmen and brokers, and we could get pretty rough in there. Billy Hill, an assistant to the provost at Wayne State University, had played point guard at Cranbrook and had triple-jumped in college, so you wanted to be on his team. He could pick up his dribble pretty near half court and still beat you to the basket. The Narenz brothers, both in their family's plastics business and on their way to becoming young millionaires, would just as soon kill you as let you take the ball away. One of the lawyers, Adam, would throw all five-foot-five of his self at you the whole way down the court and make you look really bad with his finger-roll baskets. Peter Fayroian was a fellow teacher who had once been a tennis pro, and he was as smooth and lithe as a cat when I covered him. Pete's now the head of the Green Hills School in Ann Arbor. These were intense games.

I was staying thin and healthy in those days because of the basketball and weight room work with Cranbrook kids, and I was much stronger than I used to be, getting more defined every week. I took a couple of seminars on strength and conditioning so I could instruct the kids better, and coaching them made me a better, more attentive athlete. It was fun to work off my normal frustrations in high-intensity court workouts and weight room sessions. This all kept me sane, and it also kept me from dwelling on the lack of young women in my life.

In the summer, Cranbrook ran a very interesting program called Horizons Upward Bound, or HUB. Developed around the time of the Detroit race riots of the late 1960's, it was a summer school program for inner-city kids from Detroit and

Pontiac on our campus. The students were highly-regarded members of their own urban schools and were competing for scholarships to Cranbrook for the regular school year. It was, and is, an earnest and respected program, providing a neat diversity to the Cranbrook student body. We could say that our kids came from all over the world, from Japan and Korea and England, and from the country clubs of Bloomfield Hills and the depths of inner Detroit. The interactions between these kids from totally different backgrounds were amazing to watch; there was always something in common between two 16-year-olds, no matter the upbringing or cultural, racial, and social differences. I got to watch this camaraderie develop as I taught, and every day it got easier to love these kids and our school.

In the summer during HUB, my own Marquis Dormitory became a girls' residence. Since I had no private entrance to my home, the young women had to get used to seeing a male walking through the dorm to get to his apartment. I made it a point to say hello to all adult-looking people in the dorm to explain who I was and why I was in the girls' dormitory. There was never any problem.

One day I was walking through the first-floor lounge to get to my door, completely loaded down with plastic bags full of groceries, me in a flustered hurry and having to go to the bathroom. I noticed a young woman on one of the couches, obviously not a HUB student but not really old enough to be a teacher, either. She was the most beautiful woman I had ever seen, all long blond hair and tight flattering jeans and sweet white T-shirt fitting her so nicely. My first thought as our conversation began: Definitely Out Of My League.

So I introduced myself, and she let me know that she was doing her student teaching through HUB as a part of her Wayne State University education degree. I asked Shelley how she liked Cranbrook, and instead of the usual "its okay" or "its something to do for the summer" or whatever one might expect from a college kid, she told me that she was totally in love with everything about the schools and grounds, and that she wanted to someday teach here. When I told her that I had done so for four years already, she really seemed to be in awe, which of course made me feel like quite the teacher-stud. At that point, I didn't notice or care that the grocery bags were cutting divots into my fingers and that my bladder was ready to burst. All I wanted to do was try to impress this dream of a woman just a little more. We talked about Cranbrook and teaching for a long time, until I finally had to drag myself away with no feeling left in my fingers. I made a mental note that this was a woman I should show a lot of respect for, because, maybe, I could convince her to have another conversation with me, or even go out for a cup of coffee or something. Maybe I had a chance.

As football came around again, Chuck Schmitt replaced the old Coach Dave Schuele. Coach Schmitt was all serious and stern, and everyone knew that he took football seriously, ready to take over a team that had just finished 1-8. I had been helpless in that downward spiral and was thankful that Coach Schmitt had stepped in to take the reigns. Coach Schmitt was immaculately groomed and carried his small, stocky frame like he could walk through walls, and his demeanor made our kids want to walk through walls for him. He borrowed philosophy from the great coach Lou Holtz, preaching that each player should "Do his best, Do what is right, and Care about each other." I loved those guiding principles, and even though I was just a young assistant coach, I wanted to follow those same guidelines, simply because Coach Schmitt preached them with such conviction.

The team rules stated that the players should dress alike and look good and behave well at all times. Coach gave huge responsibility to our seniors to make sure that all guidelines were followed, and they took it quite seriously. Our very small team learned a new type of offense, the "stack", where three running backs lined up in a straight "I" behind the quarterback. The opposing defense would have to guess which one of the players was getting the ball, and that gave us a distinct advantage. On defense, we relied on some good planning by new assistant coach Larry Zimmerman, a wonderful defensive coordinator who brought out talent from the meekest of kids. We lost the first three games against very good opponents, but the kids were encouraged by the way we controlled the ball without ever throwing it and looked very respectable out there. In the first game, our opponent had barely won by a touchdown after having beaten us by 40 the previous year. You could see our players coming together with each contest, believing.

We started winning and eventually got to the point where opposing teams were starting to worry about Cranbrook. We shocked the league and won the next five in a row and faced the hated Country Day school for our final game. They were bigger and meaner and had much more talent than us, but Coach Schmitt got the players all fired up and thinking they were supermen about to take on mortal enemies on the field of battle. Our stack offense was working well, and quarterback Chris Seidner (no John Edman in terms of athletic ability but brilliant as a distributor and faker) was a magician with the ball the whole game. Because our running game was looking so good, Coach took a chance and had Chris throw a wobbly pass to young Mike Howell to make a key first down. Tiny Peter Pirsch, all 130 pounds of free safety, made a key interception off a tipped pass, and Aaron Moore, the little bulldog of a running back, carried the hell out of that football, straight up the middle every time, gaining each yard with ferocity.

Freddie Scott was a star for Country Day and returned a kickoff for a touchdown and caught about a thousand passes in that game. Freddie soon went on to Penn State on scholarship and hung on for a while in the NFL. After leading for much of the game, we lost in the final minute of play on a one-yard run set up by one of Freddie's receptions. There was a lot of weeping, but also a lot of pride since Country Day had been ranked as one of the best teams in the state and we had been given no chance by anybody outside of our team of winning that game. None of our senior players, except Aaron, who gave it a go at tiny Washington University in St. Louis, ever played another game of organized football. We almost had those mean Country Day boys.

At the team banquet that fall, Coach pumped up all of us, making each player and coach feel special and excited about what he had accomplished. Coach Schmitt and Coach Zimmerman praised me in front of all the boys for the job I had done as assistant coach, though I had just run around all season being encouraging and enthusiastic, not really in charge of anything. It felt great to have these kids clap for me and know that I had made a difference. That was the probably the best 5-4 team that ever played the game, and we had come so far together. I loved them all.

Coach Schmitt broke my heart and resigned from Cranbrook in January. He never actually said goodbye to me, which hurt me, since I had given him tons of sweat and effort. But it was obvious that his stern ways and demanding tone and need for structure did not match Cranbrook's free-flowing style, and he opted for the boarding-school mentality of the East. He had influenced me greatly in only one wonderful football season, and now Chuck was off to Pomfret Academy, then settling in at Case Western Reserve in Ohio.   I was left without a mentor on the field.

During that season I had begun a wonderful courtship with Shelley. She had been hired at the end of the summer to be in the girls' dorm as a House Advisor, and she was also going to teach part-time in the Upper and Middle Schools. I was ecstatic. Since we were both house advisors, we had to attend all the pre-school dorm meetings together. We always found ourselves sitting next to each other, and it had to be obvious to everyone that we found each other interesting. The amazing part was that this stunning woman was even remotely interested in a *schlumpf* like me. Even more amazing was that I didn't say anything stupid enough to make her run away from me during our conversations. When did I learn this art of measured restraint?

Things started out slowly, and we got to know each other better, though we had not actually gone on a date. My friend Sheila, even more like a sister to me now, was also there at all of these dorm meetings and got to know Shelley and insisted that I ask her out. At one faculty picnic, a furry brown caterpillar fell out of a tree and landed on my head, all of us sitting on a checkered blanket eating hamburgers. Shelley saw it and said, later, that I looked so cute and helpless, not wanting to squish the poor caterpillar into my curly hair in an attempt to remove it. So she took it out with her own pretty hands, so delicate in my hair, my head and neck tingly where her wrists dusted my skin. Sheila told me later that she had known that was the moment of impact, when I had fallen flush on my face in love.

So I tried to learn everything I could about her. Shelley's skin was light-colored and delicate, and I noticed that she had some slight purplish marks in her arm, almost like where drug users put needles, but not really that noticeable unless one was looking intently for such things. I also detected, especially during a mixer game for dorm residents, a slight limp that she tried to cover. She was awkward when she ran, as if she hadn't run before.

She answered this series of questions for me one day at another picnic table at another school function where we found ourselves briefly alone in a gentle Michigan summer afternoon: Shelley told me she was a hemophiliac. She asked if I knew what that meant, and I said yes, sure, of course, though I only knew some little bit. Shelley explained that it meant that her joints often became swollen with blood that didn't clot the right way, but that the myth of "death by casual cut" never really happened these days. She had plenty of platelets to make the initial blood sticky enough to clot on the surface, so bleeding from a cut was not an issue for her.

Shelley added one other bit of grim news: her little brother Patrick, also a hemophiliac, had died just two years earlier, at the age of 13. Her eyes filled with tears when she mentioned it, then she shook them away and went back to cheerfulness. It was not time to ask how he had died, since she did not volunteer any more information. But it was clear that she had loved him very much and it would be an issue somewhere in our lives. There was more to this, to be saved for another time. She seemed appreciative that I didn't push.

We were starting to make little efforts to be near each other. It was amusing how we always seemed to end up at the same table or meal or meeting, next to each other. Others were starting to notice. My fellow teacher Randy saw us together and shot me that knowing glance that men sometimes share. He asked me, all wry and wily, who the pretty young blond was, and I told him that she was this wonderful young science teacher who was going to be part-time with us in the upper school. He could tell, he told me later, that I was lost in love in a big way. And he was so right.

I had questions that I could not possibly ask Shelley at that point in our relationship. I did not want to embarrass her, and I didn't want to chase her off. I had heard some things about hemophilia, that it was what had ailed the Russian Czar's son and that some of Queen Victoria's children had had it. I really liked this Shelley's guts and beauty and mind and charisma and everything about her, including hemophilia, and I needed to know more and more. And her eyes, man, her blue eyes burned into me.

Andy Cohen's dad was a provost at Wayne State and had been a professor for a long time at the medical school there. Unquestionably, Dr. Sandy Cohen was the most intelligent person I knew at that time. I had met him when Andy and Sheila had invited all of us over for Passover dinners and to celebrate the Jewish high holidays. I would ask him direct medical questions at the dinner table, and I would watch him dig deep into the recesses of his brain and draw out perfect answers. It was as if he had a filing cabinet in his head that he was able to open up and bring to the surface of his consciousness at will. I doubted if Dr. Cohen had ever truly forgotten anything he had learned in his life.

So I called him at his house one night that fall, and I asked him if he knew anything about hemophilia. Dr. Cohen was intrigued, and the pause told me that he was going through his mental "filing cabinet" for the proper answers. "Well," he said, probably amused at my curiosity and intrigued that I would call this important man at home, "I'm not a hematologist, but what do you want to know?"

I asked him to give me the skinny on hemophiliacs, what their symptoms were and how limited they were. I wanted to know what I should worry about if I were to have some sort of friendship with one. He explained that there was nothing to worry about, that hemophiliacs generally take care of themselves. He explained about the missing clotting factor that defined the disease, that a hemophiliac was usually missing Factor VIII, which was one link in the fragile chain of the blood-clotting cascade. Therefore, he said, hemophiliacs rarely stopped bleeding unless they received this Factor VIII as an infusion. Factor VIII had been a miracle cure for many hemophiliacs as it allowed them to lead somewhat normal lives with minimal caution, allowing their blood to clot normally after infusing the product.

Dr. Cohen intimated that there was more to know, and he kindly invited me to ask away. "Dr. Cohen," I asked innocently," what kind of problems would a female hemophiliac have, like, during her period or during childbirth?"

"Hold on a second there, Gary. Are you sure your friend is a classical hemophiliac? That's extremely rare for a woman."

I could picture him on the phone, rubbing his magnificent gray mutton-chop sideburns, intrigued by my naiveté. I explained, "Yes, she told me she was a real hemophiliac. She told me that her father was also a hemophiliac and Shelley was herself a rarity, a genetic mutation. The only way for a woman to be a classical hemophiliac, she said, was if Dad was a classical hemophiliac and Mom was a carrier of the gene for hemophilia."

Dr. Cohen agreed with me, and congratulated me on my knowledge of genetics, even though I had gotten all of that from Shelley herself after she had drawn me the biology-class punit squares with X and Y chromosomes.

I continued. "But, Shelley's mother is *not* a carrier of the gene, so Shelley is not *supposed* to be a hemophiliac, but she *is*. She's a genetic mutation."

I could tell that Dr. Cohen was a little unsure of my homework here, but he accepted what I had to say. He asked if she had enlarged joints, as many hemophiliacs had gotten bleeding in their joints when they were young and had not had the advantage of factor. I told him she did not have large joints, but her ankles were in terrible shape and hardly bent. She had shown me this one afternoon, the scars from the operations in an effort to stem her frequent bleeds, and I had thought it was remarkable that she did all the things she did without complaining. The needle marks in her arm could be explained by infusions of clotting factor. That made sense.

In Shelley's case, a small bit of bleeding in any joint would continue unabated until the entire joint cavity was filled with blood. Anyone who has had a severely sprained ankle can understand this kind of pain, except in a hemophiliac it could occur so frequently that the person would go months without ever bending that joint, in constant pain and unable to walk. The blood in the joint would slowly dissolve many parts of that swollen hinge, so many hemophiliacs had calcified joints and no cartilage and crazy kinds of muscle atrophy. Walking on an ankle like that was like walking on fire, Shelley later said, and changing the way you walk could result in a hip or knee bleed. Yet she fought through this pain and tried to walk normally, every day, every step. As an athlete who had, at times, suffered through pain on the field, I was in awe of what Shelley had done.

Dr. Cohen told me that there was more, and he was as factual as he could be. "Gary, there was a significant problem with the clotting factor starting in the 1970's and 80's. It seems that the blood pool from which factor was derived had been contaminated with the virus that causes AIDS."

This was when I got a tight feeling in my stomach. I asked Dr. Cohen, "Do you think that her brother could have died from AIDS?"

"Yes, Gary, that's very possible. Something like 95%, though I don't remember the actual statistic, of all hemophiliacs who had infused with Factor VIII during that time got the virus. That was before heat-treatment had been introduced to kill it. Her brother probably died of AIDS-related illnesses."

There was another question to be asked, and he and I both knew it. I swallowed, and I don't remember if I said this out loud, but his response told me that I had. "Do you think...is it possible that Shelley is also infected?"

Dr. Cohen shot from the hip. "There is a very good chance that she is infected. But, of course, you can't be sure until she tells you."

It was hard to be logical because I was in love. This was not Jenny who could not communicate with me, or Anna who was not able to have a balanced relationship, or the lifeguard in Massachusetts who blinded me with her body but had no real use for me. Both feet were on the ground with Shelley. This was a woman who I worked with and saw every day, who loved the kids and brought them out of their tiny selves and recognized the need to help them grow. And she saw, somehow, some good qualities in me. What was the risk here? A broken heart, which is a risk in any relationship? Or more?

Coach Schmitt's words to the football players rang in my ear: Do your best. Do what is right. Care. The peace these words brought to me could not be measured. And, God, I loved that beautiful woman, maybe even more now.

Chapter 7: Love and Patrick

I was done for. Shelley was in my eyes and my head and my chest and I was lost deep. She was bright like the sun, her laugh a breeze through my hair, my very breath. I knew she loved me, I knew that I craved all of her. And the one thing I knew for sure was that our road would be rough. And so what.

Even though she hadn't confided to me yet, there was really no doubt in my mind that Shelley had the HIV, the Human Immunodeficiency Virus, the virus that caused AIDS. Up to that point, my knowledge of the virus had been limited to whatever I had picked up from the news by chance. It was a disease that was so far away from me and everyone I knew, all of us naive and innocent in the fall of 1990. It was the gay man's disease, the prostitute's and drug user's problem, wasn't it? How could it ever reach us in our "safe" neighborhood, behind the stone walls and mansions of wealth and privilege?

Shelley saw me teach some of my classes. "You sure have a way with kids," she would say with sincere, sweet eyes, making my head swell. "I sure hope I can be as good a teacher as you are, Gary."

Truthfully, she was an amazing teacher in her own right. She was so organized, so prepared, and she really connected with the kids she taught. While I entertained and made jokes for the young high school kids, she focused her students and got more work from the 6th grade girls than they ever thought possible. I sometimes watched her from the hallway whenever I had a free period, and she was quite impressive with her command of the material and the attentiveness of her kids and her amazing preparation. Her own praise for me, though, was better than a kiss from such an angel.

I finally, finally, finally asked her out on a real date, at one of the fall faculty meetings. We were sitting together and listening to the heads of schools talk about how great Cranbrook could be, and we agreed with them in our heads and hearts since we loved our school, and I took a deep breath and asked Shelley if she wanted to go out for a piece of pie in Birmingham. It seemed an innocent enough offer, so she would not have to call it a date if she didn't want to, and we could just sit and chat like we did in the Kingswood dining hall at supper. She was cheerful and smiled brightly as she looked into my eyes. "Sure!" I was thrilled, way down deep inside.

On the car ride there, for some reason, I stared straight ahead and said something dumb, like, "I hope you don't mind, but I don't really feel like talking that much tonight...." Maybe I was just trying to ease the pressure, assuming she felt some. She just rolled right along with my weirdness. Once there, we ended up talking for many hours. And boy did we talk.

Her brother, Patrick, was at the forefront of the conversation. She confided, in hushed tones, how he had died of AIDS at such a young age. She got choked-up many times during the conversation, the tears starting to well up in her sweet eyes, but she pulled herself bravely back from the edge of sobs each time. Patrick had been a tremendously important part of her life, a part of her own self, and now he was gone, and it had been such a waste of a good young person.

Without making me ask, Shelley told me about how the bad blood product had seeped into the entire hemophiliac community and had infected many of her friends, the ones who she had grown up with. She had lost dozens of her childhood friends in their teenage years, all before they had tasted the first challenges and passions of adulthood.

Shelley explained that AIDS would eventually get her father too, as he was also a hemophiliac and HIV-positive. She told me some things about the HIV, and I surprised her by asking the right questions and showing that I understood the technicalities. She could tell that I had done my homework, though I could tell that she also wondered why I had bothered.

We talked about everything, mostly Cranbrook and how we both really wanted to make a difference in the world and influence young people. How wonderful it was to be a teacher! A few more tears, a lot of laughter, some mediocre soup and fabulous Baker's Square chocolate pie, and our first date was in the books. There were so many clues about Shelley that would lead me to more love for her and anticipation of what she had not told me yet. That night, I felt in my heart that she would soon tell me she, too, had gotten the bad blood and was infected.

As I dropped her off at the girls' dorm, where she was now house advisor, I asked if we could do this again, and she enthusiastically said that she would love to. I drove off with my heart pounding and no breath in my chest. Man, was she beautiful, and man was I in love. Crazy in love!

After I checked on some dorm kids back in my residence hall, I decided to make a couple more late phone calls. I found the number to the Oakland County AIDS hotline and called, feeling fairly brave. I started to wonder so many things: What kind of a man called the hotline? Was this bravery? Cowardice? Before I could consider that point further, the man on the other end of the line answered evenly and fluidly, as if he wanted to let me know that it was all right that I had called and that he was not passing judgment on me. Of course, the first words out of my naïve, sputtering mouth were, "Uh, I don't have AIDS, but..."

His professional manner helped my nervousness to dissipate quickly, so I jumped headfirst into the hard questions: How is AIDS transmitted? Can you get it through kissing? What does it do to you? How do you know if you have AIDS? The man was very patient as he explained all of the answers in knowledgeable tones. I pictured a thirty-ish gay black man, taking each question as seriously as I had intended, confident and smart and, somehow, understanding.

The man explained everything he could about AIDS and HIV. The virus is called HIV, but it causes an immune-system dysfunction that allows all kinds of bad infections to seep into the depths of the helpless human body. Many of the infections are ones that normally-healthy people could fight off, but the cells that usually direct immunity become unable to do so. When the body reaches a certain level of failure in containing the HIV, symbolized by a drop in T-cells to an established quantity, that person is said to have AIDS. Thus, people with AIDS get sick with rare forms of pneumonia and brain infections that healthy people hardly ever get. The man made all of this very clear. He was a good teacher, and I really appreciated the way he taught.

My friend on the phone explained that you could get the HIV by blood transfusions that were tainted with the virus, and it was carried in semen and vaginal secretions as well. Blood, semen, and vaginal secretions; I could remember that. And mother's milk also, he added. What about kissing? He said that saliva contained no

HIV unless there was blood in the saliva, perhaps from a cut in the mouth, but it would have to be an awful lot of blood to cause infection, and it would have to find its way somehow into the recipient's bloodstream. He said that you needed to do something drastic, like injecting a gallon of saliva directly into your veins to get enough virus in you to replicate. So the chance of getting AIDS by kissing, even really deep and passionate kissing, was infinitesimally small. But be careful of obvious mouth sores. I understood.

I learned that the test for HIV involved a blood sample that, at that time, took two weeks after the blood was drawn. It had to be sent away to a special lab where it was double-checked. The two-week wait probably seemed like an eternity to someone waiting to find out his or her infection status.

I asked who was susceptible for AIDS, and the man told me that the population was almost entirely made up of gay men, drug addicts, prostitutes, and recipients of transfusions of infected blood before 1985. I got a little chill when he informed me, though to little surprise, that this included hemophiliacs. He added that other populations, such as minority heterosexuals, had a rapidly growing infection rate because of lack of information as to how HIV could be passed from person to person. And it was all over sub-Saharan Africa, including Kenya, in alarming amounts amongst all people of all backgrounds. It was a crazily growing disease in 1990, starting to permeate every conceivable population, though education of the public was starting to make a small difference.

So how could I remain safe? What if I wanted to have a relationship with a woman who had the HIV? He could tell I needed to know specifics. "You can only get HIV if you get her virus into your bloodstream. You should refrain from getting any of her body fluids near you. Always use a condom when having any kind of sex."

Whoa, sex. I wasn't quite ready to think about that yet..... or was I? He continued, "While the chances are small, oral sex performed on her probably isn't a good idea either. A small cut in your mouth could allow the HIV from her vaginal secretions to infect you, and the virus only needs one chance to get into your blood."

Wow, I thought, this is serious stuff. No oral sex. I had never considered that. "You also have to be careful about cuts on your fingers if you are going to touch her in any sexual way. Never touch her vagina with any open wounds on your hands, no matter how small. Again, kissing carries a risk due to small cuts around everyone's gums. But that is a very small risk, and it is up to you if you want to take that chance. Nobody's been infected from kissing, as far as we know."

So I got the picture: I would just have to be smart and not allow any part of her body fluids to get inside me. That, of course, was only if our relationship ever got that far. So for the first time in my young love life, I had to think ahead about what actions I would take if the situation ever came up. Spontaneity, so to speak, would have to be planned. And sensitivity would be absolutely necessary at every turn. I wondered if Shelley had thought that far ahead about me.

I asked her out for the following Saturday, for a longer date. And I knew that soon I would kiss her, and I would happily deal with whatever happened next as long as she let me touch her lovely lips with mine. I felt safe.

She had a little cold on that day, but she was determined to not let it stop our time together. If anything, it made her charmingly vulnerable, trying to smile through her sniffles and cute little cough. How could a cough be cute? Her laugh, though stuffy on that day, was like music. She listened to me and thought I was bright and funny, and my ego swelled.

We drove around the lovely Michigan countryside where the leaves were just starting to turn orange and the late-September air was thick with harvest smoke and the end of summer. After a movie way up in Rochester Hills, we went to a cider mill for hot sugary doughnuts and crisp apple juice that tasted like pure liquid candy. It was my first time at a real cider mill, and Shelley loved explaining how trips to the mills were a part of fall in Michigan, happy to be breaking me in to that small traditional pleasure she had loved when growing up with her family.

At the mill I told Shelley about my family, about how I had a sister who was fighting to graduate from the University of Tennessee and a brother who I loved but had been mean to when we were young. I bought Marty a porcelain frog at the mill for his new house in Atlanta. We talked about Mom and Dad and how they were good people and very proud of me being at Cranbrook, and how sometimes I got mad at them. I told Shelley how important football was in my life and how, someday, I dreamed of playing again, though the chance of that happening was getting smaller.

She listened and smiled and laughed and blew her nose. She told me she knew nothing about football, and the way she said it made it not matter. I thought she was a flower, an absolute angel from heaven, sent for me. Why was I so lucky?

It was nighttime when we returned to the girls' dorm, and I pulled right up to the door. We were afraid of the boarding girls seeing us, so we stayed in my little Mazda. Everything was as right with me as it had ever been, and Shelley was radiant in the fading evening light. I asked if she wanted to do this again sometime, and she had no doubt in her voice as she told me that she would love to go out with me, again and again. I told her how much today had meant to me, and she echoed it. The dance of words was headed where I hoped it would. I asked a lovely smiling face if I could kiss her, and I dreamily heard her say, Yes, I'd like that. It was, I have always realized, a perfect kiss. I still have to close my eyes when I think of it now, years later, her warm soft lips for the first time against mine.

Shelley asked me to park the car, because she wanted to walk around and show me the secret rooms of the girls' middle school, down in the basement of Kingswood. We walked in the back way so no boarders could see us, and we went down a staircase that I had never seen before to go into the little sitting area below. The muted lights of Saarinen's ethereal design, never too direct, guided our way to a snug bench built into the wall far away from the crowds where busy students might wander during the day. We sat down and she let me kiss her again. It was just as nice. And then we knew it was time for her to talk.

"Gary, I know this is fun for both of us, and I love kissing you.... but we need to talk about this. I really like you..."

Her jaw quivered. She started to cry, and as her lips started trembling, she was forced into a pretty frown and had to look away. She had no tissue and the tears began to roll down her cheeks. My heart ached for her, partly because I knew what she was going to say and partly because she was so sweet. I calmed her as best I could, but she lifted her hand and stopped me from touching her.

"Listen, Gary, I have to tell you this. You know that I'm a hemophiliac but what you don't know is that I'm also HIV-positive. And if you don't want to see me anymore, I will understand."

Now it was out in the open, quickly and succinctly. What would I do with it, and what did she expect? A million thoughts ran through my head. How painful that must have been for her to tell me. Here was this magnificent, intelligent woman, sitting with a man she obviously liked and wanted to get close to, and she had to tell him that it was okay if he ran up the stairs, screaming, never to see her again. So I responded.

"Okay."

She was a little puzzled. "Uh, Gary, don't you understand what I'm saying? I'm saying that I have the disease that causes AIDS. You know what that is, don't you?"

"Yes, Shelley. I know what that is. I kind of figured that you had HIV since you are a hemophiliac. Don't most hemophiliacs have it?" She looked stunned.

"Do you realize that just kissing me is slightly risky for you?"

I savored the lovely taste of her still in my mouth. "Yes, but you don't have any open cuts in your mouth, do you? If you don't, it was worth it. You're just yummy!"

She seemed to want to smile but began to cry again. I put my arm around her and pulled her tight. This was going to be tough, and we both knew it. In 1990, there was minimal acceptance of people with HIV, and fear still abounded in certain communities. Not long before, Ricky Ray had his house burned down in Florida, and Ryan White was forced to move to another town in Indiana. Both of them were hemophiliacs with HIV, and Shelley had known them from camp and retreats and newsletters. Shelley's own little brother had learned to keep his mouth shut. They all had. Shelley had told no one, except me.

No teachers in America had come out with the news that they were HIV-positive. In fact, very few teachers had even disclosed that they were gay for fear of losing their jobs or being victimized by overzealous parents or religious groups. So much for the freedoms of America. Keep your mouth closed. Don't ask; don't tell. Not in our schools!

So I told Shelley that her secret was safe with me. And I told her that I would continue to kiss her, anytime, anywhere, which we soundly and roundly did the rest of that night, in the basement of Kingswood, in the reflected light and shadows of Saarinen's remarkable, romantic architectural effort. And these kisses were the real thing, let me tell you, through her sniffles and smiles and lovely loving eyes.

The fall continued and I worked with fine young men on the short lined grass, teaching them not to trip over their own fat, confused feet on their way downfield. It was still the year of Coach Schmitt, and he showed me the way to coach successfully, with repetition and quiet dissatisfaction for any effort less than 100%. It was my best season of football, as player or coach, by far. All who touched Coach Schmitt's program were blessed with success, even us assistant coaches. Do your best. Do what is right. Care.

Shelley and I kissed more often, making plans to go out on weekends and get to know each other better and better. I fell in love with her more each date, learning what made her happy. She had an amazing affinity for yucky things, like showing me chewed up food and trying to make me blow liquids out my nose in laughter. I got her good one time by folding a menu into a triangle and holding it up to my mouth like a megaphone. I asked if this was a "seafood" restaurant, which she smilingly and suspiciously admitted it was, and I said, "See? Food!" showing her the chewed up salad in my mouth through the folded menu.

That was the first, and best, time I made iced tea come out her nose, and we laughed and laughed. I had to stay with this wonderful woman, obviously.

We acted silly and carried on, and she told me stories about her family. She had an older brother she admired, now a successful banker. Mike was married to a lovely woman with two small girls. Shelley also had a sister with two fine daughters, whom Shelley adored and saw often. In the middle 1980's, Shelley had not been allowed to be near any of her nieces for fear of giving them AIDS, which had been horribly painful for her. For a time, her own relatives had forbidden Shelley to see her lovely young nieces.

Shelley cherished all of her nieces more than fine gems, especially knowing that she might not be able to have children of her own. Genetically speaking, two of them would be carriers of the gene for hemophilia. Any boys that these carriers might conceive would be hemophiliacs.

And Shelley talked to me about Patrick, her beloved little brother who had died so young. Since her other siblings were not hemophiliacs, Shelley had been the closest to Pat. He had been adopted in infancy when Shelley was 8, and all-of-a-sudden there was another child in the house who was just like her, complete with the bleeds and bruises and worries of hemophilia. She taught him everything she had already learned, showing him how to be more independent, taking him to hemophilia camp with her, teaching him how to infuse the clotting factor. Learning how to self-infuse meant, for any young hemophiliac, freedom from dependence on nurses and doctors and over-protective parents.

They went together to the hospital when one of them had a joint bleed, Shelley understanding what it was like to feel isolated in a room, alone and scared, and she never let that happen to Patrick. In the hospital cafeteria they played the same food games that Shelley and I later enjoyed, and she made him shoot a load of chocolate milk out his little nose in laughter one day. That can still make her smile, even today, remembering that time with Patrick, so happy in the hospital in the face of their trauma.

One day when he was around 11, Patrick did not feel good. It seemed like stomach flu, with diarrhea and vomiting and night-sweats. He would wake up moaning, his pajamas completely soaked through, his bed like one big puddle. He didn't feel like laughing as much, or riding his bike, or horsing around with his sister. Soon he coughed all night long, a wet and racking cough. All he did was feel sick. This lasted for months and months, and the light faded from his eyes. The whole family went to the hospital for testing, and their hematologist found that Patrick was more than just sick with the flu. Charles Main had seen children in dire situations before, and this was one of the worst.

Dr. Main, in his amazing and compassionate career, had seen too many bad things at William Beaumont Hospital in Royal Oak. He had been a pediatric hematologist and oncologist for many years, and he had known the Brysons since Shelley had been a baby, the sweet little blond girl incredibly diagnosed as a classic hemophiliac. He had seen so many children fade away right before his eyes, fighting demons with a stronger grip than his. And he never stopped trying, through all of his daily battles for the lives of children, never giving up hope. What an amazingly resilient man. With a heavy heart, Dr. Main told the Bryson family what was happening to them. Patrick had HIV.   Shelley would not listen.

They had heard the rumors in the months before Patrick's diagnosis. Shelley had talked, cautiously, with her friends at their hemophilia camp. The counselors there had started hearing about the "gay man's cancer" that seemed to be sneaking into the lives of the hemophiliacs that they all knew. But denial had taken hold quickly: they thought there was no way the HIV would ever touch any of them, no way AIDS would enter any of their lives. Shelley was 18 in the summer of 1985, angrily invulnerable. She had learned to deal with her hemophilia and was going to protect herself and everyone around her with her strength. She was independent and stunningly beautiful and fabulously healthy in those days. How could she, or her family, or her friends possibly be in any danger? And all of this was in Shelley's thoughts while Patrick was beginning to waste away.

At hemophilia camp that next summer, there had been a wonderful nurse who Shelley had loved since she was six years old. Sue Atkins had seen it all, just like Dr. Main. Sue had been witness to the kids getting sick, and she had done the reading in the medical journals. She knew what was happening, and Sue grabbed hold of Shelley one day when Shelley was 18 and indestructible and told her to face it: Patrick had the HIV, and this was no time to ignore it.

Shelley would have none of this foolishness. When Sue told Shelley that all people who had infused probably had the HIV, Shelley would hear none of that either. "Shelley," said the strong, young, beautiful nurse who Shelley loved dearly, her grip firm on Shelley's shoulder, her eyes imploring, "you probably have it yourself, and you had better learn to deal with it."

Shelley decided she would never get the virus, no way. And she told Sue she would never test for it, either, and that was final. That was also, Shelley would admit later, incredible denial. "Thank God," Shelley would also say, years after that horrible summer, "that some of Sue's words did seep in and I did make some better choices about myself and others, finally."

Thank God for Sue, who loved Shelley like a daughter and had seen her grow into a lovely woman, who had to be the one to tell Shelley to wake up. Thank God for Dr. Main, who had taken care of them all.

We dated for several weeks. And like any other dating couple, especially those in love, we were starting to breathe a little heavier with each date, to get a little more adventurous with our hands and mouths and everything else. Like any other young couple, we were passionate kissers, and there was a desire for more. I eventually became more adventurous, gauging her reactions to my loving hands. Good, she seemed to like that. She touched my chest, and I shivered too. We were both old enough, me 27 and her 23, and we had both been *there* before, but this time was different.

Indeed, had there been no issue of health, and had we been otherwise the same people we were, we would easily have been deep into lovemaking by the third date. I was that kind of guy, believe me, the healthiest of males and very realistic about it. But this was different.

One night in November I asked her to spend the night in Marquis Dorm with me, but I suggested that she would sleep on the old white couch in my living room with me in the bedroom. She agreed, amused that I would insist on sleeping separately. I did not want to push her into sex, no way, but I wanted her to feel wanted. I strongly needed to bring her some pleasure, more than what we had experienced before. We had been dating for two months and had known each other since mid-summer. It was time.

I remembered the rules: no mixing of fluids, especially getting hers into mine. So I proceeded with great caution, remembering early experiments with young girls in the backseat of a car or on a darkened band bus, almost always getting stopped before reaching magical places of the imagination. There was a similar thrill here, and a little sense of danger. I was going to be very smart and safe, at all costs, so Shelley wouldn't be afraid for me, and could enjoy.

I found a way to please her. I stayed outside of the last layer of clothing. She was worried about her fluids and my hands, but I stopped and showed her my hands: no cuts or abrasions anywhere. I looked her in the eye and told her that I wanted to do this, that I was not afraid, that I needed to bring her this pleasure of touch. She looked deeply into my own eyes, and we kissed as fiercely as we ever had. She gripped my shoulders and ran her hands through my hair as I explored and loved her, as safely as I could, and I was rewarded with the knowledge that she was enjoying my cautious but loving technique. Later, dreamily, she would tell me, that I was a wonderful lover. And so was she.

She slept on the couch, and I slept on the bed. There was a feeling of happiness in my little apartment, and I woke up the next morning smiling and peaceful. I tiptoed out and saw that she was still asleep on my old white couch, looking like an absolute angel, her golden hair a halo on the pillow. My heart swelled again as I looked on this trusting, sincere woman, asleep in my own house. Shelley woke up and found me looking and giggled. "What the heck are you doing?" she asked, cutely confused by my idiotic stare.

I apologized dozens of times for staring at her asleep, worried that she would think I was too weird for her, which further tickled her. Man, was I lost in her laugh. Later that day I called my brother in Atlanta and played for him the phone message she had left on my machine, just wanting someone else to hear her musical voice and know how in love I was.

Soon we made love, all the way, for the first time. I was so careful, and she asked me 100 times if I was okay, did the condom stay on, are you sorry you have to be so careful with me? I reassured her constantly, that everything was wonderful, that being with her like this was a dream, a true pleasure. Eventually, she was able to relax and enjoy our intimacy. There was a certain thrill to being with her, to making love, which made me want it more. Bringing her pleasure, perhaps helping her to forget whatever pain was there, made me so happy. And she needed to know that I was being very careful, that the bad things in her blood would never touch me. She cried after, and I held her close. The fall ended and we moved into our first winter as friends, confidantes, and lovers.

I had met her family at her folks' house for our first Thanksgiving together. No doubt they had been wondering what kind of guy I was, and I was eager to impress them. Her parents were warm and smiling. Her dad, Eldon, was a man with a musical voice. Just the word "hello" had several different octaves and notes in it, and his good cheer was genuine. Eldon had spent his childhood as a hemophiliac without clotting factor, so his joints had suffered from dissolving of cartilage and fusion of bone. His knees did not bend anymore, from months of lying on the couch during bleeds with ice packs on his legs, no doubt in agony. His ankles would bend only slightly. To walk, Eldon had to roll his hips as if he were walking on stilts, and it was amazing how mobile he was as I watched him move around without bending his knees. I instantly admired him. He was an engineer at General Motors, and he did much volunteer work for his beloved church and a retirement home nearby, reaching out to those less fortunate.

Shelley's mother was like most others of her generation, staying home to cook and raise the kids. She greeted me with a lovely smile at Thanksgiving and showed me great hospitality, but that did not last long. Soon after we arrived, Sharon launched into a tirade about something and could not be stopped. Shelley was embarrassed and horrified, and her father did not know what to say to me. It was apparent that Shelley's words about having a mother who was a little "crazy" were not far off: her mother was having a type of anxiety attack that had been typical while Shelley had been growing up. Undiagnosed for years, Sharon was finally found to have severe depression and multiple personality disorder. And I was witnessing, over our first Thanksgiving together, an episode of that illness.

We eventually made it through the evening and I did my best to show Shelley I was "okay" with the situation presented. Shelley had been embarrassed greatly by the whole experience. My parents were the same way, I told her, but she did not believe that. "Not like that," she said flatly.

Her mother had eventually come around to some semblance of sanity and been pleasant for the last half of the evening and we ended up chatting in their living room about life and my background. One of the interesting things I had noticed was in the pre-meal prayer. Eldon had delivered the blessing over all that had been provided for us, but instead of ending with "in Jesus' name" as was typical of their staunch fundamentalist Christianity, he closed with "in God's name we pray." This was obviously in deference to my Jewish upbringing and was intended so that I would not feel uncomfortable. I noticed, and I appreciated it. This man had shown me, with his choice of words, that I was welcome in his house and at his table. And as the evening went along, he let me know that I was welcome with his daughter, who he cherished.

It was obvious that Shelley's mother had had to live with a very grim realization for many years: that she had lost a son, and would eventually lose a husband and daughter, to something unseen and unstoppable. Maybe that explained some of her own emotional issues.

And now it was time for Shelley to meet my own family, so we rose early the next morning and got into my new Jeep Cherokee for the long drive to Tennessee, through sleepy flat Ohio, past the rising Cincinnati skyline and over the river that welcomed us to Kentucky. I was so proud to show her off, and the drive down to Tennessee, usually a boring 10-hour journey down Interstate 75, was over in a flash. I just loved being with her in the car, watching her sleep and wake up and yawn and tell me she was hungry, asking about the location of the nearest Waffle House. Every minute with her was joyous. I would look over at her in the passenger seat, curled up so tiny, so trusting of my driving, and my eyes would get misty. My one true love, finally.

We chatted about everything, and with every sentence I realized I wanted to be with her more. It made me so happy to lead her through the rolling green hills of Kentucky, watching the terrain change with greater relief and better geology as we got closer to the Appalachian folds, and she was patiently interested as I explained the features. I got that warm familiar feeling as we left I-75 at Corbin and jumped onto the smaller, twisty highway 25E. That turnoff represented the last, lovely 2-hour stretch through coal towns and the breathtaking Cumberland Gap. Finally, we ventured into Tennessee, my own state. We moved on into the friendly, wavy land, over Clinch Mountain where I pulled off to show Shelley the sunset on the TVA lakes below, into the valley where I grew up. Morristown was home, tucked into the foothills with a natural rocky protection from the outside world, the folds of the Chilhowee formation watching over us.

We pulled in at 7 o'clock and Mom and Dad were waiting with Marty and Hillary and my grandmother, Erma. Mom had made another turkey so we could have a second Thanksgiving with them, though it was really my third, having had turkey with the boarding students at Cranbrook before they had gone home for their own deserved break. I hadn't introduced my folks to a girl in ten years.

Shelley was radiant and showed them that I had good taste, and I was incredibly proud and, for the first time in many trips home, totally relaxed. Everyone could see how in love I was, and it was easy for Shelley to fit in. I carried the bags into the house as Mom, with amazing instinct for how to embarrass me in the shortest period of time, told me that she wasn't sure where Shelley was going to sleep, that she had made up the guest bedroom at the end of the hall but if I wanted her to stay with me it was okay with her, you know, whatever I wanted... How embarrassed I got! I insisted, red-faced, that Shelley would stay in the guest room. I did NOT tell Shelley what Mom had offered, because it would have embarrassed her as well. It amazed me to think that my own mother would think that I even CONSIDERED pre-marital relations! Even though I was guilty of such things anyway.... how could she THINK it!

At the Thanksgiving/Sabbath table, Mom blessed the candles and kissed each member of her family, taking Shelley's smiling face in her hands and smacking her loudly in an obvious display of affection, like she did to all of us, while Marty and I rolled our eyes. Dad blessed the wine and made a silly joke, as usual, and we sang the blessing for the bread together. My grandmother, elegant as always, took in whatever she imagined she heard from the conversation and graciously asked Shelley about herself, though she could not hear most of Shelley's answers. My Love answered slowly and loudly, having had much experience working with older people in her college job as nursing assistant at Beaumont Hospital. I was very impressed with Shelley, again, as she handled my family so warmly and deftly, letting me know that she felt comfortable with them. This was working out magically.

The next day, we all went to the Tennessee-Vanderbilt football game in Knoxville, where it was rainy and cold, lousy weather for anyone. Shelley was a good sport, pretending to enjoy the bright Orange experience at Neyland Stadium as the proud Volunteers easily kicked my sad Commodores all over the Orange checkered field. She hugged me to show her support for my poor team. We fought our way through a satisfied and wet Orange crowd and headed back to Morristown.

I had made this Morristown-to-Knoxville-to-Morristown trip a thousand times, up the lovely highway 11-E along plush farmland, through Jefferson City and Strawberry Plains, along the French Broad River, next to the anticlines of the Smoky

Mountains, which shadowed us the whole way. But this was my first trip with Shelley, and I loved to point out to her all the familiar sights that waited around each corner, and she seemed quite enchanted by the ride. Dad told stories about how he had driven us to Sunday School in Knoxville every week and sang to us to keep us occupied. He told of all the kids that, at various stages of their Jewish education, had carpooled with us. He remembered sturdy little Jacquie, who had an obsession with pigs when she was 12 and made squealing sounds the whole way, which made Dad insane, and he recalled hyper little Jeff, who insisted on flicking my ear all the way in to Knoxville, even when I was trying to sleep, flick, flick, flick. Shelley laughed and laughed.

We drove back to Michigan on Sunday, and it was a glorious and sunny trip back over the mountains into Kentucky and Ohio. Shelley told me stories of her upbringing, of her mother's insanity and her father's saintliness, and more about her brother's long death.

Patrick had gotten much sicker in 1986, never to get better. The "flu" had kept him sweating and diarrheic for the last two years of his life, and Shelley had watched him wither away into a frail old man at 13. She would lie with him on the couch, watching TV and trying to keep him warm since he was constantly shivering. He kept a silver cooking bowl nearby that he often vomited into, being that he was constantly nauseous, and it was known as "Pat's Bowl", never leaving his side. At that time, the only thing Pat could keep down was crabmeat, so there were several trips by his father to the Red Lobster each week. When the manager noticed the frequent visits by the same person and commented, Eldon explained that it was all his son could eat because of "some illness", so the manager made some kind of wonderful discount deal with him for the expensive crab-legs. Eldon appreciated it greatly. They were not rich, and Eldon was not about to go begging for meal deals; the manager presenting the idea himself was looked upon by Eldon as generosity, not charity, and he accepted, gratefully. There were good people out there, and good businesses, and the Bryson family had found them around hidden corners.

Pat had little cheerfulness in his life at that point, and there was not much his family could do to ease his suffering. One day Shelley had her wisdom teeth out, and she ended up being horribly nauseous when she came home. She and Patrick had to comfort each other as they lay there under blankets on the couch, shivering and

moaning. Patrick was unusually upbeat about someone sharing his type of misery.
Since Shelley had not eaten in a while, her father had made her a chocolate milkshake,
hoping the coolness of it would ease the pain in her jaw, and Shelley enjoyed it. But
eventually, she started to feel sick. Patrick, who had been listless for many months by
now, saw his sister ready to vomit, and he became animated. Finally, there was
someone in the house sick like him! "Are you gonna throw up, Shelley?" he asked
with glee. "Do you want my bowl? You want my bowl? Shelley, can I get you my
bowl? Huh?"

Shelley obliged him and nodded, recalling this as the one time during his long
illness that he was able to come out of his own misery with some strange happiness.
He announced to the entire house, with a smile, that Shelley was throwing up in his
bowl! One moment of joy...

As Pat got weaker and weaker, and the family's sense of helplessness
increased, Shelley's brother Mike tried to do something, anything. They were unable
to tell anyone about Pat's illness because of the stigma still attached to AIDS in 1989.
But Mike became trusting enough to put in a call to the Make-a-Wish foundation of
Michigan, and he explained Pat's situation to a case worker there, though he was quite
cautious as he spoke, not sure how they would respond to an AIDS case. Thankfully,
arrangements were made, and a trip was planned.

Since Patrick's infancy, he had been absolutely intrigued with the beauty of
Christie Brinkley. Whenever he had seen her on television or in a magazine, he would
become entranced, saying with awe, "Oooh, she's boo-ful...!" while staring wide-eyed
at her image. Her posters were all over his walls as he entered adolescence, though he
was now too weak to climb the steps to his room and look at her magnificent visage.

In June of 1989, thanks to Make-a-Wish, Patrick was to fly to New York with
his whole family to see Christie Brinkley in a photo shoot and visit with her in her
private dressing room. Even as everyone was getting excited, Pat was quickly
becoming sicker. There was no meat left on his frail bones, and there was no
medication that could stop the spread of the virus within him. At 13 and one-half,
Patrick was sinking fast.   They all boarded a plane to New York, Mike carrying his
frail little brother to his seat.

Because of the last-minute arrangements, the family could not sit together on the plane, and Shelley was seated by herself in the back row. Of course, she was worried about her brother, but, she would later tell me with some degree of shame, she was more worried about how the others on the plane would perceive her and her family if they "knew." As the plane's engines started rumbling, Shelley saw quite a commotion up ahead, in the row where her brother was sitting with her parents. She caught a glimpse of him from her seat and saw that he had suddenly turned a yellowish-gray color. In her heart, she told me years later, she knew right then that her brother was dying. But more than that, she was scared that the other passengers would find out what he was dying of and eagerly throw them all off the plane. She cried as she told me that, further ashamed of her selfishness at that time, mourning her gentle little Patrick.

Nonetheless, the plane took off and they headed to New York. Patrick lapsed in and out of consciousness, and upon arrival they knew he needed to be hospitalized immediately. The family was scared and in a strange city.

The Brysons had been told by their Michigan doctors that they needed to go to a certain hospital which treated AIDS patients better than the other hospitals, some of whom would refuse to accept AIDS cases at all. Also, the family would need to lie to the ambulance drivers who met them at the so that they would allow him into their vehicle. Shelley told me later that it took 20 minutes to convince the drivers that Patrick's ailment was not contagious and had only to do "with kidney problems", her parents eventually resorting to begging and pleading with the drivers, as lying had not been enough.

Finally in the hospital, it was clear that Patrick's situation was grave. His color was deep yellow with tinges of gray as his kidneys and bladder had ceased to function, no longer filtering impurities from his whole system. The shutdown of his frail body was now swift, though it had taken 18 months to come to that point.   He was barely lucid, no light in his eyes. What the family had been dreading was now here. Shelley told me this two years later, still in great pain and shock at the loss of her beloved Pat, staring at her own vulnerability head-on with each thought of her brother's death. Her tears flowed as we drove over the mountains in my Jeep, her anger flashing at the great unfairness. She told me the rest.

Christie Brinkley had rearranged her schedule and soon appeared in Patrick's room in the hospital. He was barely alive then, and Christie came to his bedside and hugged him dearly. Her face, Shelley told me, was heavenly, and she carried herself like a gazelle, lithe and graceful on her long lovely legs. Somehow Christie was above all this suffering, and she lifted the trodden spirits of those in the room with her presence. She gave Pat a T-shirt with her picture on it and posed for family photos and videotape. Pat stared on, fighting to remain conscious, imagining, perhaps, that he was in the presence of an angel. He tried to speak to his angel, but no words came out, just a low mumble. He tried to reach for her, though his arms were too weak to rise more than a couple of inches, and Christie stayed close to him and touched his feverish head again and again, gently, lovingly. She was not afraid of Patrick, or his disease, this beautiful woman.

Shelley told me, through tears and anger, about how Christie Brinkley did not really meet Patrick that day. Christie met a disease that had taken over Pat's body. For years after that, Shelley had mourned for her brother, remembering that he had never really met his dream-girl, but that a shadow of a boy had been there in that bed in Pat's place, pretending to be alive while beauty moved around his earthly shell.

After Christie Brinkley left, promising to come back again the next day, the family took turns in the hospital room and tried to make Pat feel comfortable in this strange place. He was unconscious most of the time, incoherent, except for one brief period when Shelley was with him, alone. In that rare moment of lucidity, Patrick said with great clarity to his sister, "Shelley, is this it?"

She told me later that, at that time, she did not cry. Instead, she looked at him as strongly and calmly as she could and said, "Yes, this is it. Its okay, Patrick."

And with that, she had given him permission to let go, which was exactly what he needed, and exactly what Shelley never wanted to have to give. But she knew that she had to. Its okay, My Brother.

That night, Shelley's mother was taking her turn watching Pat, and he was stable. When Sharon left to make a phone call down the hallway, Patrick stopped breathing and quietly slipped away. For much of his life, he had depended on his parents and family to survive and get through his everyday life. People had been cleaning him and feeding him and worrying about him for the last 18 months. Shelley noted, with considerable pride, that Patrick had done this for himself. He had died on his own terms, when his mother had left the room, so as not to bother anyone for anything else, and he had done it alone. Patrick Bryson was thirteen and one-half years old.

Chapter 8: Seeing the World With My Love

On Christmas Day of 1990, I gave Shelley a pendant made by an artist-friend in Bloomfield Hills. He was a graduate of the Cranbrook Art Academy and it was made with three small emeralds I had bought in Ecuador. Each emerald was surrounded by a square of gold and stacked one above the other, each square a little smaller than the one below it. The pyramid-like shape resembled the Saarinen-designed chimney atop the Kingswood dormitory. Shelley loved it and showed it off to everyone, her blue-green eyes flashing above the emeralds.

That January, we went to see a movie, "Green Card," about a big oaf (Gerard Depardieu) and the gentle beauty (Andie McDowell) who falls for him and his rough ways, despite her own delicate nature. I took my lovely Shelley back to my apartment after the movie, sat her on the white couch, and told her that I loved her desperately. I was so sure of this love that I wanted to marry her, I needed to marry her, as soon as possible. And she left no doubt of her own sureness as she stared into my eyes and accepted my proposal with deepest love. She said yes, with no doubts, her bright eyes smiling. I had never known such happiness. We hugged forever.

Both sets of parents were thrilled, and since we had no time in the coming summer to get married, we decided to hurry up and do it over the spring break in March, just two months after the engagement became official. And we wanted to get married on the magnificent Cranbrook campus, since it was there that our relationship had grown and blossomed.

After calling scores of "high-up" people who could give us permission to use the campus facilities, we found that such a thing was either impossible or too expensive, since everyone in Michigan wanted to get married on our exclusive grounds. We went and asked the school librarian, Jan Reelitz, who had been so nice to me over the last several years, if she could help us. She picked up the phone and went right to the top. Jan called her friend the Director of Cranbrook, Dr. Lillian Bauder, and told her about this problem, that two young teachers were not be able to get married at our own school. Well, that ended the dilemma quickly as Dr. Bauder "took care of things", made a couple of phone calls, and we were soon told that we could be married in that very school library, right across the plush quadrangle from Marquis Residence, my home. It was a beautiful room filled with tall walls of books, an ornate carved limestone fireplace, and a large bay window overlooking the quad fountain, all designed by Saarinen and his craftsmen.

The girls in Shelley's dorm were thrilled for her, as she had become a sort of stern older sister to them, and our friends, the Cohens, threw a shower for us in the magnificent residence commons room, Page Hall. There were lots of winks and nudges from the faculty, as they had all known that we had fallen for each other before their very eyes. The wedding was very small, just our immediate families, my mentors Randy and Ellen Tufts, my buddy Bob from Vanderbilt and one former student, Harold Kobrak, who had become my friend when he was a student and Resident Advisor in my dorm a couple of years earlier.

Harold had cherished his Cranbrook experience deeply, one of those rare teenagers who got the most out of Cranbrook while giving the most back. He had turned out to be the captain of my fencing team when he was a senior, and we were close enough to spend many late nights figuring out the meaning life in the dorm a couple of years earlier. He almost broke my couch when he pinned me against it while wrestling at 2 A.M. That's how boys show affection for each other, throwing each other around dorm rooms. Imagine in this day and age being found wrestling with a boarding student after midnight in an adult's residence....

We asked Rabbi Dannel Schwartz to perform the ceremony for us, since I had coached his twin sons, Peter and Ari, on the football field a few years earlier, and he agreed to do so if we attended a class on Judaism. The class was something Shelley and I could do together and it gave us a chance to discuss religion in our lives. She had been raised in a very fundamental Christian church called Bethesda over on the East side of Metro Detroit, though she had rebelled against some of its precepts and exclusivity, and some parts of Judaism appealed to her. She still held onto her Christian beliefs regarding Jesus as the Son of God and admitted that she worried that I would end up in Hell while she went to heaven. This led to more interesting discussions, where I pointed out that I had always tried to live my life in a good way and if that was not good enough for God, then perhaps I didn't need Heaven. She had no response to that, which made me smugly proud of my own logic. But Shelley did say, sorrowfully, that she'd miss me if she got "There" and I didn't.

On a rainy Saturday, March 23, we married in front of our families and friends underneath a canopy in the Cranbrook library. We had hired a flute and guitar duo to play Pachelbel Canon (which I annoyingly referred to as the "Taco Bell Cannon" just to bother my bride) as we marched in. Both sets of parents met for the first time that weekend. Uncle Jack filmed the ceremony for us, though he left the camera on throughout all of the pauses and filmed a good bit of his shoe for 20 minutes. It was a fine ceremony, even when I started wavering on my feet and Shelley thought I was about to faint. The Rabbi blessed us and had us say some vows to each other in Hebrew. Shelley was careful not to say the wrong thing because the Rabbi had told her earlier that if she got one of the Hebrew syllables wrong she would have pledged her love to the Rabbi instead of me, which I thought was hilarious. She believed him.

Shelley's parents and I signed a *Kitubah*, a Jewish marriage contract written entirely in Hebrew which neither of us could read. There was no place for Shelley herself to sign, which distressed her, as if her parents were signing her over to me like cattle. Neither of us really knew what the contract said, but from then on, whenever I balked if she wanted me to do something for her, like going to a movie she wanted to see or stopping for ice cream, she would wryly say, "You *have* to go with me... it's in the *Kitubah*!"

We had a wedding reception at the glamorous Fox & Hounds right there in Bloomfield Hills, in a room above where the truly wealthy dined. Shelley's sister Kathy made a great wedding cake, and we fed each other with little mess, though Shelley did make it a point to shove a piece into her niece Sarah's mouth in a moment of silliness. The guitar and flute duo played more, and my brother Marty made a loving speech as best man.

After the prime rib and toasts of love, Shelley and I were to leave for the airport in her little Volkswagen Fox, the wedding present that I had helped pay for with the sale of my beat-up Mazda, but the valet parking guy couldn't get it started. It was weird: the car-door alert made noise and the lights worked, but the engine was unwilling to make any connection. We couldn't understand it. We had to get someone to give us a ride to the airport hotel, but before we left, we went back into the bar area of the glamorous Fox & Hounds while some others worked on the car. There was a jazz band playing right there in the bar, and they noticed us in our wedding finery. The lead singer asked if there was a song he could play for us, and I said that "Wonderful Tonight" was our favorite, the one by Eric Clapton. So we got to dance, all dressed up as bride and groom in front of all kinds of rich people, to our song, and I sang it softly to her while we danced and smiled and looked into each others' eyes, spinning slowly around and around. We found out later that Shelley's car needed to have the seat belt hooked up before the car would start, and no one had noticed that it wasn't buckled. Gotta love that German ingenuity.

We honeymooned in St. Martin at a time-share condo my parents had given us for the week. It was lovely there, sunny and warm, all those frozen drinks with the flowers and umbrellas and beautiful smiling people. Every night we made chocolate-cookie milkshakes in the blender in our room, giggling as we made messes in the kitchen. One day, we went horseback riding across the island, but the man in charge made our horses gallop full-go all the way to the beach, so we had to clench our legs to the saddle in fear. Shelley's fake fingernail caught on the stirrup and ripped off, so she bled little drops all over her horse, a horse that she said was surely trying to kill her. On the beach we let the horses run free, and Shelley's ran straight at her so furiously that she dropped to the sand and rolled out of the way in panic. That further proved, she said with wide eyes and a very serious tone, that her horse wanted to see her dead. We vowed never to go horseback riding again, ever. Like she didn't have enough in her life to worry about.

When we returned home and spring break ended, we both had to return to our separate apartments to finish the school year. The dorm kids were mystified about how we could be married yet live apart. Shelley continued to be with her boarding girls; I loved to come over and watch them swarm to her to ask questions and bask in her presence. She really brought the good parts of these girls out of "themselves" with her generous smile and questions, and they truly liked her. We decided that we would both live at Kingswood the next year, together, and be dorm parents for the girls.

On a trip to Tennessee to see my folks that summer, we decided, on a whim, to go to the Humane Society dog pound, just to look around. In one of the cages, there stood a golden ball of fluff with four white feet, staring intently at us, ears high with a mouth that looked like it was about to say something important. She lifted a paw as if to wave, then stamped her feet impatiently. We bent down and stuck our fingers in the cage where the little golden dog tried to chew them. She saw something in us, the young lovers. Shelley and I smiled at each other, then walked around to see more of the dogs. There were no more puppies, but there were several full-grown dogs that would probably not last much longer before being destroyed. A couple of the dogs had bitten people and were kept separate. The man who took care of them shook his head sadly as he told us their stories, that they would have to be put to sleep. We imagined that he carried a heavy heart sometimes. What a sad job, to have to put dogs down.

Shelley and I left the shelter, and I drove home to my parents' house, but it was clear that we were thinking the same thing. As we pulled into the driveway and got out of the car, we looked at each other again and again with silly smiles. We walked in the house, ignoring my mother and the wonderful smells her cooking made. As soon as we sat down at the kitchen table, we said, at exactly the same time, "Let's go get her! ...Really?"

We stood up, went out the door, and drove down to the pound to bring home our little Gypsum. The people at the Humane Society weren't going to give her to us, since we weren't local residents, so we signed my parents' names to the contract and took our little dog with us. She was all over the car, jumping and whimpering and trying to nip our noses as we struggled to hold her, the cardboard box we had brought useless in the back seat. We laughed all the way back to my parents', who told us it was too soon in our relationship to have a dog, as if they knew anything at all. And then they laughed and loved our Gyp as much as we did.

Gypsum brought us closer. We spent all of our time fawning over her, Shelley trying to cradle her little puppy while getting gently chewed up. We found that those little needle teeth could hurt if you weren't careful, and Gyp tried to bite us playfully every second she was awake. We took her outside my parents' house and let her play in the flowers and trees, and she bounded awkwardly all over the yard, falling often and skidding to clumsy stops. We laughed and laughed, and my Shelley was happy. Gypsum just could not have enough fun or cause too much unashamed joy as she danced in the grass.

Gypsum chewed everything we owned, and when she wasn't chewing, she was peeing and crapping all over the house. Shelley bought her some bacon-flavored dog treats and fed her one after another, so Gyp then threw up bacon chunks all over the house too. It was my job to clean it all up, so I worked hard to housebreak her. She learned quickly and responded well to praise, and I loved my little dog as much as Shelley did, especially when she relieved herself outside more often than inside. We took Gyp for walks down in the nearby little town of Cumberland Gap, letting her play in a tiny waterfall and run up and down the trails of the nearby National Park. Gyp always came running back to us, crouching at our feet in smiling exhaustion, looking up with a smile, full of love. Thank God for dogs.

The summer ended and we returned to our life at Cranbrook. It was a new school year and we moved into the girls' dormitory at Kingswood. Football started and good old Del Walden was the new coach. He had been at Cranbrook for 30 years and had been a successful football coach in the 60's and 70's until becoming Dean of Boys. When he had been reluctantly replaced as Dean in 1991, he recovered from this unwanted shift by agreeing to follow Chuck Schmitt as head football coach. He had been a legend in coaching circles around the state and I was really excited about working with him on the field.

That year I became the first male house advisor for the girls' dorm, and while I had been able to work well in guiding and counseling young men, I was totally lost in the world of teenage women. They chewed me up and spit me out. I would come home from duty nights just shaking my head and muttering to myself because some of the girls had driven me crazy. One night I looked up from grading homework at my hallway duty desk and said hello to one of the young women who was walking past, and she wheeled around and started to scream at me, literally scream, about how unfair everything was. Then she started to cry and ran back to her own room. Through the entire outburst, I had sat slack-jawed, just watching. I had no idea of what to do, so I called Shelley, who instructed me to leave the girl alone. Sometimes girls just have bad days, said my wife, and I listened, helplessly. Bad days. I was becoming an expert in them.

The year progressed and I got no better at being a dorm advisor for girls. Even worse, the football season was quite a drama. Del had re-installed an option-style offense, which is what he knew best, and the kids were learning it well and working hard for a man they all respected. The problem was with one of the other assistant coaches. Mike, a former successful businessman who had been an assistant under Chuck Schmitt and had a son on the team, had wanted to be the head coach instead of Del. When Del got the position, Mike just asked if he could still be an assistant coach. Del innocently said yes.

Once, when Del became emotional about the importance of football and loving one's parents, he shed a few tears at a team meeting when remembering his own father from long ago. I was quite moved, as were the boys. "Somebody" told the head of Cranbrook, inaccurately, that Del had broken down and had "lost control" in front of the boys. In another instance, when our tailback fumbled into the end-zone at the end of a game, sealing a 3-point loss, I hear rumors of complaints about Del's play-calling. Del could do nothing right, according to some parents, and the kids felt the tension between Del and Mike.

On and on it went, and even though he had a successful 6-3 season, Del was fired in January by an ignorant new head-of-schools (who shall remain nameless) who clearly wanted only to please parents. Mike quickly got the head-coaching job, even though his experience with coaching football was only two years as a volunteer assistant. I was never considered for the job, the administration knowing how much I had supported Del. Plus, I was "just a kid." I learned an awful lot about politics that fall. Poor Del... he had just been trying to help the school and our kids, even after the school had dumped him as Dean of Boys, and he got the Stone and Iron Shaft.

A change was occurring in our house also. Shelley was becoming grouchy and more sullen towards me with every passing day. If I were to leave a sock on the floor, she would shock me with a lecture about how careless I was while it was only she trying to keep the house clean. A dirty dish was a slap in her face, and she let me know it. It quickly became as if nothing I could do or say would make her happy, and I was growing very frustrated, not knowing what to do to help her. I let her go on with her feelings and kept my mouth shut. There were things inside her that were making her think about HIV and her brother Patrick and her father and herself, and I needed to understand what was going on. My dream girl was turning in bad directions, angry all the time now, and I felt powerless and a little lost. I became hungry for Shelley's love, but that love had become misplaced.

In the late fall, a truly wonderful thing happened that took Shelley out of her gloom and made me forget about the pain of that year's football coaching saga. Mary Fisher entered our lives. Mary had been a Kingswood graduate back when the girls' school was still separate from Cranbrook. She had gone on to become very successful in her own right, despite growing up in the shadow of very prosperous and powerful parents. Mary had risen to become assistant to President Gerald Ford and had made an impact in many civic and social ventures worldwide. Her role as fund-raiser for public television had been legendary in the Detroit area.

Unfortunately, Mary had become infected with the HIV by her former late husband, who had been a drug addict and had unwittingly injected bad blood into his own system. Mary had become a poster for "innocent" victims of AIDS, those people, like Shelley, who had gotten the disease in a manner that seemed to be somewhat more acceptable by society. While that seems an unfair label for all those perceived to have gotten the HIV in "sinful" ways, such as through drug use, prostitution, or homosexual sex, it certainly made people like Mary's availability as a speaker on that subject desirable. There would be less public outcry towards her appearance, more across-the-board support from conservatives, and a wonderful opportunity, with each lecture, for Mary to emphatically state that there are no "good" or "bad" victims of the virus. Mary became known for setting the world straight in regards to compassion and education.

When Mary had found she was infected, instead of hiding inside her own world of wealth and privilege, she had made it clear that she would use her life as lesson. And, thank God, she offered to come to speak about her experiences and AIDS at our high school as one of her first public offerings. Shelley got permission from her middle-school head to come to our upper school assembly. There, Mary addressed 800 silent and attentive students and many awestruck teachers and administrators. For Shelley and I it seemed as if Mary was speaking to us directly.

This was the first HIV-positive person most students and faculty had ever seen up close. In 1990, AIDS was still foreign to most people, and it was still difficult to talk about the disease since it brought up the uncomfortable subjects of sex, blood, and death. Mary opened herself up and talked about how anyone could become infected, and how students and young people were particularly susceptible because of tendencies to experiment and feel invulnerable. Shelley nodded enthusiastically throughout, crying and laughing at the stories and feeling free in Mary's presence. Shelley saw students and parents and faculty embracing Mary and applauding her openness, and one could see the gears in Shelley's brain working to take all of this in. It was clear that people loved Mary, even though she was HIV+.

After the assembly, for which Mary received a long and hearty standing ovation from our very-impressed high school students, there was a reception for her at the elegant Cranbrook House, the former residence of the Booth family who had founded our school. Shelley and I went, getting substitutes to cover our afternoon classes. Shelley sat in awe while Mary spoke briefly to some dignitaries and parents of current students. Somehow, after we watched Mary handle everyone's greetings and questions with great dexterity and sincerity, Shelley found herself alone with Mary in one of the smaller rooms. It appeared to me that there were very few words spoken, as I watched from the hall. At one point, Mary reached out and hugged my wife and they both cried and smiled and hugged again, for a very long time, Mary soothing her like a mother would soothe a child. I was sure that Shelley had told Mary about her infection. Shelley later said that Mary just sort of knew, and that Mary had told Shelley to follow her own feelings, to move forward and not get stuck in the past, trapped in self-pity. Mary said that that attitude had saved her from despair, and she wanted Shelley to consider the freedom that speaking-out offered, to pull her own self up, to become a voice for those who no longer had one. Especially those who Shelley loved.

Shelley was the happiest she had been in years after that, and we once-again talked openly about her HIV-status and life and love and the future. She was not dead yet, she admitted to me, and she did not want to die without having done what she could for others. After all, keeping quiet did no justice to herself, her father, and especially, to beloved Patrick. I agreed with her loudly and often while she went on.

After a few more days' thought, Shelley sat me down at the table and said that she wanted to go public, to reveal her HIV-status to the world, but she wouldn't do so without my permission. She thought she should become a speaker on HIV and AIDS and responsibility and choices and sex, focusing on the needs of high school students. I was overjoyed with this decision, especially since Shelley was so happy to discuss this with me. I agreed that she, as a healthy-looking, beautiful blonde could certainly get the attention of her audience. Shelley looked relieved and was as buoyant as I had ever seen her. It was November of 1992, and she wanted to go public as soon as possible. She would be the first teacher in the country to openly admit that she had the HIV.

This was exciting. Our world was going to be opened up for public discussion, our lives in full view. We had no idea which questions would be asked, but we swore to each other that we would be honest and ready for anything. We were giddy and talked late into the night, scared and awestruck at the proportions of this gesture. This was uncharted territory for an educator.

Shelley went to the head of the girls' middle school, the very serious and rigid Betsy Clark, and the two of them cried together and planned the next move once Shelley disclosed her situation.

Betsy was definitely on Shelley's side and saw the importance of all of this for Cranbrook, especially for the girls' middle school. Next, the Head of Schools, Dan Behring, gave Shelley absolute support for her speaking out. Shelley fought back tears as she asked, "But what if people want to pull their kids out of school? What if you lose all that tuition?"

At that time Cranbrook cost about $17,000 for a boarding student, and one kid's tuition could make a difference in the budget. And parents didn't have to give a reason for pulling their kids out. Dr. Behring gave her a reassuring hug and told her, with absolute conviction, "Shelley, I don't care if we lose 10 or 20 or 50 families, this is the right thing to do. Do not worry."

And he meant it. Shelley was tremendously relieved and grateful.

What was next? Dr. Behring told Shelley that he wanted to make sure the word got out firmly and quickly, and that everyone in the community found out at the same time so there would be no questions or bad reactions amongst potentially fearful parents. The official letter of notification would go out on the day after Christmas Break, and the New Year of 1993 would be the beginning of Shelley's and Gary's lives as HIV educators. It would be our last vacation without public knowledge of Shelley's secret.

As if they knew we needed to get away, Mom and Dad traded one of their time-shares and got a condominium in the south of Spain for Christmas week. And they offered to give this to us as a gift! Wow... that was just across the Straits of Gibraltar from Morocco in northern Africa.   The ancient Marketplace of Marrakech! The Sahara! This was going to be a Christmas and New Year to remember!

When Shelley and I had decided to go public, we realized that it was time to tell my folks and family about the HIV, and that in itself was sort of exciting. Of course, I knew they would be worried about me, but I also knew that my folks were pretty smart and might have already figured it out. They knew about Patrick and her dad's infection and the link with hemophilia. Mom's nephew, Dr. Spencer Misner, lived nearby, and we figured that he might have known enough to caution them about this possibility, that Shelley had "it". Anyway, phone calls needed to be made, and soon.

Mom was in Morristown alone since dad was in Mississippi for the Tupelo furniture market. We called her first, and it was surprisingly easy. "Mom," I started out, "we need to tell you about Shelley's health. You know how her dad and brother got the HIV..."

We could tell she was going to be responsive by her calm demeanor and patience; she could tell we were saying something important. "...well, Shelley got unlucky too. She has the HIV also, but," I added very quickly, "she's very, very healthy."

Mom surprised me by asking about her T-cell count.   She's a very smart lady, my mother. I think she had it all figured out.

I got a little careless when she asked about me and my status. Of course, I completely meant to say that I was fine, but somehow I got the words "positive" and "negative" mixed up in my mind, and I came out with, "Oh, no problem, I'm positive..."

There were gasps from all three of us, and Shelley was quick to say "negative! negative!" Whoops.

Once we got Mom past my careless comments, we assured her that Shells and I were being very safe and smart and had decided to go public very soon. Mom said that Morristown might not be ready for such news, and that she thought we shouldn't tell my grandmother, who was now 89, as Mom thought it might upset her. Shells doubted that Erma would have been bothered, but we honored Mom's wishes and kept it from her.

Next we called Dad in Tupelo, who assured us that he loved us. Marty was next, then Hillary, and they were both super, as expected. Lots of words of love and concern were spoken. When all was said, Shelley and I collapsed on the couch and held each other. We felt great. We were doing what was right.

Christmas break came and we had cheap tickets to Spain. Exhausted, we took the plane and train and taxi to our place on the Mediterranean, which turned out to be a fabulous luxury resort right on the water. In fact, the hotel was on a little jut of land out on the Sea, surrounded on three sides by the lovely blue water, and on the fourth side were the mountains. When we checked in, we were stunned to find that we did not have a room but rather a suite... the *penthouse* suite... with a private rooftop and all kinds of space. We were thrilled to go up the spiral staircase to the roof and lazily stare out at ships that went past.

Shelley was still a bit tense, and I worked hard to make this a fun, carefree time for her. We argued on Christmas Day about something silly, then made up on the rooftop under the Mediterranean stars, her tears seeping into my shoulder as I held her. Christmas always had been, and always would be, a tough time for her, all the memories of her father and brother spilling out.

In the second week of our holiday, we decided to take a boat over the Straits of Gibraltar and go deep into Morocco for about a week. First we went to the capital city of Fez by train, after we got through the immense throng of people trying to sell us their wares by the ship's dock. They seemed to smother us with their bracelets and carvings, and Shelley was so taken by surprise that, when we got separated from each other, she actually traded her watch for a metal plate worth, well, about a dollar. I was furious about it since that watch had cost me a lot of money, which made her very angry since she had been excited to make a trade, and it remained a sore spot for many years. We got over it, though and occasionally I would pull the plate out of storage and serve snacks on it to company, just to tease her.

Morocco was strange and enchanting and mysterious. In Fez, we went shopping for richly colored Berber rugs and teapots. We wove in and out of the market stalls, drinking sweet, thick mint tea with merchants, all with giant bearded smiles and snake-like friendliness. They nurtured us and flattered us until they realized we would not buy anything from them, and then we were dropped like dirty laundry. It was fun to barter with them and see how much a merchant, in his fez and traditional Muslim long-shirt, could run around and order his underlings, loudly and with a flourish, to wrap things up and make nice packages for us. Each rug was a work of art, dappled with azure and glowing oranges and yellows in repeating patterns.

In contrast, the marketplaces were dark and smoky and filled with sideways glances around curious faces, and it was thrilling to come around each corner, not knowing who or what would be there. While the scenes were like something from an Indiana Jones movie, we felt safe in this, the capital city, because there seemed to be armed guards just about everywhere, looking angry and alert. That took the edge off our worries, though we were careful to not behave too "suspiciously."

We stayed in a cheap hotel in the downtown area, and the guards at every street-corner seemed ready for any threat or revolt. The room was tiled and clean, overlooking the dusty and loud village square. We fell into an exhausted sleep after talking late into the night about all we had seen in our day of discovery. Our world exploded at 5 A.M.

Apparently, the speakers that announced the morning Islamic call to prayer were mounted right outside our window, and they burst to life in the dark of early morning. Scary Arabic words came screeching out of the speakers (the first phrases sounding like, "HASBAROUK! HASBAROUK!") and straight into our brains as we jumped out of bed in terror. In a moment we would later find hilarious, Shelley started crying, thinking we were in the middle of a war, while I searched blindly in the dark for the source of our discomfort. In about 30 seconds I was able to wake up enough to realize where I was and what was happening, and I was able to quickly tell Shelley and calm her down. Our hearts did not stop racing for another hour, and by then we were ready to go. On to Marrakech!

The train took us there in comfort, many hours sipping tea and napping and reading in the clackety lull. Shelley always had a good book or magazine to read, and she could sleep on any moving vehicle. We went through a real desert, the fringes of the mighty and mythical Sahara, watching abandoned shells of villages drift by along the tracks. Arriving at midday, sweaty and dusty, we were anxious to find a room so we could wash. Shelley looked cute in her giant backpack, and we were proud of our appearance, not as tourists but as serious adventurers, tough and ready for any new challenge.

Our guidebook, a rugged traveler's guide with offerings of decent and cheap accommodations, suggested a quaint hotel near the marketplace. While it was small and did not have private baths, the guidebook said that the ladies who ran the place were obsessed with cleanliness, which tickled Shelley. We took the room immediately. I must admit, the three ladies never stopped cleaning things the entire time we were there, stooping over the stairs with small brooms or scrubbing the fountain at the entrance.

We settled in as evening came about and headed out for some food. The marketplace was like a carnival, though we dared not venture in too deeply as it had gotten darker and there were more places in which to get lost or get trapped by a thief. We noticed that there were very few policemen or armed guards here. We had eyes in the back of our heads the minute we stepped out the door of the hotel, which made it all the more exciting, as we cautiously rounded each corner searching for something to eat.

I loved it whenever Shelley said she was hungry because that gave me a chance to engage in my absolute favorite traveling activity: trying the strangest foods I could find. In contrast, because of the extreme dangers of getting sick in a foreign land, Shelley was very careful about what she put in her mouth. In fact, she always traveled in foreign lands with a jar of Jif peanut butter in her daypack. That and locally-baked bread meant she never had to go hungry if she couldn't find anything decent to eat. This day, however she was in luck: just a block from the hotel, towards the marketplace, we passed a man who had a little beat-up cart, kind of like a New York street vendor. He was frying sweet bread dough in a vat of boiling oil, pulling it out and rolling it in sugar and cinnamon. It looked very strange but smelled a lot like heaven. Shelley peered into the man's cart as she passed, got a lovely smile on her face, and said, "I want *that*!"

I loved it when I could offer my sweet girl instant gratification, which was never often enough. I spoke my poor Moroccan French and got her the doughnut from the greasy smiling man. We had to go back later for another one, it was so good, and yet another the next day.

In the market, stalls were lit up with candles and cheap gas light fixtures, giving the vendors an eerie glow. There was everything for sale there: clothing, dried fish, millions of spices and pickled things, house-wares, you name it. A thin, happy man threw a spider monkey on my back as Shelley screamed with shock and delight. It took my breath away as I crouched, not sure how to behave. The man made it clear that for a very reasonable fee Shelley could take a picture of me and the monkey. It was a bargain!

Now, I had never worn a monkey on my shoulders, so I had no idea what it was doing back there besides holding onto my hair. Shelley was laughing and laughing, almost unable to breathe. Suddenly I felt something wet on the back of my neck, and I flinched and crouched lower, hoping the man would take the monkey off, but he was laughing too hard to do so, and he was waiting for Shelley to take the picture, which she couldn't do because she was doubled over herself. What was the wet thing the monkey rubbing on my neck? I was contorting myself, trying to keep the wet thing away from my skin, but it wasn't working as the monkey had to cling closer so he wouldn't fall off my spasming gyrations. It was a wicked dance we did. Finally, Shelley took the picture and the man took the monkey off, and I could see that it was clutching a piece of orange in its hand that it had been rubbing on my neck. Just an orange, thank God.

Smoky, delicious smells filled our nostrils as we passed one food-stand after another, and I was very hungry now. Shelley agreed to have a soda while I sat at a picnic table and accepted a food vendor's plate of the day. I had no idea what I was ordering, but it looked like a kind of meat and collection of local vegetables in a stew. It was fragrant and filling, and there was considerable caution with every bite of something new. What was I eating? Shelley made me feel like a hero for trying all this weird stuff. "You are so daring, Gary! I could *never* do that..."

That night at the hotel, we decided to ask the ladies who ran the hotel to wash our clothes for us since we were running out of clean ones. No problem, they gestured in staccato English, with some French mixed in. *Pas de probleme.*

As with all else in this third-world country, it was expected that you would barter with the locals over everything. I loved to trade and fancied myself to be good at it, at knowing when to frown and act like the seller was crazy, when it was time to act surprised, when it was the right time to walk away. When a vendor came running down the street to stop me and agree to my price, I was always amazed and quite pleased with myself. Shelley was nice enough to let me do the trading since I loved doing it, and she always ended up getting what she wanted at a better price. Honestly, we were probably ripped off with each purchase, the vendors laughing uproariously when we turned the corner with armloads of junk. But it was so fun!

So I bartered with the woman who was going to wash our clothes. She and I haggled for a long time, back and forth, seeming to be at a stalemate. Shelley was following along with her limited French and gesture interpretation, and she realized that I was stuck on about $2.25, while the lady was stuck on $2.50. When Shelley realized what was going on, she was livid. How could I be hesitating to make this deal over twenty-five cents when that was probably the poor woman's salary for the week! And she was going to do our wash by *hand*! On a washboard! In the hot sun! Wow, was Shelley mad, and she was right, too. So I gave the lady the money and Shelley gave her a bright yellow handkerchief that the woman had been eyeing as it lay prettily on Shelley's soft white neck. The laundry came back perfect.

When our Moroccan adventure ended and we were on the way back over the Straits of Gibraltar, the little ferry boat began pitching and rolling quite violently. Shelley and I looked at each other warily, both exhausted from our long train journey. Out the window, the waves were meters high, towering over our hopeful ship. It was obvious that we were in exceptionally rough seas, the waves whipped up by the persistent Gibraltar winds. We had to cling to our seats like scared little children, and even the seasoned Moroccan and Spanish travelers seemed uncomfortable. Up and down we went, the boat seeming to make no progress as it rolled and danced, the coastline nowhere in sight. Often it seemed like the water jumped out from underneath the boat, leaving us in free-fall down to the bottom of the wave's trough. Over and over again this happened, and Shelley did not look good. I just stared straight ahead and tried to meditate.

After a half-hour of this, Shelley unbuckled her lap belt and moved hurriedly to the ship's washroom, her facial color a pronounced green. She was gone quite a while. I, meanwhile, tried to put myself in a type of trance so that I could overcome the effects of this carnival ride. I focused on a spot out on the horizon, trying to keep from getting nauseous like my lovely green wife.

Shelley came back from the bathroom and started to tell me her experiences there. At first she wasn't going to throw up, but then some horrid sounds had started coming from the sink. It was a gurgling, chugging sound, as if the water was trying to force itself rhythmically up the pipes and out of the sink like a fountain. She explained that it sounded like the sink was trying to vomit too, like it was gagging up something of its own. I was trying not to listen to her, convinced I could keep myself from getting sick. But she kept on. The water in the sink was from the ocean, so it smelled like fish, which made her even more nauseous. Then it happened: the sink threw up. It spit water into the air with a sound like a vomiting human. And, she said with mixed disgust and delight, it looked like there were chunks in the sink's water too.

Well, that did it. Any effort I had made to keep from vomiting was gone with her great descriptive ability. I had to unbuckle and make a mad dash through overturned suitcases and moaning Spaniards into the bathroom. Once in there I felt better, away from the view of the rolling ocean. That is, until the sink started to gag and spit up with those sounds, just like Shelley had said.

It was *so* time to go home.

Chapter 9: Telling

We returned home from Europe and northern Africa triumphant, tired, and happy, but we also felt the storm coming. The letters to all the school parents had gone out in the mail a couple of nights earlier, and we were going to start school the next day, January 5, 1993. There would be an assembly for each school division to discuss the teacher who had HIV, and Shelley was to be visible at the middle school, just to show that she was vibrant, alive, lovely, intelligent, and able, as she had always been, if there were any questions from kids or parents. I was to appear at the Upper School Assembly on the Cranbrook campus, to stand and be ready for questions. A school administrator would speak about our school's policies so the students could be clear on Cranbrook's responses. At the end of the school day, my wife and I would appear with the school administration at a Parents' meeting with the officers of the Dads' Club and Mothers' Council. Arlyce Seibert, our Upper School head, wanted all of the parent groups to feel involved, since this was such a sensitive matter.

There were several powerful parents in charge of these groups, many of them wealthy and used to running their ventures their way, and they obviously had a lot of pull in how things flowed around campus. How would they respond to this situation where they might not feel that they have control? What would their kids say to them at home? What would the parents say to each other in closed rooms that Shelley and I would never hear? What would they say to the newspapers or television stations if asked?

Shelley seemed subdued in our cute little Cranbrook apartment the night before the big meetings, but I was very excited and couldn't wait for the events of the next day. I annoyed her because I was full of "what if" questions all night. What if some of the kids cry? What if they ask a question we can't answer? What if there's a parent revolt? Shelley looked at me with lovely lowered eyelids and said, "Gary. Relax. We can handle it."

I was so proud of her and proud of what we were going to announce. This was the right thing we were doing, and Cranbrook seemed behind us all the way.

I had already told some of my closest co-workers. Randy, my friend and mentor who shared my office, had known for a month now, when Shells had originally made the decision to start telling people. I had only just told my officemates Bob and Russ, and since all three of these guys taught biology I didn't have to explain too much about viruses and such.

We had eaten supper with Randy and Ellen Tufts at the Kingswood dining hall every night since we had gotten married. They had taken us to their summer house in Petoskey that first July, and Randy had been a big brother to me since I set foot on campus. He had reassured me a month earlier, when I had told him about Shelley, with great sincerity, "Gary, if there's anything I can do for you.... *Any*thing.... you let me know."

He meant he would go to war for me, even with parents and administration should there be trouble. Coming from a man like Randy, that meant everything to me.

Randy had once been head of the girls' middle school. When he lost his job due to politics after the two middle schools merged, he could have been disgusted that his hard work and love of Cranbrook Kingswood had been cast aside. In fact, he almost took a director's position at another private school in Pittsburgh. But rather than uprooting his family from their home on campus, Randy had decided to stay at Cranbrook and teach Upper School science. He was a wonderful, nurturing mentor who taught me every good thing I do in the classroom. To this day Randy is a rare teacher, possessing calmness and patience with the insight of one who truly knows what it is to reach kids and make them feel valued.

Bob, the man who Shelley and I think is the most like Jesus with his thoughtful and gentle demeanor, actually got a bit watery-eyed when I told him, which was a little awkward for me. I had been trying to act cool and like "oh, it's no big deal...", but he put his hand on my shoulder with love and appreciation for what he knew I would go through. Bob and his wife Trina, an incredible medical illustrator, are great people. When I was single, they had me over for breakfast in their faculty apartment many times

Russ is the one full of knowledge and unafraid to show it. He answers the biology office phone with an enthusiastic "bugs and beetles!" Russ has to be one of the smartest men around, retaining just about everything he has ever learned. He knew everything about HIV before I did, and he was very helpful in clarifying some things about the way the human body works. He, too, let me know how much he cared about Shelley and me and would back us up all the way.

On the day of the assemblies, I stood near the front of the packed Cranbrook assembly hall, where students had, for 60 years, come to listen to deans and headmasters tell them news of war and celebration, homecoming plans and policies on dating. Now Cranbrook students would hear, for the first time, that there was a person on campus who was HIV-positive, that it was a teacher many of them knew, and that it was a young, beautiful female whom they would have least expected. It was 1993, and there were no other teachers who had disclosed HIV-status anywhere in the world. The times were changing, perhaps too fast for anyone's comfort, but this was the way things were. And Cranbrook's official statement was one of compassion and support in the world of AIDS.

While Pat Hall, Dean of Girls, was speaking on the Kingswood Campus to the half of the Upper School students who had classes on that side of the lake at that time, John Winter, Dean of Boys, stood in front of the roomful of the other half. I was there in the front, seated, looking at John, and there were 400 curious students behind me. While this group had often been rambunctious at such assemblies, today they were unusually attentive and respectful. A tone was in the air, one of kindness and even importance.

John began: "Some of you have heard by now that this assembly is to tell you about a very special teacher we have on this campus. Shelley Gerson, a middle school faculty member who knows many of you and whom many of you have had as a teacher, has bravely decided to come forth and disclose that she is HIV-positive."

It was out, loud and clear. The hall was quiet and respectful, the students' eyes riveted to the front.

John went on. "She is very healthy, she is very active, she is not contagious to any of the students she comes in contact with, and she is very happy to discuss this with anyone. Mr. and Mrs. Gerson have decided that they did not feel comfortable keeping this a secret any longer and want to use this to help educate others, and that is why they are coming forward with this, so that none of you is surprised. A letter has gone out to your families and they should be receiving it today."

The room was quiet, respectful, charged. I sat in front, slightly flushed, ready. "Are there any questions? Mr. Gerson is here to answer anything for you."

I knew that not too many questions would come out on such short notice, and this was only a 15-minute assembly, but I was glad to hear this presented so nicely and received with student seriousness. A few hands went up.

"How long has she known?" asked one of our more responsible young men. John deferred the question to me. Up until then, I had probably been just another young teacher to the kids, just another guy at the front of the classroom droning on about weather and climate and rock formation. All of a sudden, my words had become important to the whole student body. While the question was innocent, I was unsure about how deep the kids would dig here. I figured that they all probably wanted to know how she got it, and I had a chance to get that out of the way. I hoped my voice would sound strong as I stood, turned, and faced them.

"Shelley is a hemophiliac, and many of them were contaminated in the early 1980's from bad blood products that they had to inject. We're not exactly sure when she got it, but she figures she's had it since 1981 or so. No later than 1985, though, when they started treating her medications and getting rid of the HIV. Most of her hemophiliac friends were infected then too, as were her father and little brother, her uncle, and a cousin."

A good, concise answer, a good beginning, and I felt okay. Another question, surprisingly personal, though it was time to be ready for anything. "Did you know when you married her?"

"Yes. She decided to tell me on our first date so I could change my mind about seeing her if I wanted to." I smiled. "Obviously, I didn't want that."

That got a few appreciative giggles, taking the edge off. I knew then that every one of them, while perhaps not greatly informed about HIV and AIDS, realized that the question of sex would have to fit in there somewhere, but nobody was going to ask, at least not then. There would be time later, in a more intimate setting, and we would be ready. The next statement from a student surprised me with its affection and candor. It came from a sharp young lady in the far back, a young Ivy-League-bound woman who had the respect of her peers all the time.

"Mr. Gerson, this isn't a question but rather a statement. I think that your wife's going public with this information is incredibly brave and that your sticking with her is wonderful."

The entire auditorium suddenly erupted in cheers and applause. I was not expecting that at all, no way. Holy Cow. They really cared about my beautiful wife and me. They had cheered for us! I looked with disbelief over at John, who also was clapping.

John had to conclude the brief assembly. "There will be time for questions and discussion later. Please do speak to the Gersons or anyone on our Care Team if you have any concerns. Please go to your third period class."

The kids were buzzing as they left, and many came up to me before heading to the exit. Each had a supportive comment. Several football players came up to me and looked me in the eye and shook my hand. "That is so cool," one of them said. "I could never do that. Wow, Mr. Gerson..."

Wow, indeed. I loved this! Who knew they would be so nice?

I went right back to our little house after school. Shelley came in a few minutes later, glowing. Her experiences, she told me with delight, had been awesome, even better than mine. She had gotten a standing ovation from the other half of the Upper School and about a thousand hugs and lots more tears from the Middle School girls who loved her so. They had totally embraced her.

Shelley had had to tell each class of middle school girls, all of the 6th, 7th, and 8th grades, separately. Each time she had cried just a little and explained that she just could not keep this information from them any longer. She told them that she had lost her little brother to this disease, and that she was dishonoring him by keeping her own status secret. While many of them did not know very much about AIDS at that age, all of them had heard of it and had known that it was a horrible, horrible thing, once so far away and foreign. Shelley had brought it home to them, right into their young consciousness, and was telling them that they could decide how to handle this news as they wished. She had been prepared for them distancing themselves from her, which would have broken her heart. Instead they all, every one of her students, moved closer and closer to embrace the beautiful, brave teacher they all loved. When she told me about all this, she was ecstatic. All of the girls she had spoken to, and all of the teachers, had cried for her.

We hugged forever right then in our little apartment. My wife, my Shells, was triumphant... and she was now free. While she had been prepared to explain over and over that HIV was not contagious, her 6th grade girls surprised her by expressing no concern for themselves. Instead many pointed out that they had to be careful to wash their hands and not sneeze near Mrs. Gerson or *they* might make *her* get sick! When Shelley told me this, I loved those girls! Any doubts we had had about doing the right thing, about speaking out, had vanished in the faces of our Cranbrook kids.

At the parent meeting that night, outpourings of good wishes overflowed the small meeting room. Everyone wanted to tell Shelley how brave she was, and I got to sit next to her and watch her glow. There was lots of crying, lots of statements of support from the strong parents. It became evident that so many of them had come in contact with, or read about, people with AIDS, and they had wanted to reach out to help in some way. Shelley was giving them that opportunity by showing the HIV in a familiar face.

Dan Behring, the Head of Schools, voiced his support unequivocally in front of the parents. I was proud of our school and the way they were all embracing my wife so firmly right then. A few more questions came out, though people steered away from sex inquiries. I volunteered to them that Shelley and I would be speaking at various times to small groups and would speak frankly about condom use and safe sex and would not hold back anything. All these prominent parents nodded in approval at everything Shelley and I said. What a great feeling. They knew that we would help their kids, and they were being as appreciative as they could in the face of such a horrible illness.

Sure, a few anxiety-tinged questions eventually trickled into Dr. Behring's office over the next few days: Where would Mrs. Gerson use the bathroom? What if she had her period? What if she cut her hand? Shelley wrote out answers to each of these and actually typed up a list of precautions that she would take: she would only use the faculty restroom and would always "inspect" for stray drops of blood, and she would make all students move away from her if she did anything to cause body fluids to be exposed. She would always have access to a container of bleach to spray on anything that looked "dangerous."

Dr. Bauder stated in a letter that universal precautions would then be explained to all teachers and administration, as well as all maintenance workers. Everyone would know what to do if ever in contact with stray body fluids. All of the athletic coaches would receive further instruction and would have to travel with protective gloves and bandages. The Cranbrook community was moving ahead, proud of its responsibility in this new era.

Meanwhile, our home life got good in a hurry. We kissed a lot more, and there was much more happiness in everything. I felt Shelley open up to me, and we were proud of each other. Shelley would say, "Hey, you know that I'm getting famous for this, but *you're* looking like a real hero here."

Man, did that pump up my ego. I was so proud of her resolve and posture through all of this, and everyone treated us with so much love and respect. The school seemed pleased with the way things were going. Then the newspaper people came.

Frank Bruni had already gained fame with his very personal stories in the *Detroit Free Press*. He had been amongst the nation's first to have written about such sensitive and controversial topics as gay marriages and priests who had abused children, and he had won many journalistic awards. And now he was calling on Shelley to tell her story. Frank had to work fast because he had heard a rumor that he was about to get scooped by the rival newspaper, the *Detroit News*. So he came around and interviewed us all, including some of her students and the administration, and he brought lots of deep questions for Shelley and me.

The article came out on the front page of the *Free Press* on a school day in mid-January, and it was huge. There was a big picture of my beautiful wife right smack in the top half of the page, her hand tucked under her lovely chin as she looked straight and strong into the camera, behind her the long school hallway and students with books in their arms, blurry as they hurried to class. The headline was steady across the top of the page: *Beyond the Burden of a Painful Secret: A Teacher Speaks*

Out About HIV and AIDS. If the newspaper was trying to get everyone's attention, it sure did just that. We were amazed at the bold front-page coverage.

The phone calls started soon after that, from her friends and people who had known her long ago... Was Shelley *that* Shelley? She heard from many people she had never met, those who just wanted to reach out to her. We got $20 in a letter from a man who lived in the city who "just wanted to help out a little" with whatever expenses were going to come. School parents from all divisions wrote or called to tell her of how proud they were to be associated with Cranbrook. It was quite incredible and flattering, and it made our beloved Cranbrook look good.

The article went into great depth, showing that Frank had done much research in a short time. There was a section about her parents, and he wrote a thoughtful summary of Patrick and his slow death, and about how Shelley had the need to go public with her story so that she might honor Patrick and her father and all of her fallen friends. There were long stretches about the love her students felt for her, and how they had cheered when she had gotten her T-cell count from the doctor's office, and how they all felt responsible for helping her to be happy by working hard for her and trying to learn as much as they could.

And then there was some mushy stuff about me and how I had fallen so definitely for this lovely, passionate woman, about how I had pursued her and had been supportive when she had disclosed her private secret to me. It made us both out to be crusaders for truth and education, which seemed like quite an exaggeration. The pictures of her were superb, but the photo of me on page 9 was pretty lousy. I told Shelley that it looked like she had married the poor goofy-looking guy out of pity, and she loved that. Her laughter, again, was music as she heard me "horrified" at my puffy, thug-like mug-shot.

Only one interesting conflict involving Cranbrook came from the whole affair with the *Free Press* article. In a section about living in the dormitory and speaking very frankly with girls about life and love and drinking and sex, Shelley was describing her relationship with these girls and how she thought she needed to help them move past some dangerous feelings of immortality. Shelley had learned through conversations with kids that, at age 17, not many of these girls had ever thought that the HIV or any sexually-transmitted diseases would enter their lives. Why should the virus bother them? Teenagers often have false feelings of invulnerability. These conversations in the dorm came during her first year there, before anyone even had a small thought that Shelley might be infected, this lovely young woman with the serious intent in her voice, this big sister. Reflecting on Shelley's secret illness and her concern for the girls, the article stated:

> "She thought about the conversations she heard among the high school girls when she monitored the Cranbrook dorms at night. Some of the girls talked about getting drunk, getting sloppy and sleeping with boys.... she knew they weren't being careful."

Some administrators were not pleased that there was an open suggestion that Cranbrook girls might be sexually active and might get drunk. One response from a Cranbrook official was a bit of shock and anger at this bold statement about the types of girls who attended our school, and that really hurt Shelley, to think that her words might have been offensive to anyone from our school. But soon enough, this article was soon seen as an opportunity to open up a new area of discussion and communication in our dorms. In her own words to girls of the age of sexual curiosity and activity, Shelley always said, "I want my face to haunt you. I want you to remember me when there is a chance you might make a bad choice."

Other than those small complaints, the response from the rest of the school, especially her students, was amazing. Any worry of rejection faded away. Many of Shelley's 6th grade girls started to come earlier to class just to be with her, and several began the habit of hugging her as they left class for the day. One girl made hundreds of dollars by making red plastic AIDS ribbons in her home craft kit and selling them to other students; all of the money was given to AIDS charities. When I would go to visit Shelley in her classroom, which was a former home-economics room from the 1960's now filled with atomic models and colorful science posters and a guinea pig named Cookie Dough and a ferret named Rafiki, Shelley'sc girls would also gather around me and smile with the same love they had for her, all in appreciation of the support and care I also had for my beautiful Shells. Their teacher.

In the letter she had written to the parents, all of her goals for speaking out had been outlined so well:

"I fell in love with Cranbrook the moment I stepped foot on campus. My biggest fear was not of dying, but of losing the job and the home that I loved so much. I have reached a point that my need to be the voice for my brother and friends, who no longer have a voice, has outweighed my fear of the possible rejection I might encounter.

I have begun to understand that if I continue my silence, I am allowing their suffering and pain to be buried and forgotten. I have begun to understand that I am doing an injustice to my profession. I have begun to understand that I have been doing my husband, a man whom I love with all my heart and soul, an injustice by keeping this all inside."

And so, there was now a purpose to my getting screamed at for leaving socks on the floor and for enduring some senseless tirades and periods of moping and finger-pointing. Having Shelley validate my confusion and pain was wonderful for our marriage, especially when she made public her respect for me and my tolerance levels. The letter made me sound so noble all over again, while she told me with every word on the page how much she appreciated me. It was the beginning of 1993, and my life was coming around the right way, full of reason and reward and a woman whom I *knew* loved me. I had been at Cranbrook for six years.

My co-workers at the Upper School seemed to have a new respect for me. The older, more respected members of the faculty spoke me to in serious tones. When I stood up at faculty meetings to voice my approval of a student project or offer a thought on assemblies, everyone looked at me and listened with intent. I felt so wise, like I was suddenly somebody important. I ate it up, even though it seemed I hadn't really earned it.

Meanwhile, my life was getting ready to take yet another turn. This time it would involve my secret dreams of success on the football field. It started with my last attempt to become head football coach. In 1993, Del Walden had been removed from his job as coach, and I thought it might fall into my lap. Del had gotten caught on the short end of parent/school politics, and he was not only pushed out of the head coaching job, but they had also forced him out as athletic director, a position he had never really wanted after being the respected Dean of Boys for so long. A parent group, it seemed, had punched some buttons and found that our school had played a hockey game against an illegal opponent. For that minor offense, Del was fired, and I was very sad for him. He had taught me a lot about standing strong in the face of adversity and represented every good thing about our old school, and his troubles stemmed from the pettiness and ambition of those who had more power than him. Del was a victim, and he was also a symbol for all of us working at Cranbrook to have caution: if it could happen to Del, it could happen to anyone, so be careful.

I had been interested in the vacant football head coaching job, but no one asked me if I wanted it, even after 6 years as an assistant, a year playing football in Europe, and four years of Division I ball. The Cranbrook Parent, Mike, got the job quickly after having been an unpaid assistant for two years at Cranbrook. He was a very powerful man, quite popular with the parents and boys because he had told them all what they wanted to hear and spent a lot of his own money to improve the weight room. He had earlier made a fortune when he had sold his many car dealerships and had made a second fortune investing in a dental laser corporation, so money was not an issue. All in all, he was a pretty amazing businessman, and his chrome-like luster had dazzled me too.

I remained part of Mike's parade until I realized that he had no desire to let me help him in his effort to coach the Cranbrook team the next year, and that I would be pushed aside like an annoying little kid, perhaps offered a job as assistant to the assistant coach in charge of water bottles. There was no way I was going to stay around for that. I had a flashback to a parent meeting he had called in the weight room to show off how much he had worked with our kids while it was actually I who had done all the grunt work, teaching the kids how to lift and spotting them and yelling encouragement. At this meeting, he called me to the front and rubbed the hair on the top of my head as if I was a little boy looking for praise. I was 28 at the time. While I had smiled good-naturedly, with an "aw-shucks" grin, I was horribly embarrassed. How dare he treat me like a child in front of all those parents! It was obvious that things would get no better, and I did not want this man in charge of me in any way. It was clear that I needed out of the Cranbrook coaching scene.

So, I went to the college counseling office and got the phone number of a little school in Windsor, Ontario, just across the Ambassador Bridge from downtown

Detroit. The University of Windsor indeed had a geology program and would be a perfect match for me in an effort to pursue my Masters Degree. I found out that it was expensive for Americans to attend, but they did offer some graduate assistantships if you were willing to teach a lab class, and that would cover all of the tuition, plus a small stipend. And they offered credit for classes taken elsewhere, such as the 12 hours of grad classes I had taken at Vanderbilt in 1987. Obviously, it was worth further probing.

And there was an ulterior motive. Something had happened that winter and spring that had turned me back to the football field in a different way. Andy Cohen, my great friend from Vanderbilt, had been asked to play touch football in a Sunday league with some young lawyers and doctors and businessmen, and he asked me if I would be interested. I hadn't played regular football in many years, but I had stayed in good shape by lifting every other day and playing basketball four times a week, so I said that I would love to play. Football was still very much in my blood, this silly game of pretend war, and I thought that my coaching had made me better, maybe even a little smarter, on the field.

So we went out to play touch football with these guys, many of whom had played basketball at night at Cranbrook with me. These were fellows who had made some money out in the professional world and had also been intramural stars at their respective colleges, and they just knew me as a mediocre pick-up basketball player who was fairly unimpressive, athletically. It was a great challenge to try to get these guys to notice me, especially since few of them realized that the football field was a very comfortable place for me.

In our first game, on a cold Sunday in mid-winter of 1993, we took our positions out on the field. I was lined up at receiver, but they threw no passes at me all day, which was disappointing. No one, except Andy, had any idea I could catch a football, and the two brothers who had formed the team spent most of the day passing the ball to each other, one at quarterback and one at wide-out. About half the passes, some very easy, were dropped, and I held my tongue, still thankful for the invitation to be out there with these guys that I respected.

The bad part was when I was on defense. I knew how to play the defensive back position, but I got beaten pretty badly at least twice. On one of the plays, the opposing quarterback faked a short pass, so I came running forward as I bit on his fake, and he threw the ball long, right over my head, for a touchdown. That was humiliating for a former "big-time" football player and current football coach. On another play, I stayed deep and had a chance for a big interception that might win the game, but the ball bounced off my ready hands and, by dumb chance, fell into the arms of the receiver, who scored again. That was almost too much to bear. The guys on the team were horribly upset with me, and I felt that I had let them down in our loss.

After the game, none of the guys would speak to me, and I felt terrible. Andy came over and told me not to let it bother me, but I was really shaken. Here were these guys giving me a chance to play "my" game again, and I had not given them anything back. While I had done well in many ways, setting blocks and covering my zone on defense, it was not what I had expected of myself. I went home and thought about it all week, wondering if they would let me on the field again.

Every day that week I got into the weight room after school and lifted to absolute fatigue on every set. I worked on my lower body with plyometric jumping like I had taught the kids after school, and the upper-body coordination was addressed by catching heavy medicine balls. I went out and sprinted the beautiful Cranbrook stadium steps, getting these old legs back into game shape. I remembered what it had felt like at Vanderbilt, when I had been truly ready for practice, and I got out there and did what I could to get that feeling back on short notice. My body responded hesitantly at first, with soreness and stiff legs and no flexibility. One of the high school quarterbacks threw footballs to me all afternoon three days that week. By that Saturday all the stiffness was gone and I was ready to play.

That next Sunday was warm and perfect, and I was thankful that we ran some drills before the game to loosen up. I was catching everything the way that I had learned to, the way I had taught my kids at Cranbrook to catch, with the eyes and the hands and the steps, coming to the ball and taking it out of the air as if it was mine and nobody else's. I felt great, tall, fast. For the first half of the game, however, nobody even thought of throwing the ball towards me. I didn't touch the ball until there was only a minute left in the half and we were tied with the other team, far from the end zone. Things changed quickly.

The new quarterback, a young steel executive named John who had actually punted for Ohio State, had called a play where I was to go deep to the middle of the field and act as a decoy while someone else ran "underneath" me for the catch. But John got into trouble and had to scramble, and the other receiver was covered, so John heaved the ball towards me, deep and far outside. I sprinted for it and made a leaping, diving catch just short of the out-of-bounds line. One of my best catches ever, like in my dreams. I landed on my right side, fully extended, and hung onto the ball, feeling like a stud. In the defender's disgust, he trotted past me, helplessly shaking his head. This was a mistake. Forgetting our rules, he had neglected to tag me, and I got up and sprinted down the sideline, untouched, for a 60-yard touchdown. It was my first reception of the year, my first in many years during a real game. It happened fast and left some people with open mouths.

In the second half John starting throwing me the ball, seeing that I was willing to work hard to get to it. Quarterbacks like that sort of thing, so I made sure I was all over the place. He threw me three more touchdown passes and I also intercepted four passes while on defense, one after another. Everything was so clear now on the grass, and the ball was soft as cotton, a beach ball ready to be taken from the air. Our guys truly owned the field that second half and just thrashed the other team. When the game was over, these lawyers and professionals I respected swarmed me and slapped my hand and squeezed my neck and told me how great I had played. Granted, I was the only one on the field who had once played receiver at a high level of college football. But let me tell you, I loved being the hero, even just a hero to Sunday-morning thirty-something yuppies. It had happened so rarely in my life that I ate it up like a rich dessert. That evening I went home to Shelley all excited and did not sleep all night, reliving each catch and route over and over, especially the long ones where I ran full speed down the short lined grass faster and faster and faster, chased in futility by men who could not touch me. It was wonderful to be a receiver again.

The season went on into the spring and I was the go-to guy, catching at least 3 touchdown passes in every game and intercepting a whole bunch of balls on defense. The opposing team stopped throwing to the side of the field I was on because I was so "threatening". I was patient and disciplined and played the way I had taught the

Cranbrook boys. The ball was a little stuffed animal on a string as it came into these ready hands, and my eyes were big and clear and focused each time.

In the finals of the league championship, we faced the same team that we had played in the first week, the team that had beaten me and made me look like a beginning pick-up football player. When I caught my first touchdown pass of this game though, they couldn't believe it. One of their players yelled out in frustration to his beaten teammate, "HE can't catch a touchdown pass against us! No way! Not HIM!"

I loved that, because I was the poor fool they had abused so much a couple of months earlier in the opening game. They were equally chagrined when I got a couple of interceptions that changed the game, especially the one-handed pick-off that I ran back for a long score. Total vindication: they had dared to throw to my side of the field. They had never seen me as a threat until the game was over, and by then it was too late.

I realized, from that small league of once-pretty-good intramural athletes, that I could play this game at a higher level. I would be 30 in April. If I was going to make a move, it had to be now, and it sure wasn't going to be easy. I needed to try to play *real* football one more time.

I had heard, long ago from my archaeology friends in Canada, that I still had eligibility to play football in Canadian Universities. I had no idea if that was true, but it became obvious that I had a need to find out. It was now April of 1993, and I had never caught a pass or made a block in a real North American football game, where you wore pads and got hit on every play and had to look out for your brothers in the same-colored uniforms. I needed to find out if I could still do it. A phone call to the geology department in Windsor started the ball rolling, me full of hope and dreams and inspiration from my wife, who had been freed from her own confines of secrecy.

Chapter 10:   One More Season

Coach John Musselman took my call in his little office in the human physiology building. A bulldog of a man, Muss had been head of the football program at the University of Windsor for several years, but they had not had a winning record in forever. He listened to me tell my story, and he said that I might have a chance at some eligibility, but I could tell by the tone in his voice that he never believed that he would see me in a Lancer uniform. I guessed that, probably, a lot of Americans had called him for a second chance to play football, but they had never followed through or couldn't get accepted to the University or had found something better to do. So I had to pull information out of Muss a little at a time, hoping he would believe me in my sincerity to play the game again. This was my last shot, having no eligibility left anywhere in the States, and I probably sounded desperate.

Muss said that it was possible that I could have a couple of years left if I had only played three years at some other school. That is, in Canadian universities, you had 5 total years to play college football, and it did not matter where you played or how you transferred. There really was no "red-shirt" year like in the NCAA. However, one must play his fifth year at the same school he played his fourth year. For me, that would be the defining factor, as it seemed that I had already played my fourth year in Nashville. I told Muss I had played 4 years at Vanderbilt, and he said that that was too bad and would keep me out of Canadian university football. Sadly, I volunteered that, well, I had not actually played, rather I had just been on the scout team, and that I really wanted another chance to prove myself in a major program and would do anything to live that dream. Muss stopped me and asked, "Wait, you mean you didn't actually play in the games? Did you dress for them all?"

I told him that I had not dressed in uniform for most of the games, including the entire season of my second year on the Vanderbilt team due to a broken leg. That interested Muss a little more. "The whole season?"

Yes, the entire season, first game to last, no uniform.

"Well, that makes you eligible. In Canada, you have to dress for a game to use your year's eligibility. You still have two years here. Gary, if you're interested, I'll check into it and you can come join us in the fall."

I was eligible! Wow! I promptly told him that I had not been very good, or very fast, but that I would work my butt off for him. I told him my scant football history, breathlessly. Muss was either unimpressed or disinterested, probably waiting to see if I showed up at all.

When we hung up, I was soaring. I was getting another chance to play in an established, respected program! Real football!

I knew I had better get busy quick, in so many ways. The questions flooded my brain: Could I get back into shape? Could I catch a football fired at full speed from a young gun's arm, looking through a helmet? Was I fast enough? Was my head right? Would anyone laugh?

I needed to find out more about my academic eligibility for the Windsor geology program, so I went over the bridge to Canada in late April of 1993, ready to dig out what I needed to fulfill this dream. At the University of Windsor, I was directed to Dr. Terrence Smith, an older member of the faculty who was regally British, athletically fit, and smelled of very nice after-shave. He invited me into his office and told me that he would be happy to guide me through a masters program in geology. He told me that I should have no problem gaining an assistantship to cover my tuition, and there would even be a $4000 Canadian stipend each semester. Of course, that was only about $2900 in United States currency, but I didn't care! They were going to pay my way! It was obvious that they needed good teaching assistants there, and my classroom experience at the prestigious Cranbrook Schools was very important and suggested that I could handle a class or two. Of course, that part was true; I could certainly teach a few lab classes on mineral identification and analysis of rocks under microscopes. Doing the thesis work, however, seemed like it would take forever and, quite frankly, scared the hell out of me.

Dr. Smith told me that he would be happy to offer me guidance in the study of some rocks he had brought back from the Caribbean. No ordinary rocks, these were cumulate blocks that had formed from crystals stuck together inside a magma chamber deep under the surface of one of the islands in the Lesser Antilles. Neat, I thought, I would love to do some work in this area of igneous petrology. That kind of study would be obviously challenging, but I was willing to try with this esteemed professor's help. It was guaranteed that I would learn a lot about geology in the process, and that would certainly make me a better teacher. Could I handle the thesis? It was worth a try. It meant that I could play football.

So, I started the whole machine going. Ms. Seibert offered to let me take the year off from Cranbrook, without pay of course, but she would allow me to continue to do dorm duty in exchange for our campus housing. I told all the other teachers and my friends that I was taking a leave-of-absence to work on my master's degree, but I didn't have the courage yet to tell anybody I was going to play the real game.

I worked out the plans with Shelley, and she was lukewarm to the whole idea. She was content to "support" me for a year while I worked on my masters program, but she had absolutely no words of encouragement for the football scheme. I tried to explain to her that it was something I felt that I needed to do for my own satisfaction, but she was not buying that. It was strange to me that she would not offer blind acceptance and undying encouragement for my plans, but I was going to have to deal with that. The way I saw it, Shelley had never played on an athletic team or taken part in a competitive sport, and she had no idea of the benefits of such things or what it could possibly mean to me. She had never really known a football player, and here she was married to one, and I could not expect her to embrace football the way I did. So, I churned on without her, which was sad to me, but necessary for my own self. I would have done anything to see her excited for me then, but it was time to work on my own self, and I learned to live with her indifference.

That spring, I started working out after school with religious fervor. It was fun because the high school athletes were encouraging to me and impressed that this "nerdy" teacher could bench and squat and throw around the steel so well. I worked hard on the areas I knew would be tested, and I was able to, for the first time, bench-press 225 pounds. This weight continues to be a standard in the world of lifting and conditioning because it consists of a 45-pound bar with two 45-pound plates of steel on each side. It looks impressive sitting alone on the bench, balanced and centered and slightly bent down by angry gravity. It is even more impressive when someone is able to lie flat on the bench, slowly release and lower it to his chest, and extend it back up again with force and a hefty grunt of success. I felt triumphant in my efforts, and after all those years of teaching and studying weightlifting, I could back up what I had taught the young men. I got to the point where I could do this lift several times, even with my seemingly scrawny frame, which could not muster up any more than a 185-pound press when I was at Vanderbilt.

I did a two-day rotation of lifting, which meant that on one day I would work hard on chest, shoulders, triceps, and abdomen, and on the other day I would do legs, back, and biceps. I did this rotation 6 days a week, each exercise with the best form I could muster and to total exhaustion. The idea was that by challenging my muscles to their limits and attempting to go past my previous best each time, the muscles would grow back stronger in the next 48 hours. As they say in biology class, if you strain an organism, the organism either dies or adapts to the strain over time. It felt like I was just short of death with each lift, as the aches each night proved, but my body was growing and adapting to the daily challenges. I could literally feel it all working as my muscle tone tightened after each workout.

I also did the plyometric exercises with the boys after we all finished lifting, every other day. I would direct them to jump on and off a variety of wooden boxes, up and down, over and over, and as quickly as possible. The trick was to touch the ground between boxes for just a millisecond, then back up again to the next box in line. After ups and downs, we would do quick drills where we would again jump but change direction with the jump, left, then right, then left again. This was to help us make gains in *proprioception*, or "knowledge of body in space". I loved using that term; it was very impressive to throw it around like a weight-lifting scholar. "Let's work on our *proprioception*, shall we?"

These workouts went on every day for at least two hours after school, and the kids and I were really making some gains. I also was starting wind sprints out in the yard at night where no one could see me. It was kind of embarrassing since 30-year-old guys don't usually run back and forth in the darkness at full speed, but no one ever saw me. I was a sweaty mess every day, and it felt great!

In June I called the coach from Windsor again and told him that I was still coming, but I don't think he remembered who I was at that time, or at least he gave no indication of recalling me. So I reminded him, and I made plans to come see him and discuss my possibilities. On the day after our final school meetings at Cranbrook, June 15, I went down across the bridge and found Coach Musselman's office. I wore the tightest shirt I could find, a thin black T-shirt from my Vanderbilt days, which now made it a size too small for my growing frame, perhaps making my biceps appear a little larger than they deserved to be. I found myself in the office of the head coach of Windsor, hopeful and nervous.

I wasn't sure if he was surprised, confused, or even disappointed to see this skinny old guy in front of him, but when I met this meaty, honest-looking fellow, I knew I liked him. He had been an old football player himself who seemed like the kind of guy who would give you a chance if you were worthy of it. By then he had found out that, indeed, I had some eligibility left. And he offered me the chance to earn a spot on his team. No promises, no deals; just a chance, like everyone else. I assured him that I would be ready. I asked Muss if there was anyone I could throw the ball with over the summer since I would be coming in to work on my rocks for Dr. Smith just about every day to get a head start on my thesis. He told me of a backup quarterback and punter named Andy Vasily who could be found in the gym pretty much every day, "Working oot," he said in his Canadian accent.

So, I went to the reception desk of the workout facility, a very nice complex with decent weights and a great training room for rehab and teaching. The gym was huge enough to have indoor track meets and 20 different basketball games all going on at the same time, very impressive by American standards. Lots of Canadians went to Windsor to get a degree in physical therapy or human kinetics, and they certainly had the facility to do good work right there. At the desk I left a note for Andy (seemed everyone who worked there knew who Andy was) saying that I would be back at 4:00 the next day to talk to him and throw the ball around. I mentioned that I was a former U.S. collegiate receiver, which was left open for interpretation. I don't think he interpreted it correctly at first.

When I came the next day, there was a really good-looking blonde guy with a tan at the counter chatting with the lovely young ladies behind the desk, getting a football from one of them and flashing a winning smile. He was about my height, trimmer and younger, with cutoff sleeves and a playboy look, like a high school stud. I came over and asked in general if anyone knew the quarterback Andy Vasily. That stud took one look at me and knew I was the American college receiver, and the expression on his face could only have been one of disappointment. I knew what he was expecting when I saw the look on his face: a tall, lithe, lanky fellow with long arms who could lope downfield and run under whatever long ball was thrown. Here was me: 5'11", unimpressive, little bit of a belly. White. Old.

Well, Andy quickly wiped the disappointment off his face and smiled his sterling smile (Shelley later told me it was the first thing she noticed about him: a smile that could sail ships and send hearts aflutter). He told me that he was really excited that I was going to be playing for the Lancers, and it quickly became obvious to me that this kid was a winner. We went outside to run and throw the ball around together. I stretched for a only a short time so he wouldn't think I was out of shape, put on my cleats, and we lightly tossed the ball around on the football field in the hot afternoon sun. Even though this was a time for casual tossing, I always made it a point to step towards the ball before I caught it, then I looked it in from my hands to a tucked position next to my ribs. I did this with each and every catch, just to show that I meant business: there were going to be no catches taken for granted by this old guy. Quarterbacks, I had learned, appreciated that kind of thing: make sure you catch the damn ball and put it away. And be serious when you do it.

Andy then told me how some of the routes were run at Windsor, the quick slant and the out route, and I started out with the short ones. Three steps and a quick look-in to the quarterback was the route known as the 83, and I did it as Andy said I should. On the first try, I ran it hard and made my experienced head fake at the end of it, which I had taken from Chuck Scott at Vanderbilt and taught all of the kids I had coached at Cranbrook, just to cause the "imaginary" defensive back to hesitate for a split-second. I turned for the ball, not looking too soon so the quarterback had time to set up for the pass.

Let me tell you, Andy brought that ball in there like it was shot from a cannon. It became quickly obvious that, as much as I wanted to make an impression on him, he wanted to make one right back on me. The kid had a howitzer for an arm, and it came in to my hands on a straight line. Gravity stood no chance of working on a short throw from Vasily, for sure. I quietly reached out and grabbed his first perfect pass like it was nothing, kept my stride, and turned up-field for a practice touchdown, prancing in full gait like a gazelle, or at least as close to a gazelle as I could get. It felt so right, so smooth, no sound as the ball sucked into my hands. He pumped his fist at me and smiled big. We impressed each other enough over the next few throws to relax and enjoy the pitch and catch between two guys who knew what they were doing. He had proved himself to me, and so had I to him. The connection between two men working for a common goal on the football field is an awesome thing.

We did this all afternoon, for an hour and a half, and that is when we became friends. He started praising me with, "Hey, nice catch, way to go, oh that was pretty," and I gave it right back to him, "Wow, what a throw, nice pitch there, oh that had a touch on it." The dance that men make was on.

As I walked gingerly off the field next to him, knowing that I had given him everything I had, I asked the question that needed an honest answer, "Do you think I can play for Windsor?"

I loved him for his quick answer, the lack of hesitation a compliment. "Absolutely. You look like you could start at two different position, wide-out or slot. But you need to get faster."

"Really? You really think I could start?" I needed more, my poor ego hungry and me trying hard not to sound desperate.

"No question. Gary, you have better hands right now than anyone on the team. I can't wait for next fall. You're really gonna help us, ay?"

"Such a winning smile on that kid!" I thought.

Well, that was the fuel I needed. For the rest of that summer, I would drive to Windsor in the morning, work on my rock thin-sections all day, find Andy in the afternoon to throw the ball, and go work out every evening with the leftover Cranbrook boys, the ones who had not gone to Europe or camp for the summer. The kids and I got stronger together in the evenings, and I loved the results from my hard work in the weight-room.

Vas and I would eat supper together some nights down in Canada when Shelley was busy, and we became fast friends. He was a great punter and it was fun to try to catch his high, booming kicks. I knew he dreamed of playing quarterback, but it was going to be hard to beat out the current starter, a kid named Rob Zagordo who the coaches seemed to like a little better. I eventually knew that Vas was working through this; he was a guy who thrived on coming from behind, rising to the challenge, winning over the enemies. This was a tough battle for him.

So the hot summer moved along and steamier August came and Coach Musselman became friendlier to me, which made me wonder if he had been getting reports on our throwing all summer, and my confidence grew. I had no idea what to expect, but I was going to be ready for everything they presented on the field and in the meeting rooms. There was a type of focus there that I had not known before, certainly not at Vanderbilt when I was just learning how to play.

I kissed my wife goodbye, and soon after she offered whatever little encouragement she could in her effort to understand my infantile desires, I moved into the dorm at Windsor for our five-day preseason camp. Vas was my roommate.

The first thing we had to do was the strength testing. For the bench press, 3 racks were set up, one with 135 pounds, one with 185, and one with 225. We were to try to do as many repetitions as we could at whichever weight we chose. Most of the backs and receivers did a few reps on the lower weights, while the linemen tried to do multiple reps at 225. When it was my turn, Coach Gerald Hlady, an old Windsor Lancer who had once been drafted into the CFL as a lineman and was quite huge, asked me what weight I wanted, and I casually told him I would try 225. Coach Hlady looked at me with a sideways glance, probably wondering if I knew what I was doing. So one of the linemen got behind the bench to lift the bar off the rack for me, and I waved him off; I wanted no help. So with a self-start, I quickly threw up 13 repetitions at 225 pounds, each rep done with a convincing yell of power, Bam, Bam, Bam! The little old receiver, against the young studs, had pressed 225 for 13 reps on the bench. That opened up a few eyes, and I sensed some of those glances shift over to me. I felt like a serious stud, knowing that the boys and men in that room were asking amongst themselves, "Hey, who's that guy?"

When practice began that afternoon after all the testing was done, the coaches told me to go run at slot-back, which was a totally foreign position for me. It could be compared to a position in America that combines tight end with running back. The big difference, however, was that I was allowed to be moving towards the line of scrimmage before the ball was snapped. In America, no one is allowed to move towards the line before the snap, so I had to get used to this new concept. On the plus side, it meant that I could have a head start by being allowed to run at full speed at the start of a play rather than standing stock-still, and that could be advantageous for a slower guy like me.

I was to position myself on the opposite side of the other slot-back, a strong and talented Ontarian named Norm Casola, undoubtedly one of the best athletes with whom I had ever stepped onto a football field, including anyone from the States. Norm caught everything, looking better than any Vanderbilt player I had known, and we all knew he was great. So did he, in fact, but he walked the walk of greatness, and in football that means you can say whatever you want about yourself. Norm eventually ended up with the Toronto Argonauts of the CFL.

So I learned the plays and ran the routes and worked as hard as I could. Most importantly, I kept my mouth shut and let my actions speak. Coaches, I had learned, liked that sort of thing, when you stayed quiet and let them yell at you and you looked right into their eyes like they were telling you the secrets of the universe. They like it when you say, "Yes sir!" even if you don't totally believe what they're saying is helpful.

When I was timed in the forty-yard dash, I came in at a respectable 4.90, which was pretty fast for me but very slow for a world-class wide receiver. Then again, I didn't need to be world class here; I just had to do my job. And right now, my job was to work harder than the 18- and 19-year-olds and show the coaches I knew what I was doing more than anyone else. With each catch and block, I was proving my case. Every night, I returned to the dorm room and collapsed, full of aches and exhaustion and new bruises, but satisfied that I had not left anything inside me that I could have spent on the field.

Vas worked as hard as he could too, and I loved it when he was throwing passes to me, but Rob was a good quarterback too, and he put the ball where it needed to be, though with much less velocity. Every time I saw Vas during practice, he would remind me that I was living my dream, that we were doing what we loved doing, flashing me that smile with a pumped fist. His timing of comments was impeccable and his enthusiasm lifted me all the way through pre-season. Before I knew it, it was September, and I was still on the team. In fact, in the season opener on our home field against McMaster University, I was to start at the position of left slot-back on our beautiful field. I would wear a uniform of blue and gold with my name stitched across the back, and the coach had even pulled a few strings to let me wear the number 23, my old Vanderbilt number and the date of our wedding anniversary, which was supposed to be a number for a defensive back. I returned to Michigan and my Shells after camp, ready for whatever came in between the journeys back and forth over the bridge every day. I had missed her lots.

School started at Windsor and I ended up taking a couple of very tough classes on igneous rocks and thermodynamics, two areas that I had never before attacked in any depth. Dr. Blackburn taught the thermo class, and he was brilliant as he solved equation after equation on the board. I looked around to the other grad students to see if any of them comprehended the complex ideas floating about the room, and from their expressions it seemed they were in the same boat of ignorance as me. I took notes and more notes so I could later match what Dr. Blackburn said with what appeared in the textbook. Luckily, it did match, and I started to understand about the rules that governed the temperature and pressure of stability of minerals as they formed. I wondered, constantly, what I was doing in such high-powered study, but I was also thrilled by it.

I spent a lot of time looking at my rock thin-sections under the microscope to see what they were made of and in what order the minerals crystallized. They were beautiful to look at under polarized light of the powerful microscope, like tiny stained glass windows of bright pink and gold and teal. And each mineral told a story about how and where and why it had formed. The days went by in a great series of documentation and hard work and constant wondering about what a dumb guy like me was doing in such a smart lab.

The week of the first game was like a wonderful dream. The starters got most of the reps in practice, though I was going to split my position with another fellow and we would take turns bringing the plays in to the huddle. There were so many differences in the Canadian game still to learn! The field was 10 yards longer so that there was a 55-yard line in the middle of the field instead of a fifty. The end-zones were 20 yards deep instead of 10, which made them huge enough to run all kinds of pass routes in, and the whole field was several yards wider.

The two really big differences for me were these: there were 12 men on the field for each team instead of 11, and 3 downs instead of 4 to gain 10 yards. The 3-down rule made the punting and kicking game much more significant than in America, especially since your team got one point, or a "single", if you kicked or punted the ball into the end-zone and it was not returned out. I loved the new rules and, of course, I loved my running start at slot-back.

I also loved my teammates. Sure, Norm could have played at any school in America, and so could a few linemen and a couple of the linebackers, though perhaps lower down the depth chart. But most of the Windsor players were guys with huge hearts who loved the game enough to get all beat up for free, lacking enough great athletic ability to have been offered an American scholarship. They cared about each other and loved the feeling of flying around on the field, backing each other up in battle and trying to get the elusive win. They saw the value in the game and all the work that went with it. And the feeling that I would be allowed to try to win a game with them each week was worth every bruise and pulled muscle.

The game approached and I was ready for everything. My legs were charged and eager. Vas kept checking on me during the Friday pre-game workout, which was light and fun as we just stretched and jogged through the plays. He would look over and mouth the words, "You did it!" while waving me a clenched, triumphant fist. I ate all that up.

On game day, I got up early and drove in to Windsor so I could have a big breakfast with Vas at one of the local joints. We were going to make this a game-day tradition. One of the bonuses of playing football was the chance to return to the days of eating anything I wanted since all I did every day was run and run and run. My body was back to looking decent, like in the early days at Vanderbilt, but with even more muscle. I ordered pancakes and eggs and toast and everything, thinking I needed lots of fuel for the day ahead. I saw that my meal came with something called pea meal bacon, which I had never heard of before. I asked Vas what it was and he explained, "Well, Gers, you've heard of a he-male, which is what you are, a manly-man, and you've heard of a she-male, which is a cross between a man and a woman, like in the porn movies you always rent, ay?"

I was chuckling with him now. "Well, a peameal is right in between the two, sort of like a she-male pig."

He said all this with a straight face, and I fell off the chair I was laughing so hard. College-boy humor, ay? Glad to be here.

We went over to school at about 10:30 to relax and get taped before the game. I put on my game pants and a T-shirt and went into the weight room to do some curls and triceps exercises because I found that that made my grip stronger for catching a football. I did all this wearing my game face, a focused grimace where no one would come bother me, and I loved looking all tense like that.

We were out for early warm-ups on the field by 11:45 in just helmets and pants, no shoulder-pads, and the ball was looking good to me as the receiver coach tossed us light passes on the jog. In a few minutes we went back in for full dress. I was relaxed and ready to play, but I could also feel the excitement of the situation creeping into my bones and muscles. In full gear, I went to a mirror and saw a Lancer football player in blue and gold. I was so proud to be with these men, to be in uniform, to look like I belonged on this good team.

When Muss gave the call at 12:35, we headed out to the field for a team stretch and the final preparations. As one unit, we marched to the edge of field from the dressing room, and then as we crossed the white line onto the playing surface we gently broke into a jog, moving to our stretch positions. Fans were starting to fill the stands on this lovely day, and I saw my wife on the far side of the field. I gave her a big thumbs-up sign and saw her smile back, seeming to sense my happiness. I almost leaked a tear then, thankful and a tad choked up that she could see my joy and reflect it back to me, but I quickly got back to the business of being focused. After the stretch we ran some practice plays and the guys were pumped up.

When we broke to the sidelines, Vas ran over to me, grabbed my shoulder pads, stared into my eyes and asked if I was ready. I told him I would kill for this chance, and we hugged like the brothers we had become. The team lined up on the sideline for the national anthem. My eyes grew misty with the words for a country that was kind enough to let me in to reach for the stars. The True North Strong and Free. I had to wipe my eyes as the beautiful song concluded. O Canada, I stand on guard for thee!

If the emotion of the preparation weren't enough, now the team gathered around the starters as we were introduced. I couldn't believe they were going to say my name over the stadium loudspeakers, and I was the second name called. "At slot-back, number twenty-three, Gary Gear-son!"

My teammates were clapping for me and patting me on the back as I ran through them to a spot on the field where Craig Poole, the fast wide receiver, greeted me and slapped my hand. The rest of my teammates were introduced in a blur, then there was the kickoff, and before I could come to my senses we were out for our first offensive series. I was on the field to start and was mostly a decoy on pass plays though I had to make some key blocks on running plays. We had some success moving the ball, but we had not scored yet.

At the end of the first quarter the play was called to my side and I did a deep corner route. Rob released the ball on his sprint towards the sidelines, and it floated right into my chest where I cradled it with my whole body. I was far from the sideline myself, but I wasn't sure if I was getting ready to go out of bounds, so I dragged my feet on the catch and went to the ground. It was complete, 12 yards worth, and the fans cheered. On the way back to the huddle, I heard the announcer: "Zagordo's pass complete to Gear-son for 12 yards. First down, Lancers!"

The catch was complete! I had a statistic! It was now in the books and could never be removed. I had played the game as hard as I could since I was 19 years old, and at the age of 30, I had finally contributed to my own team's success, a real team. When I came off the field, I was saying out loud, to myself, "I did it! I did it!"

Vas was waiting to give me a huge hug and congratulate me. Having him there to share in this, so happy for me when I knew he wanted to be out there too, not just as punter, was quite stirring, especially after all of our summer work together. What a great guy.

The game went on and I was on the field when we scored our first touchdown on a running play, which was so exciting. Our defense held them and we went on to win by a couple of touchdowns. I found Shelley after the game and gave her a big hug and thanked her for being a good sport and coming all the way to Windsor for the game, and she was so sweet to me. She headed home and I had a beer with my teammates in the team room, an event called the "Fifth Quarter," and there was plenty of high-fives and back slapping. The offensive coordinator, a really decent older guy who was nearing the end of his coaching career, came over and said, "Good game, Grampa!" Vas loved that.

The season went on and I caught a few more passes in the next couple of games. They knew I was a guy who would not make a mistake when on the field, and it was a nice feeling to be counted on by the coaches and team. My parents, who by now were quite amazed and impressed that I was giving football one more try, asked to come up for a game. I suggested that they come up to Ontario in the first week of October for our game against the University of Toronto, one of the oldest football programs in North America. So they made plans, with my brother Marty, to come up for that weekend and enjoy the sights in that amazing city before our Saturday game. How exciting, and especially moving, that my parents, who had come to every game at Vanderbilt and had watched me stand on the sidelines for entire games, who had given me so much encouragement when they saw I was going to stick to the game of football even though I might never get to play at Vandy, were going to come up and see me as a starter.

It was raining and messy for the game, but there they were in the stands. There were only about 200 fans there in this great old stadium in the center of Toronto, where they had used to play the Grey Cup game, the championship of the old Canadian Football League. My folks were obviously thrilled to be there, video camera and umbrellas in tow, all bundled up against the chilly drizzle. They were there for the warm-ups and everything!

In the first quarter, I caught a couple of passes, one for about 20 yards up the sideline, slipping and sliding until the "middie", the free safety, knocked me onto my butt about ten yards out of bounds. We were holding our own against the defending national champions. Our speedy little running back, Ozzie Nethersole, had a 100-yard punt return to tie some ancient record, and we were within one touchdown of the mighty Toronto in the second quarter. That was when the call came to my side; I was to do a short curl to the outside, about 12 yards deep. Easy play. The ball was snapped and I moved into position, knowing I had run a good route and I could feel the linebacker separate from me as he went to cover a different zone. The pass from Rob was high and fluffy, and I was a little off-balance as I went up for it.

I caught the pass up high, having to leave my feet, and before I could come down there was a huge, loud collision. The linebacker had recovered and come towards me, and the strong safety had not yet left my area and had a chance to respond to the pass, so they sandwiched me while my arms were still up. Each of them drove his helmet into me, one into my chest and the other into the center of my back. They bounced off with equal and opposite force, the result of one of Newton's laws. I, meanwhile, had been in the middle of these two massive men. Had I been positioned differently, perhaps I would have bounced off them and continued my journey downfield. As it was, however, I got crushed.

I went straight down as if shot, my legs flopping around like a rag-doll's as I hit the ground. I could not breathe, and I could hear one of the other players yelling for the trainer to come onto the field, "He's not breathing! He's not breathing!"

But I had hung onto the ball, and an official came over and took it from the crook of my arm as I lay spread out on the muddy forty-yard line.

God, my chest hurt as I lay there on the field. It was like a boulder was sitting on my lung. A big damn boulder. I still hadn't breathed and was getting more scared with each millisecond, knowing my parents were in the stands, imagining them standing and watching helplessly, hoping I would get up. I thought my ribs had been crushed and splintered. The trainers from Windsor ran out onto the field and knelt down. The head trainer, a wonderfully no-nonsense woman named Kathy, looked at me and very sternly said, "Gary, calm down and take a slow breathe! Do it!"

And slowly, I took one in. It felt as if my lung was re-inflating like a crushed aluminum can. The next few breaths came a little easier.

I sat up on the field with the trainers' help after lying there for what had seemed like a half-hour. I could barely talk and had no strength at all, but I gave a thumbs-up signal to my folks in the stands, and soon after I was able to stand up, though I was hunched over. When I straightened up all the way, the middle of my chest gave off a crackling and popping sound like gravel in a sink disposal. Just before I jogged off the field, I turned and pointed to the opposing Toronto huddle, where they were all clapping for me, the injured guy, and I yelled to all of them, "Great hit! Great hit, man!"

I found out later that my Windsor teammates had thought that I was taunting the guy that hit me, and I never told them that I had just been trying to show that I had no hard feelings for the helmets in my chest and back. After all, that was part of the game!

On the sidelines my teammates gave me high-fives and slaps on the back, and I felt better with every minute that passed. I waved to my folks and they were obviously relieved. They had it all on film, I noticed, as Dad had brought his video camera along. It was also on local television in Toronto, so some channel-surfing Canadians had seen some great hit by their home team. My chest still hurt a bit, and it felt really weird when I spread my arms out to the sides. A deep breath made me recoil and gasp, but the trainers checked me out and told me I was fine. Kathy suggested that I couldn't be hurt because the opposing football players, one on each side of my ribcage at the time of the hit, absorbed all of the impact and I should have felt none. I thought that was silly, of course, since that implied that hitting your finger with a hammer while resting it on a table wouldn't hurt since the hammer and table would absorb the force and the finger would remain passive. But I didn't have the heart to point out that error in front of the other ballplayers, so I let it go, and I entered the game once again at our next possession.

I tried my best to go downfield and make blocks, but it was clear that I was not hitting with full force and was too tentative to do my job efficiently. The first half of the game ended soon after that, and on the way to the locker room I had the need to cough. It was a bloody cough and had come up from my lung, so I told the trainer in the locker room and she got the Toronto team doctor, who told me to sit out the second half. I agreed with him, knowing that something was wrong. It was very disappointing to take off my shoulder pads and go back out there in just my game shirt, and I walked over to tell my folks what had been decided. Mom, of course, thought that that was the best choice, looking all concerned as if I had been sixteen again and that she might have had some say in the matter. I just smiled and thanked them for being there.

When I got back to Shelley the next day (she had had a speaking engagement and could not come to Toronto), she was very upset about my injury, telling me her worst fears had been realized. She broke into tears and told me how thankful she was that I had not been more seriously damaged, and I was very impressed by her show of concern. I realized that I had not really understood how scared she had been for me, and I was saddened that I had not had more empathy for her earlier. To make her happy, I went to the hospital for X-rays and a check up. The doctor in the emergency room told me that I had slightly separated my rib cage, had damaged the cartilage around my sternum area, and had suffered a collapsed lung. He also told me to never play football again, though I did not take that advice so seriously.

The next week I had to sit out most of the practices since my chest was so sore, and my sternum crackled every time I stretched my pectorals. But by Thursday, there was no more pain or discomfort, so I dressed for the game anyway. I didn't play, but it was nice to be out there with my teammates. The following week, I was moved out to wide receiver so that I wouldn't be "in traffic" so much in the middle of the field. This meant that I was back to a standing start at the beginning of each play since wide-outs can't go in motion, but that was ok. I liked the feeling that I was "anchoring" the far left side of the field.

As the season continued, I caught a few more passes and really appreciated every chance to be out there doing what I could do to contribute. My total for the season was 12 receptions for 220 yards, not an impressive set of numbers for an all-star, but certainly satisfying for a 30-year-old high school teacher living a dream. The team only won a couple of games, which was sad, but we made great strides and came together as a group of men. Vas and I were now lifelong friends, and I came to love so many of the other guys over there, the linebackers Rob McElwain and Rob McIntyre who ate nails, the receiver Craig Poole, the kamikaze reserve John Redman who only played on special teams, Mitch the free safety who weighed only 155 pounds and hit like a sledgehammer.

It was time to get back to my thesis and try to complete my class-work so that I could get back to Cranbrook in the following fall. Coach Musselman asked me if I would use my final year of eligibility to come back as an experienced receiver, but I told him that it was now time to put away my childish dreams and get back to real life. I said this with an affectionate smile, and he winked at me and thanked me. I had really enjoyed all of the coaches there, most of whom received very little pay for doing what they loved. Of course, it was interesting that I was older than almost all of them.

I had not scored any points, but I had lived my dream of playing one more year with great men. Now, perhaps, I could move on to the call of life and adulthood. It was time to go back to Cranbrook and my lovely Shelley full time.

Chapter 11: The Score

While I was working towards that long-delayed Masters Degree, it became obvious (if only to me) that I was outmatched in this academic realm. I thought that Dr. Smith had given me problems to solve which I had no idea how to begin, and I wondered how in the world I was going to create "answers" out of the smokiness that filled my brain. What was all this about crystal growth and geo-thermometry and natural barometers? Where was I supposed to look to find the answers? Football had been over for months, and I was still scrambling to make sense of my Caribbean rocks and the thesis they were supposed to whisper to me. My head was spinning. I felt like I had only really learned that there was an awful lot I did not know.

Something interesting also happened while I was working to complete my year away from the high school. The head coaching position had become open again after Coach Mike had served his one year at Cranbrook. The new athletic director, Mark Zalin, had seen through Mike's ambitiousness, and before Mike could push his way into the AD position, which he clearly coveted, Mark had made sure that Mike was gone after the season. It was like a chess game, with Mark anticipating and documenting every questionable move Mike made, and he was easily out after the season's final plays were done. Mark made sure to note that there were some problems with team behavior, such as urinating in public view at an away football game, practicing on a day when practice was not allowed, and other such minutiae that added up to a firing once the season was done. Mike went on to a different private school, became a coach and administrator there, and that little school quickly went out of business. He has not coached since.

Shelley was very excited at the idea of me coming home after my year in battle at Windsor, and she said that I should certainly apply for the vacant head-coaching job. Why, I was a shoo-in! Or so we thought.

The huge college linemen sat slack-jawed in the back of the room, tears rolling down their massive cheeks and dripping on the floor. The sniffling in the room was loud and unashamed. Even the coaches were wiping their eyes and breathing deeply. Shelley paused in the front of the room as she dabbed her eyes with the one tissue I was able to salvage for her. She never had a tissue when she needed one, which was every time she spoke about Patrick. She was telling my teammates about how she and her brother and her father had never had a choice. About how these big, strong, fast, handsome athletes had a future in front of them that Patrick would never have. About how she had seen how much I had loved being amongst these young men, how worried I was that they often drank and made bad decisions and put themselves at risk. By seeing her face, she knew that they would think twice about getting drunk and having unprotected sex. We wanted them to be safe, and Shelley told them about her own pain and let them know that they all had choices, choices, choices. I was so proud, so full of love, when she spoke to my friends, my teammates, and made them cry for her and their own huge selves and the chances they would have to grow up and be men. Chances that Patrick, her little brother, never had.

I went to Mark, the athletic director, and told him that I was thinking of applying for the head football coach position when I returned to Cranbrook in the fall. He told me that it was a fabulous idea, that I would be perfect for the job. In fact, Mark told me I should get a good start on my pursuit of the job by taking on the weight-room monitoring position for the spring. I could then start working with potential football players right there with the Cranbrook weight machines that had truly saved my life when I had played at Windsor. Of course, I would be helping out Cranbrook since they had always had a hard time finding people who knew anything about weights to run the place, especially in the spring. I told Mark that I was his man, to sign me up, even though I needed to do more thesis work.

So I put together a letter and sent it in to Ms. Seibert and Mark and whatever other people needed to see it, expressing my interest in the coaching position. I met with the parents who ran the booster club and told them how excited I was to finally be considered as head coach. To be honest, I thought they would just say, "Glad to have you, Gary, the job is yours."

But interestingly, there was a delay. March became April and I worked with kids in the weight room, just assuming I would be named head coach any day now. My studies at Windsor suffered a little as I had to leave the University at 3:00 every afternoon in order to get back to Cranbrook in time for strength training, but I knew that I was preparing for the next phase of my life. Finally, in mid-April, I got a big surprise.

Shelley called me during the day in my University of Windsor office. She was sobbing loudly as she began to speak, and I thought something terrible had happened. She stopped sniffling long enough to tell me that Ms. Seibert had just called and had told her that I had not gotten the football job. I found out that it had been offered to a recently-hired history teacher as part of a package deal to lure him here from California.

I came home to Shelley and we cried together and I wrote a long, angry letter to the interviewers, particularly the parents who had been on the selection committee, telling them what a mistake they had made in letting someone who did not love Cranbrook the way I did come into the picture. I knew what a responsibility it was to be in charge of these young men, teaching them about what is just and right, about the importance of athletics and teamwork and academics in context. Chuck Schmitt had shown all of us the importance of demanding that kids do their best, do what was right, and care, but that didn't seem to matter to the administration and parents. I had never been so mad, even going back to not being named drum major in high school. I haughtily informed the school to forget about having me as an assistant coach, too. I needed the fall to myself.

I had been lifting with the Cranbrook kids that spring since I had started working in the weight room, and my ouchies from the previous season had started to diminish. There had been time to reflect on my experiences at Windsor, and Shelley had seen how much joy I had gotten from throwing on the old pads one last time at the age of thirty. The previous year had been a marvelous ride. One thing had bothered me, though, throughout. If this was truly to have been my swan song in football, was I to go out without actually scoring a touchdown?

Shelley had been speaking publicly about her HIV status now for a couple of years, and it had made her feel better to speak about her brother's death and her own situation, about how unfair things happened for some unseen reasons. She pointed out that God did not give us things we could not handle. Her talks were wonderful, full of very sad stories and a tinge of humor and the inevitable effort to have young people take a good, long look at Shelley's youthful prettiness. The face of AIDS, she would say, could be yours. "My brother did not die in vain. I look pretty good right now. But looks can be deceiving."

Shelley and I had decided early in our decision to "go public" that no question would go unanswered, that it was important to be forthright about our marriage and sex and love and showing affection in a safe, responsible, caring way. When faced with a room full of 16- and 17-year-old boys, however, it was important to let them know that they could not possibly offend me, so I often prompted them to go ahead and get personal in their questions.

The first time I addressed the juniors and seniors in the boys' dorm, while Shelley answered questions from the whole girls' dorm over at the Kingswood campus, I had no idea what kind of questions they would ask. We both knew that our respective audiences had not had much experience with AIDS in those days, that it was still a disease that was "far away" from them. We figured that these young, seemingly-invulnerable adults, many of whom had already experimented with alcohol or marijuana and had had some kind of sex before, needed to know that this disease (and any sexually transmitted disease) was going to touch all of them in some way over the next few years. And we knew that we needed to, with this opportunity, teach them how to be careful.

Shelley always told her crowds, "Look at this face. I want it to haunt you. I didn't have a choice, and neither did my brother or my father or all of my friends. This disease sneaked up on me, and it doesn't fight fair. You are a potential victim not because of how you behave or what you believe but solely because you are a human being. This virus loves humans, no matter what kind. Don't think that it can't happen to you."

And they listened.

The statistics at that point were overwhelming. Many African nations were hugely infected with the HIV, and it was spreading almost unchecked in the sub-Saharan countries. AIDS was the fastest growing cause of death in our age range in North America. People were dying all over the world, and right here in Michigan the disease had descended upon so many before they knew what had hit them. AIDS was an epidemic, a pandemic, and permeating every population. Though it was all around, most of us humans had not taken notice of it yet, way back in 1994. It was nowhere near "us".

While Shelley was naturally a good speaker, I had to find my place in front of a crowd, since I had no idea what these young men wanted or needed to hear. I anticipated squirrelly behavior and lack of focus.

So, the first time I spoke I told them who I was and that I was married to a lovely woman who had become, rather passively, infected with HIV. I was quick to point out, as Shelley had instructed me, that there were no "innocent" or "guilty" victims, that all people with this illness were to be left un-judged until God was ready to do so Himself. That usually got their attention, Shelley had said, and she was right.

So I told the resident boys about the disease, how it was spread through unprotected sex and blood products, that it couldn't be "caught" by casual contact, that alcohol and drugs impaired decision-making to the point that they all could be at considerably higher risk if they were drunk or high. Of course, they listened hard then, when drugs and alcohol were mentioned, and they were amazingly respectful throughout. I told them that Shelley and I had gone public because we cared about them and figured that being a teacher was about teaching what one could teach best. We had that unique opportunity, and we did not want to waste it. Boys of that age, we hoped, could appreciate that honest commentary.

After fifteen minutes of talking and noticing some good, respectful attention, I decided to let them ask some questions. To be honest, I expected them to ask about my sex life, to be giggly and silly and posture for their friends the way many boys do. I was very surprised by the first several questions, since they had now had weeks to think of some things to ask as we had announced the chat session well ahead of time. They were very serious, very cautious.

"Why did you marry her if you knew she was going to die?"

That was not what I expected to hear, but it made a lot of sense. Wouldn't a young man, full of life and energy, be curious as to what would make me put myself in a position of inevitable pain? I answered that I felt so in love with her and so appreciative of what she had to offer that a few years of joy would be worth the sorrow. "Just look at her, guys," I said with a sly wink. "She's wonderful."

"What will you do when she gets sick and dies, because that's what will happen, right?"

"Well," I admitted, "I don't really know what I'll do immediately. Hopefully I will have had many years with her to think about."

I threw a question back to the audience, hoping to bring them in to my way of thinking: What does any husband or wife do when a spouse dies? I answered my own question, "It is very painful, of course, but that sort of pain goes with the ending of any relationship due to death. I'm just more aware of it, maybe, than other spouses my age. What am I supposed to do? Does any spouse really know what to do, when he or she loses a true love?"

I was very pleased at the way this was going, how respectful this room full of high school juniors and seniors was being towards me. Shelley had not even been worried about the girls, but I had had no idea what to expect. Be honest, she had told me. Bring them into the conversation. Make the terms and situations familiar. Get into their world.

"How does it feel knowing she can't have children?" one asked.

"Well, that's one of the reasons we live with you all at Cranbrook. Our children are you guys, kids in the classroom, and we like that. With her health in questions, adopting would be very difficult. But that's okay. We have you, and we have each other. To be honest, she gets sad about not having her own kids sometimes. It's my job to help her through these feelings of longing and loss and all that she goes through. And we have a great dog that we treat like a baby. We take her everywhere and hug her and make her feel all of our love. Poor dog!"

They laughed at that one, me shaking my head in mock sorrow.

After a few more questions of this type, surprisingly focusing on the areas of children and mortality, I realized that no one had asked a question about sex. Since this was a room full of teenage boys and hormones and curiosity, I figured I should bring up the subject. It was a good time for some light humor because I did not want to speak the entire time in a dark cloud about the shroud of death. "Gee," I asked loudly, in mock chastisement, "doesn't anyone wonder about my sex life? Who wants to ask if we have sex, raise your hand!"

They all smiled and nervously laughed a bit, and I think they were appreciative that I had brought up the subject. In those days, there still was not a lot of public discussion of sex and condoms and body fluids. In fact, before the age of AIDS, I don't recall anyone saying the word "penis" or "condom" or "vaginal secretions" out loud. And that's why this was all so important. I went on.

"Of course we have sex! I'm a healthy male with male needs, and she's a lovely, gorgeous, sexy woman! But what we have to do is be very careful. We look out for each other. We never let any of our body fluids mix. And I always use a condom during intercourse. I should buy stock in condom companies! Next question. Go ahead, ask anything. You can't embarrass me!"

"Aren't you scared to have sex?" asked the next tentative senior boy.

"I'm not scared because I'm smart. And this whole deal can be exciting, too. Every time is like a first time, with real caring for each other, very deliberate thoughts and actions. And we try to take a lot of satisfaction in just holding each other, too, without sex becoming an issue. But let me tell you, all of the protection is worth it. She's a wonderful woman, in *so* many ways." I said that last bit with a sly stage wink, which they loved.

"Can you, like, have oral sex?"

"To put it bluntly, she can on me but I can't on her. Vaginal fluid is a place where the virus is found in great amounts and all of our mouths are full of tiny little cuts, so I don't take that chance. I'm not too worried about her mouth, though. Saliva doesn't seem to have very much, if any, HIV, and she won't even kiss me if she thinks she has a sore in her mouth. She looks out for me, and we trust each other."

I felt the responsibility from these conversations in a giant way. I liked telling teenage boys that their questions were good, that it was important to be safe and smart, that it was valuable to stop passing judgment based on this disease and people's lifestyles and practices. These may have been their first and only questions about sex asked in an open forum, and I wanted to get it right, to be a good teacher.

"Who is more likely to get HIV from sex, a man or a woman?"

I had to be careful here. I did not want any of these young men to think that they could exclude themselves from risk in any way just because they were male. "Well, I'm not sure that it matters. How much of a chance are you willing to take?

While a woman is often the "receiver" during sex with a man, there is always the chance of having the virus find its way into a male at any time that her body fluids come into contact with a cut, an opening, or mucous membranes that are quite permeable. And even if the female were to be more susceptible at some point during sex, isn't it our responsibility as men to make sure they are not *ever* at risk?"

Do your best. Do what is right. Care. Be good men.

Shelley also had a great experience talking to the girls in the high school dorm about her life, about the importance of being smart and safe in all things circling around sex and relationships. The young women loved Shelley and responded to her statements with affection and tears and many hugs. After her talk, the high school girls would stop by her classroom during the day, even though she taught in the middle school, and laugh with her and confide in Shelley their fears and hopes and risks. And Shelley always had time for them, sharing her great love with them always. That woman was amazing in her ability to connect with students at such a deep level.

Late in the spring of 1994, we took a trip to my home in East Tennessee. Though my parents had been fearful of some public anger from ignorance when it was made known that Shelley, their daughter in law, was HIV-positive, we had all agreed that it was necessary to educate as many people as possible about HIV and how to handle AIDS in today's society. As a result, Mom made arrangements for Shelley to do public speaking in Morristown, first at my old West High School, then over at East High, and finally at Walters State Community College to nursing students and the general public. This was a big deal, as Morristown had not really had an HIV-positive persons come forward with his or her condition. Homosexuality had barely been acknowledged as having existed in East Tennessee and no teacher there are anywhere else had ever come forth to admit sexual preference or disease. This was big, since the HIV had a strong association with homosexuality in many people's minds. Many of the churches there had taken firm stands against homosexuality and AIDS, saying they were both abominations against God.

Shelley was superb. We talked to the kids in the STARZ leadership program at West High, then to the entire student body at East, and they ate it up. The principals of both schools, brave in letting us come into their auditoriums with so controversial a subject and warning us that these kids could "get kind of rough on speakers", were astonished at how mesmerized these students, even the tough ones, had been in the light of Shelley's beauty and wisdom. These young men and women seemed ready to listen to anything involving the drama of sex, death, danger, and a lovely woman! One principal said it was the best program they had ever had at that school in his many years there. I was proud to show some of my old teachers that I had chosen so well and so wisely in my life. And that I was not quite the goofball many of them had written me off to be, no matter how deserved the critique at the time.

At Walters State, Shelley talked and wept in her most emotional speech yet, dwelling on how friendly and loving my family and all of the Morristonians had been, and many of our old family friends were there in the audience. After she talked about life with HIV and Patrick and her dad and not having children, they were all so ready to embrace us both. Her talk was videotaped and shown over and over on the local cable channel. She got dozens of letter from total strangers, offering love and blessings and comfort to this woman that so many of them wanted to touch in some way. Ah, the people of East Tennessee. I love them, my homies.

As the summer moved along, I continued to work out and run. After I had done my straight-ahead wind sprints, I would get my dog Gypsum to play with me out in the lower fields. I would chase her and she would run in tight circles and figure eights, never allowing me to catch her. That dog was quick, let me tell you, and she could change directions better than Barry Sanders. I found that this was a great extra workout which kept me balanced and ready to cut and spring to the side, leaving us both breathless and full of joy. After our workouts in the hot summer sun, we would sprint back to the house down in the Cranbrook Valley, me heading for ice-pops from the freezer, Gyp crashing into the bathroom for some delicious water, fresh from the toilet.

I called Coach Musselman in July after camp and told him that I was re-enrolling to work on my thesis in the fall. I told him I wanted to play one more year of football. He was noncommittal. I figured he had already planned on letting someone else play wide receiver, thinking that I was not going to return. That was okay, as long as he would give me a chance to earn a spot. He agreed to that.

When I called Andy Vasily and told him I wanted to come workout with him, he was ecstatic. We fell right back into our workout routine, inviting Craig Poole, the super-fast receiver who would be playing on the opposite side from me, to join us. Craig shared all kinds of track drills since he also ran for the Lancers in the off-season, and we all looked like we knew what we were doing. My chest was still a little sticky from the injury at Toronto, but I could lift almost as much as before.

Shelley hated the idea from the start. This would mean more time away from her, more moaning from me about how sore I was, more chances for me to get my lung knocked out of my body. I was being selfish. But I was going to go ahead with this dream one more time, spend all of my energy, get it out of my system, and emerge drained and empty of the need to play this silly game. I knew she would not understand, and why should she have? Running down a field probably seemed like an awful waste of time to her, such a childish game, when there was so much more to be done in so short a time.

In August I reported to camp and checked into the steamy residence hall, a former motel next to the McDonald's and across from the practice facility, rooming with my buddy Vas. He was fighting for some playing time at quarterback while still being the best punter in the league. It didn't look good for him as Rob Zagordo was returning for his fifth year as QB and seemed to be "in good" with Muss.

Staying there for the preseason was a blast, though it was extremely hot with the Detroit/Windsor humidity permeating everything. In some concession, Shelley made cookies for me to share with my friends in the residence, a nice gesture seeing that she didn't really want me to be there, away from her, close to the raging hormones of goofy 19-year-old football players.

Every night after practice we would sit in the sweltering heat of our room, munching cookies, Vas trying to play that poor guitar of his while we loudly sang Eric Clapton and Pete Townshend songs, an endless stream of "rookies" coming in while we threw cookies at them and laughed at their shyness as they tried to catch and eat the free treats. One big defensive tackle who was built like an executive desk hung out in our room every night. His name was Morris and we mockingly called him "The Cat" for his lacking grace, and he would sit on the floor between the beds all night, a silly grin on his face while Vas teased him and tried to make him sing for his cookies. It was fun trying to help these young puppies have fun in the pressure of football camp. They were all so nervous! Vas was in charge of camp spirit, it seemed, and he loved his job.

We had a little refrigerator in the room which we kept stocked with cold drinks, and Vas always had a carton of delicious milk in there to quench his thirst. One afternoon I noticed that the fridge had gotten unplugged, and everything inside had gotten warm. No big deal, I thought, as I simply plugged the machine back in and went back out to the field. That night, Vas and I came back to the room and ate a couple of cookies after supper. He opened the fridge and took out his carton of milk. "Nothing like a cold swig of milk after a cookie..." he happily spouted.

Before I remembered to tell him about the unplugged refrigerator, he upended the carton and took a couple of giant swallows. I will never forget the look as he lowered the carton, a huge scowl on his chiseled and sunburned face, his jaws actually chewing the soured milk solids. I started laughing so hard I could not breathe, whereas Vas quickly ran to the bathroom, gasping, "Oh my god, oh my god," chunks of milk now streaming down his sweaty T-shirt, while I rolled on the bed, then the ground, howling with laughter. I knew that it was not right to laugh at another's misfortune, but I could not stop picturing the absolute look of shock and dismay as he chewed the milk, even as he alternately yelled at me and gagged off in the distance. For some reason I have always found the sound of vomiting quite hilarious. Vas must have brushed his teeth for an hour that night, then eaten about a million breath mints, fistfuls at a time, while I struggled to catch my breath and hold my aching ribs.

I passed all of my training camp tests, making it through the 350-yard runs with no difficulty, still able to bench-press 225 pounds 8 times, even after that chest injury from the season before. On the field, I just plain caught everything. But the coaches seemed to have other plans, and they kept putting a very fast rookie in front of me in the drills, a kid who always wore red socks against the rules and did not want to take my advice or encouragement. I tried to understand where he was coming from and what the coaches needed, so I continued in my role as reserve through much of the preseason while the Red Socks kid sped across the field and dropped half his passes. My teammates knew what was going on, that Muss was building for the future and needed to keep the youngsters interested in this non-scholarship environment, even the reckless ones, and my buddies continued to encourage me as I caught everything and made the routes look easy and practiced. I could handle being on the second team, if that's what the team needed, but I was going to spend everything I had to break back into the starting lineup.

I seemed to keep getting banged up around the fingers and toes, but my body stayed mostly in-place for the entire preseason and I was thankful when August ran out and I was still right there in the running for major playing time. At the end of the two weeks we had the traditional Blue-and-Gold game, pitting half of the team against the other half in a live scrimmage with game-like situations. This was when the men stood out from the boys and final decisions would be made for the season. I was pumped and ready. Red Socks Kid was on the Gold side and I was on the Blue with Zagordo, the quarterback, who knew I wouldn't drop any of his passes and would make him look good. So things were right and ready.

I got passes thrown to me all day. Down-and-out routes for 12 yards and little five-yard hitches where I would catch the ball, spin around, and take on a linebacker full go. On my second little hitch, I wheeled around with the ball to stare into the eyes of Rob McIntyre, a hungry bastard who I loved but knew would knock me back into Michigan if given the chance. Instead of making a head-fake or some other move, I took him head-on as he bore down on me, putting my facemask into his chest and driving him a yard backwards before he tackled me. My thumb got caught in his jersey as I fell and I felt a twinge in my hand, but it was soon forgotten. On another play, a 15-yard out, I spun a rookie defensive back around so hard with a head-fake he almost fell down and couldn't recover enough to catch up to me. I caught the pass for a first down and fell out of bounds.

All day, passes like this fell into my hands, I got more yards after each catch, and I was fired up in a big way, yelling at my teammates with intensity and encouragement. The coaches were loving me then and the old Lancer offensive coordinator, Coach Larondeau, was the head of the Blue squad. It had always seemed like he was on my side. I continued to dive ahead for two or three extra yards after I first got hit, trying to show how grateful I was for one last shot. How many 31-year-old men get a chance to live a dream like this, again?

Late in the scrimmage, my thumbs were swollen and my nose was bleeding from a couple of rough hits, one where my helmet was knocked clean off, but I was flying high with eight catches for some 120 yards. The gold team had put in a tiny defensive back with tremendous guts, Pat Kocsis (who we all called Psy-Kocsis, like in *Psychosis*), and Coach Larondeau's mouth started watering at the prospect of throwing over this poor fresh player. The play was in, Coach sending me into the huddle with glee, the call being a Stop and Go. When the ball was snapped, I acted like I was catching a short hitch route and Kocsis came right up like a little puppy to intercept the ball. Zagordo faked that throw and I sprinted down the field, Kocsis lost but trying to get back onto my heels, while Rob throw it long over Kocsis's head. I almost never saw the ball.

The sun was low on the horizon by this time, over the McDonald's and the residence hall, right in the path of the ball. The opening in my facemask was filled with bright sunlight as I struggled to look in and find that elusive football. But I had seen the ball leave Rob's hand as he threw it, so I just kept running. I figured the ball would make it on down the field, so I just hoped it would appear out of the glare in time for me to get to it. All of a sudden, there it was under the sun, just away from my body, within reach. I had to slow down a little and do a bit of a high-step in order to keep from falling, but I managed to haul it in and keep moving, off-balance. Kocsis dove and I stepped right onto his helmet. My ankle turned to 90 degrees from the rest of my leg and I went down hard, feeling the ankle pop. Great catch, and great recovery by Kocsis to stop the touchdown. Trainers, get out there and help Gerson.

I managed to smile and eventually limp off the field, but my ankle was shot. I could feel the blood pulsing as it filled up the joint there and pushed at my skin, hot and heavy and sickening. As the game ended, I was on the bench with an ice bag on my leg, happy at my great day but miserable at how my ankle was starting to feel. Vas came over to check on me and he told me I was now starting for sure, and so did Zagordo, which I thought was a nice touch since he knew how close Vas and I had become. Coaches from every position came by and told me I had had a great game. I was smiling broadly even as my thumbs started to hurt too. Both of them were swollen so that it looked like golf balls were under the skin where each thumb met the rest of the hand.

I was named starting wide-out right there in the locker room after the game. Everyone was slapping me on the back and hooting, and our team had really clicked out there. McIntyre, the big linebacker, came up and asked me what drugs I had been on, taking him head-on like that. What great guys; I was so honored to be in the Windsor blue and gold, so proud. My ankle was like a gallon jug by now, and my thumbs were so sore I had to get help taking off my shoes.

There would be one more scrimmage early next week, which I would obviously have to sit out, and then we would open the season at home against McMaster in twelve days. Twelve days. That was how long I had to fully recover. On that realization, I wondered with some frustration why I had not bothered to tape my ankles that day. Silly me.

I started back teaching at Cranbrook that next week, and by then I could barely put any weight at all on my sore ankle. It had turned purple and green and was still as large as my thigh. My thumbs had continued to stay swollen, so I went to a hand specialist up in Rochester who told me that I had two "gamekeeper's thumbs," where small bits of bone had broken away from the main part of the thumb, still attached to the ligaments. Great, two broken thumbs. The doctor put a cast on my left one since it was more severely separated, but he let me have just a removable splint on the right one. Shelley was very sad about my injuries, though she made sure to let me know that her ankles always felt like that anyway. Hemophiliacs, she explained with diminishing sympathy for me, always had swollen joints. She could be so smug, that girl, though I deserved it. God, I loved her.

I started going in to the Windsor trainers after school every afternoon that first week. Kathy, who was a genius at athletic recovery, took a very strange substance that smelled like kerosene mixed with hot sauce and rubbed it into my bad ankle. She furiously mashed all of the retained blood and fluid out with her thumbs and palms, which hurt like hell but, even during all of that suffering, I *knew* was necessary for healing. Then she would put me on a balance board and have me try to regain some of my proprioception, the ankle's "knowledge" of body in space, of balance and natural reaction. It was very hard to stand at first, but as the days went by, I could feel the muscles re-learning their purpose, could feel the nerves once again telling my brain how to adjust the ligaments so I could stand, walk, turn. All that week, I missed practice, but I worked harder than I ever had, going back into the weight room after my sessions with Kathy, keeping my body ready, my mind in the game.

Finally, on Monday of game week, I was given permission to join practice, though not in any form of contact. I went back to the doctor and had my thumb cast cut off. My ankle was still discolored and fairly sensitive to direct pressure, so I went to Kathy and had her tape everything as firmly as she could. I think it was exciting for her to have gotten me back into shape so quickly, but she never let on her enthusiasm as she was always stern, all-business, and not about to reveal her sensitivity to all these little boys swarming around the training room. I could appreciate that. I still loved what she was doing for me.

I went out and ran my Monday routes smoothly with the first unit, uncontested, still able to catch everything. The Red Socks Kid had faded into the background after an uneventful second scrimmage. On Tuesday and Wednesday it was more of the same, my ankle holding up well and getting stronger as I rejoined the rhythm of sprint and return, catch and move, dancing with my teammates against imaginary opponents in preparation for Saturday's battle. My thumbs ached and I managed to pull a muscle in my right thigh, probably due to subconsciously favoring my recovering ankle. But during the flow of the practice nothing hurt, nothing bothered me. Perhaps it was the naproxen, and perhaps it was the adrenaline coursing through me. Thursday preparation, when I finally put on shoulder pads with the rest of the team, was a blur of repetition and crisp action for all of us. Friday, all of us in shorts and game jerseys, was full of simple reminders and last minute adjustments. I was going to start on Saturday in the season opener against McMaster at left wide receiver. It was my position. Everything was held in place with tightly wrapped tape, but nothing *hurt*.

I remembered a poem I had written five years earlier, when playing real football seemed an impossibility, when my shoulder still ached and crackled with every movement in the shadow of a couple of small operations to glue things back in place and take out the seaweed. It had been published in the *Cranbrook Review*, the faculty periodical, with very few people understanding what it had meant to me:

Woke up again, stiff with that pain
Jabbing crooked to my soldered bone.
That place once fluid lies rusted now;
A shoulder ball hovers crackly in a dirty socket.

Angry tears come at night, trying to rest my old self.
Sleeping hunched over, now jamming awake as
Simple flesh-weight pulls clear with fiery jabs
The ragged-webbed muscle bands,
Dead leathery by the scalpels of my own decisions.

To this day I spy my lithe figure
Flag-bound in the short lined grass.
While numbers in my speed decrease, I am
Fed the ball as bullet from trusty strong arms.
Fingers clasp projectile as commanded.

Falling followed no fear then; now
Some forty years on and down a different field
I cringe lifting cushions to a gray and aging head.
Yet. And yet, I *would* lope downfield again
Even knowing this price, this costly fine.

Yes I would swing out and go one last lovely time
Yes spending all I had for another earned line.
And afterwards, grateful, breathless, and proud,
I would finally, gracefully, thankfully decline.

On Saturday I rose and kissed my wife, she still snuggled deep in our feathered comforter, lovely, peaceful, full of beauty. She told me to be careful, to have good luck, as she sneaked back in a sweet way to her dreams of running with me. Gypsum gave me a gentle wag, her head now on my pillow as soon as I rose, her feathery tale rising slightly at the tip, over and over, as she smiled at me with her eyes and promised to watch over my Shelley. I knew my wife would be there at game time. I got in the old silver jeep and headed south to Canada, first on Woodward, then to the interstates 696 and 75, and then over the Detroit river. No traffic on Saturdays. 35 minutes. Clear skies.

Again I left my own country for another one I loved as much. At the top of the Ambassador Bridge was the competing view of both cities, Detroit and Windsor, succulent in their own ways, I thought with joy. My thumbs were still puffy, and I could not even open a can of pop without hurting. My ankle was a fading greenish color, the purple gone now, some muscle back and ready. My shoulders were ready after the two arthroscopic surgeries years earlier (and two more yet to come), fastened in place with rubber bands and masking tape. This was going to be the first game in my last dance of a season, a place to which I would not be allowed to return after this year, not ever.

I met Andy Vasily at his apartment where his girlfriend sleepily waved to me. His thick hair was still wet from the shower but, as always, he was bright-eyed and ready to go. We went to our usual place for our pre-game breakfast and silliness, such comfort in that little ritual where we dreamed of greatness and ate a meal of glory. We relaxed each other with dumb jokes, talked of a great season, ready to go one more time. The air was special. I had peameal bacon with my pancakes.

In the training room I got some heat on my bad quad and let Kathy, only Kathy, tape my ankles. She did it silently, knowing we had worked hard for one last chance, one good try for the football player who was as old as she was. I knew she wanted me to have my rewards on the field, perhaps knowing I *needed* it, that she herself looked for me to have a few moments of success after she saw me nearly losing it all. We quietly cheered for each other as she tucked my thumbs safely into a maze of foam and tape. My ankles were secure. My mind was firm.

In my practice pants and game jersey, I took a quick trip into the little student weight room nearby. I did a few quick reps of curls and push-downs to get my biceps and triceps full and ready for action. My hands were ready to grip and my arms ready to push. It was good that the uniform jerseys were tight in the arms and made my little muscles stand out. In the mirror, I saw the stern look in my own eyes. I was not an old man. Not quite yet.

The grass exercises before the game made me feel comfortable, watching my teammates do their little rituals to prepare for their own one-on-one battles with the opponent. McMaster was on the other side of the field, and I tried to see who would be covering me but couldn't tell who the starters were; they all looked so young and ready. Vas came by me as often as he could to tell me I looked great and ready and tough, and I told him I hoped he would get in at QB, though we both knew it wouldn't happen that day. Zagordo threw to me in our practice plays, and the ball arced crisply on a tight spiral.

To the sidelines we trooped at a little before 1:00. My position coach had a talk with us receivers about staying focused in the game, and Poole eyed me, knowing we were going to go out there as brothers and hold down the far ends of our line of scrimmage on offense. He was a wonderful athlete and I was honored to be stationed opposite him for each play. There were TV cameras scattered about as this game was to be broadcast on cable through much of Ontario. Turning, I saw Shelley rise into the stands, behind the fence, settling into a seat with about 500 loyal students and parents, and I waved proudly. When she smiled and waved back I had to turn away, my eyes starting to fill from being overwhelmed with what I was doing and where I was, once more, one last go-round.

We stood on the sideline for the national anthem, the first time of my last season, and I stood next to Vas and we tapped our held helmets together as we stared at the red and white banner, the big red maple leaf proudly displayed. *The true north strong and free. We'll stand on guard for thee.* Again I almost cried, stifling a bit of a sob with my friend there beside me, ready for a new season, a final chance. I knew he understood. A cheer went up. The starting lineup. "At wide receiver," bellowed the lusty voice of the Windsor announcer, "Gary Geeeeeer-sonnnnn!" Goose bumps, a quick thrill, a sprint through my teammates' arms, a closed fist instead of an open hand so their sweat wouldn't get on my new receiver gloves, a turn on the yard marker to face the cheering fans and greet my fellow starters. Alone but for a second on the short lined grass, ready to welcome anything. Give it to me.

We got first possession and returned the kickoff to the thirty, and then our offense went out. Zagordo called the play in the huddle, and I was momentarily stunned that the first pass of the first game of my last season would be to me. We clapped and went to the line, the backs going in motion away from me to Poole's side, leaving me alone, one-on-one against a big blond defensive back, having no idea how good or bad he really was. The ball was snapped and I did a five-yard hitch. Rob threw a strike, and I sensed the defensive back closing in on me, my back to him as I snatched the ball out of the air and gave a move as if I would turn to the inside. The young DB bit on my fake and I felt his surprise as his sure tackle turned into a miss and I spun out of his grasp and saw open field. To his credit, the DB was able to clip my heels and make me stumble as I turned away from him, so I was off-balance and lunging forward. I could see the first down marker in front of me as I staggered downfield, a huge linebacker bearing down on me. I dove forward just as he got there, stretching the ball forward past the down marker as he stuck his entire massive body through my ribcage in a hard and legal tackle after an eleven-yard gain for the first down. Our huge offensive lineman, Dan Comiskey, had run downfield after the play, hoping to flatten some little middie had I gotten loose from the tackle. He came over and pulled the linebacker off, tossing him aside like a rag-doll, and then he gently lifted me off the ground to my feet. "You okay, Gerse?" he asked with genuine concern as we jogged back to the huddle.

I assured him that I had never, ever felt better. This was a good man to have on your side during battle, believe me, all 6-foot-7 and 310 pounds of him. He's still in the CFL, last I heard.

The kids at hemophilia camp were gathered around the campfire. After five years away, five years of denial and anger and healing, five years of the slaughter of all of her friends from the bad blood, Shelley was back. The smile on her lovely face was wide and full of energy as she sang the camp songs and made them all join in, pried them from their inner-city staunchness and back into the freedom of the Bold Eagle. They loved her, the kids, and they were like her own. She went around the circle, to each of their shining eyes, and implored them to yell and clap and stomp their feet, made them forget for a while the darkness from where they had come. Her eyes met mine, only for a moment as she danced and spun, and there was a touch there for me too. Welcome to my home, she said with her glance. Welcome to my freedom, to *my* place of no pain.

It took me a couple of plays to figure out the defensive back's tendencies, and we soon ran a pitch play to my side, our running back sweeping out wide behind some pulling guards, intent on getting up-field. I ran right at the DB so that he would backpedal away from our point of attack, making him think this was a passing play for as long as possible. Once he saw it was a run to his side, he stopped going backwards and tried to make his way to our ball carrier.

By then, as I had been taught and had taught others, the cushion between us had closed and he could not get around me, so he tried to push me out of the way. I ducked and thrust my shoulder at his outside thigh, catching him perfectly, and he flipped over on top of me, absolutely out of the play as our back ran on through for a twenty-yard gain. That felt just as good as catching a pass, doing a fine stalk block to free our tailback for a long run.

The game went back and forth, with Vas keeping us ahead with some fabulous punts and a good punt-fake that he ran for a first down. We went into the locker room ahead 14-8. I had three receptions for 34 yards and felt like twenty million dollars, Canadian. We looked good as a team, and McMaster was lucky to have their one touchdown. Though I had gotten hit pretty hard for the first time in two weeks, there was no pain. The second half would show what we were made of, and the whole team was up to the challenge, ready to get back out there onto the field of battle.

I came out for the third quarter and jogged past my wife, who was now down on the track that surrounded the field, taking photos. She gave me a winning smile and I mouthed the words "I love you" right at her, hard.

We stretched quickly as a team, and then went to the sideline while the defense went to work. I caught another pass in the third quarter as we worked on running out the clock and making short gains up the middle. Both teams ended up punting the ball to each other over and over, hoping to pin the other team deep in its own territory. We got the ball back at the last part of the fourth quarter at midfield and huddled up, prepared to do what we could to get another score and try to lock up the win.

On first and ten, the play was called to my side. Our flanker, Raul Banton, who was a quick and dangerous little football player, came in motion behind me before the play, parallel to the line of scrimmage. My defensive back switched over to cover Raul, just as Coach Larondeau had predicted, and I was left with the big old linebacker to cover me. When the ball was snapped, I just ran right past the linebacker, offering him half of a head-fake to get him turned around. Zagordo saw it all, dropped straight back behind his trustworthy line of men, and let the ball fly.

I saw it release right off his arm, arcing up and over to a place I was going to be soon, far up the field, behind the defense. The linebacker and my former DB were now chasing me, hoping something would happen before I got to the ball, that I might fall or the ball would blow out-of-bounds. It was on its way down, spinning closer to the sideline ahead, wanting to come to me as my legs worked as hard as they could, feeling like pistons churning my old and young body downfield, faster, faster, faster.

If I put my arms out for the ball on its final motion, I could reach it in full stride, just inside the boundary lines. It spun into outstretched hands, the thin sticky leather of my glove grabbing the ball, stopping its rotation, me hearing and feeling the skin of the ball give a little pop as it was halted and held. I could not tuck the ball away for fear I would drop it as I ran and ran, the yard-lines passing in front of me as I ran and ran and ran, and suddenly there were no more lines to speed over and the boys behind me stopped chasing and I was in the wide side of the end-zone, holding the ball in both hands like a prize bird. I looked around as I came to a stop, not believing it had happened.

The ball went to my right hand as I slapped my other flat against the top of my helmet, stunned. A touchdown. My first one, ever. I was thirty-one years old.

I turned to face my teammates, hoping there was no yellow penalty flag on the ground. There was none. Suddenly Vas was there, out to hold the extra point, his facemask against mine in a glorious hug. "You did it, Gary! You did it!" he screamed into my beaming face.

Soon the whole team was there, swarming over me, yelling my name. I could have died right then and been complete. Where was my wife? I had no time to look for her, but I was sure she had seen. She told me later that she knew, right when I scored, everything about why I had done this, why I had tried this silly game one last season. In that moment it had all made sense to her. We missed the extra point attempt.

McMaster went on to quickly score another quick touchdown on a broken play, and all of a sudden they had the ball again and were driving for the winning score. They went right down the field and had time for one last play before the clock wound down. From the twenty, their quarterback threw into the end-zone, and the ball was intercepted by our own Wayne "Soupy" Campbell, who ran it out to midfield before being pushed out of bounds.

The game was over! We were 1-0 on the season! Vas came running up to me after we all had hugged Soupy, and Vas said something I had never thought possible. Beaming, he whispered in that Vasily way right into my ear, "Gary, you scored the winning touchdown!"

No way. Yes. The winning touchdown.

We shook hands with the opponents at the fifty-five yard line, and I went to find my wife while everyone around me danced and yelled in glory. The pep band resounded off in the distance somewhere.

There she was in front of the goalposts, tears in her eyes, a huge beautiful smile. I hugged her hard, too hard against my pads, making her gasp through her sniffling smile, my own eyes brimming. She breathed into my ear, her hair tickling my neck, sweetly, "My hero."

Nothing hurt in my wracked and wrecked body. I had put points up on the board, and they would never be taken down. Finally, it was time to go home.

Gary Gerson teaches conceptual physics and geology and coaches varsity football at Cranbrook Kingswood Upper School in Bloomfield Hills, Michigan. He has been married to Shelley for 17 years and they have three amazing children, Madlyn, Elijah, and Isaac. He wouldn't mind some feedback at ggerson@cranbrook.edu .

Eli, Maddie, and the Lorikeets, 2008

Shelley and Maddie, Spring 2008.

Isaac, Spring 2008

Cover photo and back author photo taken by Maddie Gerson… no kidding.